GARDENING
WITHOUT POISONS

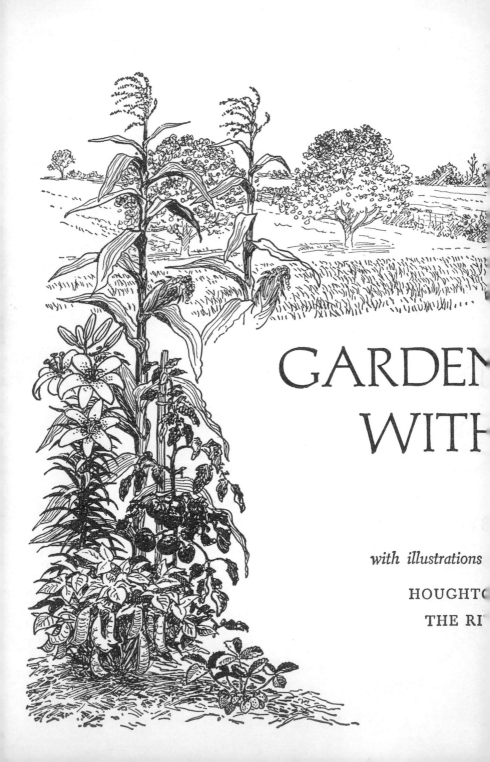

GARDEN
WITH

with illustrations

HOUGHT
THE RI

NG

OUT POISONS

BY BEATRICE TRUM HUNTER

BOB HINES

MIFFLIN COMPANY BOSTON

DE PRESS CAMBRIDGE

TO HERBERT S. ALLEN

ACKNOWLEDGMENTS

THE AUTHOR wishes to express appreciation to Friends of Nature, the organization which published the pamphlet that was the embryo of this book, and to: Rudy and Mickie Haase, Jeannette Kingsbury, Penelope Turton, Marjorie Spock, Mary T. Richards, Herbert S. Allen, Mary Peabody, Helen Hadley, and Helen Marer for their encouragement and assistance; also to governmental agencies, especially branches of the United States Department of Agriculture, United States Fish and Wildlife Service, agricultural experiment stations, and universities for supplying many helpful publications.

Special thanks go to Dr. A. M. Heimpel, Insect Pathology Laboratory, Beltsville, Maryland, on *Bacillus Thuringiensis*; Dr. Alexej B. Bořkovec, Entomology Research Division, Beltsville, Maryland, on chemosterilants; Professor I. Barry Tarsis, Department of Entomology, University of California, on sorptive dusts;

Professor Walter Ebeling, Department of Entomology, University of California, on antimetabolites; Dr. G. Edward Marshall, Department of Entomology, Purdue University, on flour and buttermilk spray; Professor John E. Bier, Forest Pathology, University of British Columbia, on tissue saprophytes; Dr. Bryan P. Beirne, Director of the Entomology Research Institute for Biological Control, Belleville, Canada, and his staff for many courtesies, especially Drs. J. S. Kelliher; H. L. House on insect nutrition; P. Belton on ultrasonics; P. Harris on weed insects; H. E. Welch and L. J. Briand on Nematode DD 136; G. M. Maw on static electricity; G. E. Bucher on insect diseases; J. M. Mackauer on ants; A. L. Turnbull and T. Burnett for manuscript suggestions; Dr. D. A. Chant, Officer in Charge, Research Laboratory, Vineland Station, Ontario, and his staff for many courtesies, especially Drs. R. W. Fisher on polybutenes; J. H. H. Phillips on population dynamics; A. B. Stevenson, J. A. George and G. G. Dustan on biological control; Dr. E. J. LeRoux, Department of Entomology and Plant Pathology, MacDonald College, Quebec; Dr. Visvaldis Slankis, Laboratory of Forest Pathology, Maple, Ontario, on mycorrhizal association.

I should also like to express my thanks to industry: Donald P. Wright, Jr., of American Cyanamid Company, on Anti-Feeding Compound 24,055, and to the American Chemical Society for kind permission to make an abstract of this information; J. J. Hager of Amoco Chemicals Corporation, on polybutenes; Harry L. Patrick, of Dow Chemical Company, Dr. D. M. Yoder, of Union Carbide, and Dr. Harold E. Aller of FMC Corporation, Niagara Chemical Division, on cellulose polymers; Fred Howe, of Packaging Products Department, Union Carbide Corporation, on polyethylene netting; and Monsanto Chemical Company on silica aerogel.

Special thanks are extended to Jerome Olds, Editor of *Compost Science*, and Executive Editor of *Organic Gardening and Farming* Magazine, and other members of the staff at Rodale publications for valuable assistance; Jorian E. F. Jenks, Editorial

Secretary of The Soil Association's *Mother Earth*; Lawrence D. Hills, Honorable Secretary of the Henry Doubleday Research Association; Spencer Cheshire, Secretary and Editor of Land Fellowship; Frederick and Alice Heckel, Dr. H. H. Koepf, Josephine Porter, Richard and Evelyn Gregg, and John and Helen Philbrick, on Bio-Dynamics; Dr. Frank E. Egler, of Rightofway Resources of America, on roadside weeds and brush; and Jack Gothard, of Trik-O, on trichogramma.

I am also indebted to the following for help in various ways: Ted P. Banks, Anne Barrett, S. H. Barton, Joseph A. Cocannouer, Ruth G. Desmond, Marion S. Gans, Ruth Hapgood, Mildred Hatch, Hugh MacDonald, Helen Perry, Miles and Ruth Robinson, Leonice Taft, and John Tobe. Thanks also go to countless numbers of gardeners who have been willing to share the fruits of their experience. Lastly, deep appreciation goes to my husband, John, who has offered encouragement and valuable suggestions.

CONTENTS

GARDENING
WITHOUT POISONS

PROLOGUE

MANY OF THE TREES on the citrus ranch were topdead, and hundreds more were dying. Upon examining the trees closely, Hugh MacDonald saw that they were heavily infested with many insects and diseases to which citrus trees succumb: cottony cushion scale, citricola scale, soft brown scale, thrips, rust, wilt.

He examined a spadeful of soil. It was hard-packed. There was little evidence of earthworms or other beneficial organisms.

As he gazed around him, his eyes rested on the deep canyons bordering the ranch. All brush and small trees along the canyon had been cut clean in attempts to eradicate small predaceous creatures. The area showed shocking signs of erosion.

As he walked he plucked a small poor quality orange from a tree and held it in his palm. He had heard that the yield on this ranch had diminished each year, despite the desperate attempts at applying fertilizers. The produce of the place had acquired a poor reputation. He had even heard it rumored that workers were reluctant to pick fruit at this ranch, knowing that their earnings would be meager.

He stood back and surveyed some of the four hundred acres he had just acquired. There certainly was work to be done. It was a biological desert. The former owners were probably hard-working people. They had used all the conventional methods of cultivation and fertilization and followed faithfully the spray program to keep the trees thriving. Yet they had failed. The ranch was favorably located at the southern tip of the Imperial Valley of California. Was this region not world famous for its growth, and the weather favorable for crops? Yet the people had failed. Why? Hugh MacDonald stood there, facing the barren wasteland of 1955, and vowed to make changes.

In 1962, Hugh MacDonald proudly surveys his enlarged 555 acres of Border Ranch. In the brief span of seven years he has restored it to fertility and health. The place has achieved an enviable reputation as one of the showplaces of large-scale organiculture.

As he examines his trees he observes that some of the thirty-year-old ones have attained a height of sixteen feet, and are bearing abundantly. The dead trees have been removed, and dead branches from formerly diseased trees pruned out. New growth has developed. Young trees have been planted to replace those removed.

As he plucks an orange he handles it proudly, aware that it is prime fruit. From the yearly production in 1955, of only 20,000 boxes of miserable specimens, the yield has now soared to 125,-000 boxes of quality fruit.

When he examines closely the fruit, bark, and leaves, it is rare for him to find insect pests or plant diseases. Control has been achieved without resorting to any poisonous chemical sprays or dusts for the past seven years.

When he spades the soil, scores of wriggling earthworms turn up in the springy friable earth.

Looking at the deep canyons, he can see the brush and small trees which have been encouraged to grow once again. Scars of erosion have been healed. The foliage of the canyon offers a haven for many quail, doves, and rabbits which are protected on the ranch.

These are some of the sights which greet his eyes and offer him a deep sense of satisfaction.

Just what has Hugh MacDonald done to achieve this radical transformation within such a short space of time? The answer is not one thing, but a combination of many.

He has set aside fifty acres of Border Ranch farmland for raising cover crops and grain crops. When the grain heads form, they are cut and traded to a nearby beef-fattening ranch in exchange for valuable manure. The standing stalks and leaves of the cover crops are mowed and raked into long windrows which gradually convert into rich compost, which is then trucked to orchards and spread under trees.

Cover crops of Espana, wild mustard, vetch, and maize had been planted everywhere and disked under. Thousands of tons of manure were spread. With adequate organic matter turned under, there has been no need for any addition of chemical fertilizers on the land for the past seven years.

Fortunately water is plentiful. It comes from the All-American Canal and is delivered by contract in cement chutes run from the canal to the ranch.

Twice a year, at the time of the spring crop set, and in early fall to size the fruit, Hugh MacDonald adds to the water a liquid fish emulsion from cannery wastes. He also adds a biological soil conditioner extract made from prickly pear, yucca, and greasewood plants, rich in enzymes and their catalysts. These materials, released into the water, are carried by ditches to irrigate the trees. The orchards are disked and furrowed so that the tree rows are set in square blocks with foot-high ridges which impound the valuable water.

Five acres of land are set aside to raise and improve citrus tree stock. This is used for replanting on the ranch, and the surplus stock is sold.

Two apiaries, each containing one hundred hives, nestle in the canyon, sheltered from wind and sun. The bees help pollinate the fruit.

Members of the Biological Control Division of the University of California have introduced vedalia beetles on Border Ranch to control the cottony cushion scale. They also released *Metaphycus luteolus* against the citricola scale and soft brown scale. These predaceous and parasitic insects have been helpful against the scales and infested areas have been aided with other biological measures. The absence of poison sprays allowed the beneficial insects to work more efficiently. As soil fertility was improved and the vigor of the trees increased, plant diseases were brought under control.

Dr. Blair Bartlett, of the Citrus Experiment Station, Biological Control Division, remarked:

Beyond a doubt, Border Ranch is the world's largest organically run citrus ranch. When Mr. MacDonald took over the property it was very run down, the soil, the trees. He has brought it back remarkably to health. He won't allow an orange or other piece of citrus fruit on the place from an outside ranch, because of the danger of bringing in red scale . . . Mr. MacDonald is operating his Border Ranch without insecticides, and he's getting by. I've been down there inspecting things. The cottony cushion scale is only a problem where there is insecticide or plane dusting drift from a nearby orchard — drifting onto another orchard and killing off the beneficial insects. Of course there are some harmful insects and scale at Border Ranch — but the beneficial insects keep them under control . . .

This is the notable achievement of one man, not in a lifetime, but within seven years. It has been made possible through understanding and wisdom. The helpful forces of nature have been utilized rather than combatted. Hugh MacDonald appreciates the prime importance of fertile soil for plant vigor and control of insect pests. He recognizes the interdependence of living organisms in the environment which contribute to sound agricultural practices.

Border Ranch thrives in the middle of a citrus belt where the annual crop is slowly declining from the dying out of trees attacked by virus, scale, thrip, aphid, mite, and other telling signs of an ailing agricultural economy. Border Ranch, without pesticides, prospers in a state in which $100,000,000 is being spent yearly for poisonous pesticides.

The experience at Border Ranch can be duplicated elsewhere by many other examples, ranging from large-scale farming down to the small backyard garden. In each instance, the developments have been made possible by the same underlying principles. In the following chapters we shall explore them in detail: first, the way in which natural forces work to keep all the elements of the plant-animal community in balance; second, the way in which these ecological principles can be applied now, by every gardener, in overcoming the insects and diseases which attack growing things; third, the remarkable new methods now being developed which give promise of safer and more lasting control than we have yet been able to achieve.

The changes in gardening and farming practices which this book advocates will not be realized until an aroused public understands the issues. These problems concern not only those who till the soil, but are of utmost importance to every consumer of food — which means all of us.

We are beginning to understand that present agricultural methods, with their dependence on artificial stimulation and strong poisons to counter the scourges of plant diseases and insect pests, have spiraled us into a dilemma which yearly grows graver. Our practices are producing soils with lowered vitality; plants grown on them have less vigor, less natural resistance, and reduced nutritive value; garden pests thrive in these unbalanced situations, and a continuous assault with newer and stronger poisons in turn encourages the development of more and increasingly resistant pests.

We do not have to be scientists to perceive that a drastic change is needed. Gardening without poisons, in a backyard garden or in a large-scale commercial operation, is possible if we make good use of the knowledge and tools we already possess.

We are presently aware of the general problem of pesticides, but lack a blueprint for action. Agricultural officials must be urged to explore many existing possibilities of safe and effective alternatives which have either been ignored or partially studied but not fully developed. Divisions for biological control within departments of agriculture, on all levels of government, need to be established. Basic research, long overdue, should be conducted systematically by these groups. Ultimately, such studies will have practical results. These divisions for biological control can wean us away from self-defeating measures and can initiate programs such as "integrated control."

The goal before us remains what it has always been — food for the hungry. World demands are more pressing than ever; a rapidly expanding population is coupled with diminishing arable land and topsoil. The achievement of our goal appears elusive and tantalizing. Soil drugs and chemical pesticides have been used as a panacea, and they seemed to offer a bounteous cornucopia of good food for all. But we now understand how these spurious aides disturb normally functioning mechanisms of living soil, plant growth, and insect survival. We have been guilty of applying an oversimplified approach in complex situations. We must learn to use a variety of techniques. We need understanding and skill to manipulate the environment so that it produces what we need. This will require a sound biological knowledge of living organisms in soil, insects, weeds, plant pests, and crop plants, and their relationships, one to the other. We will rescue ourselves from our present dilemma when we substitute intelligence for force.

1. THE REALITIES OF BIOLOGY

The acceptance of a philosophy of [pest] control rather than eradication does not minimize the technical or economic importance of a program, but acknowledges the realities of biology.

— *Report on* Use of Pesticides *by the President's Science Advisory Committee, May 15, 1963*

"WOULDN'T YOU rather eat an apple with a little bit of poison than one which is riddled with worms?" This question is posed on the assumption that only two alternatives exist: an acceptance of modern agricultural practice with its full panoply of poisonous pesticides, or a complete do-nothing approach in which noxious insects and plant diseases would lead to mass starvation.

In reality it is not necessary for us to choose between two evils. It is possible to grow a sound apple, or other crops, in farm or garden, without resorting to the extremes of either position. This book attempts to explore the middle road of safe and effective alternatives. No one approach can answer all problems. The situation demands a combination of approaches, using knowledge rather than brute force. And if we use all the knowledge that is available to us, we may succeed not only in growing the apple without poisons or worms, but in growing it with far greater vigor and biological quality as well.

We have reached a critical period. The harm done by the widespread use of poisons is becoming increasingly apparent and grave. At last the public has been aroused to some realization of problems which have been disturbing the scientific community for years. But there is a lack of general awareness of the middle road between the two extremes of poison and famine. Agriculture has been dominated in recent years by the rapid development of a wide range of economic poisons. The overemphasis on the chemical approach has obscured many biological, cultural, and physical controls which have either gone out of fashion or await development.

NEWER BIOLOGICAL UNDERSTANDINGS

Yet modern science, which has given us the chemical pesticides, has also given us deeper insights into basic biological laws that govern all living organisms. We can begin to use in a logical and effective manner those natural forces which earlier generations were vaguely aware of but which they did not comprehend. Effective pest control demands a team approach of entomologist, geneticist, biologist, agronomist, horticulturist, forester, pathologist, public health physician, food and drug administrator, and others who may share responsibilities for various aspects of the problem. We begin to appreciate how outbreaks of infestation by noxious garden pests may be far removed from their causes which germinate in modern agricultural and sociological practices. These problems cannot be divorced from present widespread practices such as poor land husbandry, overgrazing, monoculture, lack of crop rotation, oversimplification of the landscape, or failure to maintain soil fertility.

A new approach to these problems is necessary in which biological factors are given prime consideration. They must be supplemented by good cultural practices and physical controls which offer no hazards. Doubtless there will be instances which require limited chemical control, as long as unnatural demands are made upon agriculture. But hazardous materials should be considered after all other possibilities are exhausted, and viewed as emergency measures to be used sparingly. As someone expressed it, chemical pesticides should be handled as a "stiletto rather than a scythe."

NATURAL RESISTANCE TO INSECT INVASION

As our biological understanding has broadened and deepened, we have come to appreciate more fully some basic principles governing insects which are directly related to pest control. What happens when insects invade, and what natural resistance do they encounter? Through the years there have been many invasions of all types of living organisms, not only insects but viruses, bacteria, fungi, plants, and animals, sometimes resulting in population explosions. The present century, with its faster and larger transport, has brought about a worldwide exchange of organisms and, gathering momentum, has gradually broken down former distribution of species.

Most insect pests have been introduced inadvertently, often in spite of strict quarantine measures. At times they are discovered in imported farm machinery, such as used tractors which still have soil adhering to them. In 1961, some of the world's most destructive pests were intercepted at United States ports of entry at the average rate of one every sixteen minutes. Although quarantine and eradication attempts may have powerful direct killing power, they are quite different from permanent control through ecological methods which attempt to keep any insect in the community from becoming dominant, and to lower or level off completely the major fluctuations and outbreaks of insect populations through natural forces as well as artificial means.

Before attempting such manipulations, ecologists must understand the nature of invasion. The immigrant insect tries to enter an area where there is a complex and varied community of different populations competing for the basic needs — breeding sites, food, and shelter. The newcomer meets resistance from these native species. In addition, each habitat shares part of its fauna with neighboring ones. Relationships among soil, bush, tree canopy, marsh, stream, fallen log, and bird's nest may affect the balance among populations already present. Does the invading insect establish itself or does it perish? If it remains, does it add another species to the list or replace some natives and reduce their numbers? These are typical questions which must be answered in order to understand the nature of ecological resistance.

Gardeners may lack a general appreciation of the astonishing variety of species and the vast number of living organisms which comprise any community. To a large extent, many are hidden under cover as protection against enemies. Dr. Charles Elton and other ecologists devoted more than a decade to an intensive study of Wytham Woods, an area of less than two square miles of typical English Midlands countryside, surrounded on two sides by the Thames River, and varying from forest and marsh to field and limestone with a few patches of grass on top. Within those bounds, more than 2500 species of living organisms were found, perhaps thousands of millions of individual creatures.

How is this significant for gardeners? Whenever a rich variety exists within a biological community, the community has a good chance of remaining stable. There is little likelihood of population explosions of native insects, or invasions by newcomers. This keeps pests within bounds; infestations are not apt to build up.

But our present practices are what Elton terms "simplification for efficiency." Driving through the countryside, we see vast acreage planted yearly in corn, wheat, cotton, beets, tobacco, or other single crops. Man has created forests of pine or garden beds of tulips.

Invasions or outbreaks of pests occur mostly on cultivated or planted lands which man has oversimplified. We are guilty of practicing monoculture, of using crops of foreign plants unaccompanied by their full fauna, and we intensify the problem by trying to kill all other species thought to be harmful, incidentally killing or suppressing a great many more. Insecticides and fungicides do not act merely on the single species we wish to control, but may affect the survival of other species such as competitors, parasites, and enemies. As a result, the entire population within the plant-animal community may be altered or dislocated. The chain of events can go further. At times the residues of the pesticides change the metabolic activity of the soil community and reduce the productivity of crops. The yield of seeds may be reduced. The balance of soil insect life is changed significantly and upsets natural controls.

Can we learn to combine the simple culture of crops with the natural complex of nature? We must learn to explore all methods of keeping or creating sufficiently rich plant and animal communities within our landscapes, a practice Elton calls "conserving ecological variety." We can create diversity through intercropping and rotating crops. Even highly managed landscapes can be aided by hedgerows and roadside borders which can be extraordinarily variable and stable communities.

THE REALITIES OF BIOLOGY FOR EVERYONE

All of us must play a part in developing a bold new approach. Gardeners and farmers need to recognize insect infestations and plant diseases as symptoms of poor practices in need of correction. As consumers we should realize that not every apple in the basket can be unblemished and of the same size, shape, and color. This is not part of nature's plan. We must learn to demand inner biological quality of our food, nutritional value and flavor, rather than the standardization which results from assembly-line factory production.

In the Senate investigation of pesticidal hazards conducted in July 1963, Dr. M. R. Clarkson, Associate Administrator of the Agricultural Research Service, made the following statement:

> It is vital to expand our basic investigations in such areas as the mode of action and long-range effects of pesticides in animals, plants, and soils; on the life processes of insects, and their biology and behavior; on the nature of plant resistance to disease; and on the microbiological inhabitants of our soils.
>
> From studies like these will come the principles for pest control techniques that are even more effective than those now employed, and even safer to use. Some of them will undoubtedly lead to further improvement of human health, through eradication of disease-carrying insects.
>
> I would like to emphasize that it's not enough to say that there may now be hazards in the use of pesticides — or even to demonstrate what those hazards are. We must move forward to develop more ways of combatting pests without hazards and still keep on living and producing.

Large sums of money and the talents of many individuals are being used at present for the development of each new chemical pesticide. According to *The Wall Street Journal*, the pesticide industry's expenditure for research in 1963 is expected to be close to $40 million, which represents more than 10 percent of industry's sales. If such resources and creative abilities were diverted to many projects described in the pages that follow, we could embark on the program recommended by Clarkson to combat pests without hazards and still keep on living and producing.

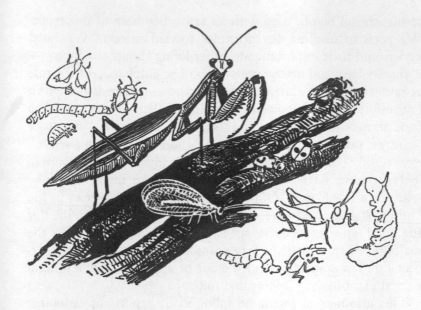

2. THE VITAL ROLE OF INSECTS

A full history of noxious insects hurtful in the field, garden and house, suggesting all the known and likely means of destroying them, would be allowed by the public to be a most useful and important work. What knowledge there is of this sort lies scattered, and wants to be collected; great improvements would soon follow of course. A knowledge of the properties, economy, propagation, and in short of the life and conversation of these animals, is a necessary step to lead us to some method of preventing their depredations.

— *Letter #34 by Gilbert White of Selborne, March 30, 1771*

MANY PEOPLE have been conditioned to the philosophy that "the only good bug is a dead one." Any winged creature that alights for a moment is apt to be pounced upon as a mortal enemy which must be destroyed. Any crawling insect is regarded as malicious and immediately crushed underfoot. This is an age of the aerosol bomb, used with an arrogance born of ignorance. We need to readjust our attitudes toward insects. We must understand their importance to other living things.

Insects have had a poor press which has emphasized their role as ravagers, disease carriers or as nuisances. There is always an uncomfortable undercurrent of opinion that insects, in some fiendish manner, are trying to inherit our planet.

Insects need an articulate public relations man. Such a spokesman could do much to change the public image. There is ample material for a fertile mind. For example, he might begin by releasing a few figures. Out of some 86,000 insect species in the United States, 76,000 are considered beneficial or friendly. Of the total number of pest species throughout the world, the majority are under satisfactory natural control, with only 1 percent listed as pests of agriculture out of approximately a million named plant-feeding insects and mites.

This information might be followed by reports of economic interest. Certain insects are valuable commercially, by providing honey, beeswax, shellac, dye, and raw silk. They may be a rich hidden source of antibiotics and fungicides.

Insects are vital to the very existence of higher life. Without them, possibly the endless cycles of life, death, decay, and birth could not function. Even in temperate climates it is doubtful that microbes and bacteria, unaided by insects, could cope with the enormous mass of dead plant and animal materials. But the larvae of many wood-inhabiting beetles, ants, termites, and springtails shred the leaves, chew up the twigs, tear apart the trunks of fallen trees, and devour dead animal tissue, which is then further broken down by soil organisms and returned to the soil to serve as nutrients. In turn, the insects die and become food for predators. In the tropics, this breakdown process is even more important. If it were not for the work of insects, the forests would soon become choked by accumulated dead timber, vegetation, and animal life.

Some insects improve the soil. Through the burrowing of

ants, grubs, beetles, and wild bees, air penetrates the soil, improving its structure and drainage. Insects bury decaying matter and bring up earth, rich in valuable elements, from the depths of the soil to its surface.

Some are weed controllers. Chrysolina beetles on the Klamath weed and cinnabar moths on tansy ragwort are two notable examples.

Of all the vital functions that insects perform, one of the most important is pollination. Without this, much plant life on earth, as we know it, could not exist. Honeybees, wasps, and other insects are recognized for their indispensable services as pollinators. In addition, they indirectly improve soil fertility by pollinating leguminous plants and trees. When such valuable insects perish from poison sprays, less valuable wind-pollinated plants flourish instead.

The concept of "insect friend" and "insect foe" is relative; insects may be helpful or harmful to man, depending on circumstances. Termites, for example, have had a particularly bad press, but in the tropics they are helpful scavengers that dispose of filth and rottenness. As wood feeders, they reduce the trunks and branches of dead trees to pulp or powder. Not until man builds houses low to the ground in wooded areas and provides central heat are termites considered pests.

Fire ants, too, have been much maligned. Although there have been massive attempts to eradicate them in the Southern states, in South America they are considered to be beneficial predators. Also, the venom of the fire ant inhibits the growth of fungus infection and can repress some bacterial infections of humans.

Moderate insect pruning of plants may be more helpful to the gardener than harmful. A moderate amount of root-pruning by insects may be beneficial, provided the plant has inherent vigor. Similarly, if plants were completely exempt from the attacks of insects above the ground, too many leaves might be produced, resulting in an excessive accumulation of weakened fruit or vegetables. Remember that leaf-chewing by insects is part of the normal and constructive cycle which keeps the landscape alive. Certain larvae, feeding on the buds of a fruit tree, actually assist the tree in fulfilling its physiological needs. For instance, some apple trees are unable to support more than 5 percent of their blooms without having branches break. Apparently an internal mechanism allows about 95 percent of the blooms to fall off. The bud moth, which destroys many apple buds, assists in this work.

No insect is all "good" or all "bad." If an introduced plant is, for some reason, considered desirable, we think of insects feeding on it as injurious, and parasites and predators that feed on these insects as beneficial. If a plant, however, is regarded as undesirable, then we view the insects feeding upon it as beneficial, and their parasites and predators as injurious.

Gardeners may be concerned with certain creatures, in general considered beneficial, who consume "good" insects. For example, the praying mantis, spider, raccoon, or frog may all eat a variety of insects without distinguishing between those we consider good and those we consider bad. This should not cause undue concern. We must realize that *all* insects increase so rapidly that we must have many means of keeping all populations within bounds. The number of individual insects, good or bad, which perish is less important than the total impact of balanced life within the community.

HELPFUL INSECT PREDATORS

Predators are those insects which move about and in general feed upon other insects. They are the lions and tigers of the insect world. Far from being the gardeners' worst enemies, such insects in the garden perform a helpful function. We can encourage them or even introduce them into the garden if they are not already present.

One of the most effective of all predaceous insects is the tiny lady beetle, also called ladybug and ladybird. It dines on soft-bodied insects such as aphids, mealybugs, whiteflies, and spider mites, on eggs, larvae, and scales. When supplies of these preferred foods are scarce, it will eat corn borer larvae and egg masses from corn plants, potato aphids, Colorado potato beetles, alfalfa weevils, and bean beetles.

Under favorable conditions, lady beetles can be highly efficient. They can crawl to the underside of leaves, into the tightest corner of nasturtium leaves, into the hearts of chrysanthemums, or inside young rosebuds, or leaves on a young lemon tree. They succeed in getting to places which would be difficult to reach by spray. It is estimated that in an orchard a larva of the lady beetle is capable of devouring up to twenty-five aphids daily, while an adult can eat as many as fifty-six; it can sustain this record for several weeks. In view of aphid populations, this number may appear small, but high densities of lady beetles can result in effective control.

In the spring you can find the eggs of lady beetles on the underside of leaves, near their early food supply — aphids. Standing on end in clusters of five to fifty, lady beetle eggs are generally yellow or orange. The larvae are alligator-shaped, blue-black, and orange-spotted.

You as a gardener do not need to leave it to nature to give you a plentiful supply of ladybugs in your garden; you can import them. If you want more of these useful beetles for your garden or greenhouse, they can be purchased commercially through the mail and introduced in the spring. (See List of Suppliers of Materials.) It is not certain that the introduced ones are as effective as the natives, but they will remain as long as the food supply lasts. They are economical, if you realize that a female, after one mating, will produce from two hundred to one thousand offspring.

Make certain that you introduce enough lady beetles to control the area. If they arrive when it is raining, keep them in their transportation container, and place them in the refrigera-

tor. If necessary, they can hibernate for several days. Merely
sprinkle a little water on the screened side of the box. Keep the
lady beetles in the container until late in the afternoon or till
sundown. Then dampen the ground and place them, by the
handful, on the ground. If they have been packed with excelsior
or other packing material, allow them to remain on it. By the
following morning they will begin to forage. Newly emerged
female lady beetles are dependent on their hosts. They must
find aphids in sufficient quantity to keep them in the vicinity
and to assure reproduction.

The vedalia is a lady beetle in California which displays a
voracious appetite in preying on a specific target, cottony cushion
scale, a pest which feeds on a variety of fruit and nut trees, ornamentals, and vegetable crops. (See Appendix A for a partial listing.) At times, the vedalia perishes for lack of food because it
has devoured all the cottony cushion scale present in an area.
It is possible to purchase vedalia through the mail and propagate
them artificially on a regular schedule for areas threatened by
this scale.

Aphis lions are found in gardens everywhere, among them
the ant lions or doodlebugs and the golden-eyed lacewings.
They are valuable as general feeders, and destroy many moth
eggs, all stages of plant-feeding mites, caterpillars, scale insects,
whiteflies, thrips, aphids, and mealybugs. Adult lacewings are
especially attracted to plants with honeydew secreted by aphids
and whiteflies. A single aphis lion, observed destroying approximately sixty aphids within an hour, showed no signs of surfeit.
It is estimated that in the short span of ten days, between the
hatching and development into an adult, an aphis lion may consume millions of plant lice. You can buy green lacewings by
mail and introduce them in the garden. They are active search-
ers and will move continually over plants.

Despite its ferocious appearance, the praying mantis is another
insect beneficial to man. It is an insectivore and will not harm

any vegetation in the garden. When young, it lives mainly on soft-bodied insects, the cutting and sucking insects such as aphids and leafhoppers; when mature, it eats flies, spiders, tent caterpillars, grasshoppers, chinch bugs, crickets, locusts, bees, wasps, beetles, or practically any others.

If you carefully examine thorny bushes, brush, hedges and berry bushes in autumn after leaves are fallen, you may discover the hardened froth mass egg cases of the mantids; these are their insulated winter homes. You can collect some from marshes and waste areas for your own garden, field, or greenhouse, making certain that you do not strip the area clean. Or you can obtain mantid egg cases commercially, through the mail, between November and early May.

To introduce them, allow one egg case for each major shrub, or four cases for each quarter of an acre without shrubbery. Tie or tape each case securely to a shrub, stick, or tree, from two to four feet above the ground. If possible, select a spot sheltered from the wind. Once the cases are set out, your work is done. They are winter hardy and the rays of the sun will incubate the eggs. The mantids will emerge, usually in bright sunshine, from early May to late June, at a time when a large variety of insect fare is apt to be available. The insects come out through the median band, the only part of the egg that gives them an outlet, and they will tug, sway, bend, and straighten up. Each creature is fastened to the egg by a tenuous cord which it must break. Freeing itself, it will drop and climb to surrounding foliage. Since praying mantids are poor flyers and slow movers, they usually remain in the vicinity as long as they continue to find food. In the absence of a plentiful supply of other insects, they may resort to cannibalism among themselves.

Once mantids are introduced to an area they usually multiply and extend control. Each female deposits several egg masses, containing from fifty to four hundred eggs, in a season. Although many of the young may perish, enough may survive to perpetuate themselves.

A large family of predator beetles, the carabidae, is another aide to gardeners. They are active from twilight to daybreak, searching for cutworms, cankerworms, brown-tail moths and many larvae. The caterpillar hunter, one of the carabidae, in its larval stage attacks and feeds on caterpillars of the gypsy moth and tent caterpillar. U.S. Department of Agriculture entomologists estimated that Aleochara beetles destroy up to 80 percent of all cabbage-root maggots. Soldier beetles have been observed puncturing nests of webworms and destroying the immature caterpillars. The fiery hunter beetle seeks out cutworms, cankerworms, and other injurious larvae. The rove beetle feeds on decaying organic matter but does not harm plants.

Fireflies are actually beetles, so useful in pest control that in Japan high school students breed them on farms for later release. In their larval stage, fireflies consume cutworms which they find underground and in rotting wood. As adults, they crawl over the ground and climb onto grass blades and other plants in search of snails and slugs. Once they locate their prey, they inject a powerful anesthetic and then secrete digestive fluids which liquefy the tissues. After the firefly drinks this liquid, all that remains of the snail is the empty shell.

Gardeners should acquaint themselves with other predaceous insects endlessly at work in their gardens and about the countryside, such as the shield bugs that attack white grubs (May beetles in their immature stage), and the stinkbugs that eat caterpillars and smooth beetles. Over ponds, lakes, and swamps, the graceful gauzy-winged dragonflies are a familiar sight. What may be less familiar is their remarkable equipment for catching their prey of the soft-bodied insects. Their enormous eyes search in all directions at once during their speedy flight. Their legs form a basket-like net as they fly and small insects are scooped into it, to be eaten on the wing.

The damselflies, more delicate relatives, also have lusty appetites for small soft-bodied insects. In the nymph stage, the young of both damselflies and dragonflies destroy mosquitoes and other water insects so effectively that there have been projects to rear them for mosquito control.

Gardeners sometimes think of ants as the source of trouble with aphids, mealybugs, whiteflies, scale insects, and leafhoppers. It is true that ants feed on honeydew secreted by these insects, and in turn protect them from their natural enemies, the predators and parasites that would normally keep them down. But it would be a mistake to think that, because of such activities, we should try to eliminate ants. Many species of ants rank high as natural controllers of insect pests of both agricultural crops and forest trees. For centuries Chinese citrus growers have made a regular practice of placing certain ants in orchards to prey on caterpillars and other pests. The orchardists even provided the ants with bamboo pole runways from tree to tree.

Today in Europe the red ant is used as a predator in forest management. Colonies of these ants are cultivated to be liberated in forests where they play their part along with birds, bats, spiders, and soil bacteria in controlling the insect pests of the forest.

Ants feed extensively on many insects that pass all or part of their lives in the soil. They destroy a high percentage of the larvae of fruit flies and houseflies. Because they will attack any insect that comes within foraging range of their nests, they have a great influence on insect populations over and above what they eat.

Some mites and spiders, which are arthropods related to insects, should be recognized as natural predators. They are less well known than insect predators because of difficulty in studying them, but we have valuable allies in these creatures. For instance, a predaceous mite controls the two-spotted mite, a well known greenhouse pest. Other predaceous mites have also been used to control plant-feeding species on citrus and avocado crops in California. The diet of spiders consists mainly of insects and mites.

The defensive secretions of arthropods are now under study. The structure and operation of their glands as well as their chemical composition may give us another helpful tool in pest control.

HELPFUL INSECT PARASITES

Unlike the predators among the insects, who dine on what they catch, parasitic insects do not devour their prey immediately. The larva of the parasite enters the body of its host and feeds on its tissues until the larva is nearly grown. When the host dies, the parasite may continue to develop within the dead body, or it may emerge and pupate on or near the remains of the host.

The polistes wasp is such a valuable parasite that nesting boxes are set out for it on tobacco plantations, where it has been known to achieve over 60 percent control of the tobacco hornworm. Corn earworm and armyworm are also subject to its attack. The ichneumon fly, actually a wasp, is another valuable ally. Its long ovipositor is capable of penetrating tree bark to deposit eggs in wood-boring caterpillars. It parasitizes tomato worms and has been estimated to reduce up to 90 percent of a population of Oriental fruit moths. An ichneumon fly was observed parasitizing young caterpillars of prominent moths which emit a blistering secretion. Although the parasitic fly was forced to withdraw frequently to clean its face and antennae, it returned to the caterpillars until every one of them had been parasitized.

The ichneumon fly is described as a parasite, but it belongs rather to a group called "parasitoids" which eventually kill their hosts. An adult parasitoid may not feed upon its victim, but neither do all predatory wasps. Sometimes it carries it back to its young, or to the nest in which it will later lay its eggs. Adult parasitoids may lay their eggs near or on the bodies of their prey so that the emerging larvae can find food easily. Or, they may lay their eggs within the bodies of victims by means of their ovipositors. The larvae, in hatching, feed internally and leave the vital organs for their last meal prior to their pupating. The larvae of the parasitoids first work as parasites, and do not kill their hosts. But later they become predators and destroy them.

Many flies are parasitic. Tachinid flies, which resemble large houseflies in appearance, prey on a wide variety of insects, including such pests as caterpillars, Japanese beetles, European earwigs, gypsy moths, brown-tail moths, tomato worms, and grasshoppers. Syrphid flies help pollinate crops and also prey upon aphids.

There is one parasitic wasp, trichogramma, which needs introduction to many gardeners. The adults are among the smallest of insects, having a wingspread of about 1/50th of an inch. Despite its size, it is an efficient destroyer of the eggs of many moths and butterflies which are leaf-eaters in the larval stage. These wasps disperse readily in their search for eggs to parasitize, and as many as three adults can develop within a single egg of a corn earworm. (See Appendix A for a partial list of some two hundred species of insect pests parasitized by trichogramma.)

The trichogramma seeks out eggs, but does not feed on or harm vegetation. It is a particularly effective control agent because it kills its host before the plant can be damaged. Under natural conditions, the trichogramma often destroys up to 98 percent of the eggs of a host.

It has taken nearly a century of concerted effort to develop an effective yet economical program based on the artificial liberation of these tiny but beneficial parasites. The methods developed for the mass production of egg parasites represent an outstanding contribution to techniques in biological control. The early work was done by Dr. Stanley E. Flanders at the University of California. Today this parasitic material has been developed to the point of practical application for gardeners. Trichogramma are reared at a private insectary and are shipped in host eggs which may be obtained through the mail. The cost is so low that it is feasible for gardeners and farmers to purchase them for massive release.

When you are buying trichogramma, you will receive the larvae almost ready to hatch out as adult wasps. All you have to do is place the opened containers in the areas to be controlled. Trichogramma emerge from the cards and seek out a variety of eggs which they parasitize and thus destroy. One package, containing some two thousand to four thousand of these microscopic parasites, will control up to five acres! One to three liberations annually are usually enough to give control. Remember, however, that all garden aides must be used judiciously. Merely because they are considered safe biological agents, do not attempt to blanket the countryside with trichogramma. By so doing you might succeed in reducing this insect group so much as to deny birds an important food source, as well as to destroy many butterflies we cherish.

Trichogramma has achieved eminent success with cotton crops. Checks on fields where heavy releases of trichogramma were made showed from 60 to 95 percent better control than in adjoining fields without releases. Many cotton growers have used trichogramma over the past several years and report effective control at a nominal cost. Field service is provided by the distributor of trichogramma, including systematic field checking to determine egg and host counts. Egg and host counts can be made immediately and will determine whether or not a liberation of trichogramma is advisable, and if so, how large a liberation is required.

Many millions of trichogramma have been shipped to Peru to control cotton pests. The success was so outstanding that the Peruvian government took steps to outlaw the use of chemical insecticides on cotton. One growers' association, having spent nearly two million dollars for insecticides during the 1955–56 season, used parasites exclusively during the following season at a small fraction of the sum previously spent for chemical control.

A DIVERSITY OF INSECTS

These are the main predators and parasites which are likely to be encountered in the garden. Their numbers are great. The rich diversity of insects is but another aspect of nature's plan and should not alarm gardeners. A balanced supply of insect life, both in the soil and above the ground, is one means of preventing any one insect from growing in numbers to pest proportions. In California avocado orchards, for example, studies have shown the presence of many insects and mite pests that could be very damaging. But they are generally held in almost perfect biological balance by native beneficial insects and introduced parasites. In experiments, when these controllers were excluded from avocado trees, damaging populations of various insect pests and mites soon developed.

With the possible exception of disease carriers, we must abandon the idea of *eradicating* insects. Instead we must aim for *control*. Even if an insect-free garden were within the realm of possibility, it would be self-defeating.

Frequently the use of chemical pesticides has interfered with the populations of native predators and parasites normally found in gardens. Many of these beneficial insects have been destroyed along with the pests they controlled. Often it was not until we attacked the one or two obvious "enemies" that we discovered how much we had depended on "friends" we had known nothing about.

The problem of spraying is not confined to the area treated with spray. Adjacent areas also suffer. The beneficial insects may disperse to the area which has been made barren and the effectiveness of normally high controls may be weakened. Thus, your garden practices and those of your neighbors interact for good or ill. Education and community action will help to develop an environment in which insects are recognized as helpers as well as destroyers.

3. BIRDS AND OTHER CREATURES
IN THE GARDEN

The health of plants depends upon a living network of bacteria, fungi and earthworms underground—and a proper balance of birds, insects and animals above ground.

—*Dr. Fairfield Osborn, President,*
New York Zoological Society

WHO HAS NOT marveled at the sight of a swallow constantly soaring through the air, searching for insects? Or of the phoebe, sitting on a favorite perch, watching eagerly and darting forth to capture some unwitting prey? No one needs to be told that birds can play an important role in keeping down insect populations. This is a natural control, which functions without man's interference. But the gardener, aware of the value of birds, can create an environment which assures their effectiveness.

INSECT CONTROL BY BIRDS

Over a century ago scientists recognized the practical economic importance to farmers and gardeners of the insect-eating birds. Under both state and federal legislation studies were conducted to determine their feeding habits throughout their range and during all seasons of the year. The standard method was to learn what the bird was eating by identifying the stomach contents. This was only partially successful, since it failed to show the direct effect on the insect population. It has since been supplemented by other methods, including visual observation. Although the work is far from complete, we know today that birds are essential to insect control. Frequently an outbreak of insect infestation funnels a bird population to an area as though an S.O.S. signal had gone out. Although birds may not be able to control severe infestations by themselves, usually they can exert sufficient pressure on moderate insect populations to maintain community stability.

Half the food of some 1400 species of North American birds consists of insects. In the spring most of them, even seed-eating birds such as cardinals, feed their young a diet higher in insects than that which they themselves eat. Through the early summer, many birds will rear their young entirely on this fare. Week after week, from early dawn until the last rays of light, there is a constant search for tremendous numbers of insects to be pushed down the gullets of fast-growing fledglings. The figures are almost incredible. For instance, it has been observed that:

> a house wren feeds 500 spiders and caterpillars to its young during one summer afternoon
> a swallow devours 1000 leafhoppers in 12 hours
> a pair of flickers consider 5000 ants a mere snack
> a Baltimore oriole consumes 17 hairy caterpillars a minute
> a brown thrasher can eat over 6000 insects a day

Richard Howe Forbush of Massachusetts, one of the pioneers in American economic ornithology, estimated that a yellow-throated warbler could destroy more than 10,000 tree lice a day, and a chickadee could destroy more than 138,000 cankerworm eggs within twenty-five days.

There have been many recorded instances where bird control has averted insect plagues. In the early days of the Salt Lake Valley settlement, gulls were credited with saving the crops from Mormon crickets. During an infestation of coulee crickets in the state of Washington, western meadowlarks appeared in such great numbers that plans for an official control program were scrapped. In 1925 a plague of locusts in Nebraska was averted by birds converging on the vicinity.

Woodpeckers have frequently demonstrated their vital role in woodland economy. In 1937, Kootenai National Park in Idaho suffered a severe infestation of spruce beetle which was brought under control largely by woodpeckers. When an outbreak of Engelmann spruce beetle threatened the White River National Forest in Colorado in the summer of 1947, three species of woodpeckers were credited with preventing serious losses. Throughout our forests they are one of the chief enemies of codling moth larvae, accounting for the destruction of more than 50 percent in a winter, while by stripping the bark from dead trees they prevent the spread of carpenter ant colonies to nearby sound trees.

The U.S. Department of Agriculture had a dramatic experience concerning the effectiveness of bird control. Massachusetts experimenters had set out netting bags filled with gypsy moth larvae. Upon their return they were chagrined to discover that the bags had been pecked open by birds and more than 60 percent of the larvae removed. The experiment was ruined, but officials had witnessed control by a bird which is sometimes undeservedly despised — the starling.

Many accounts tell of the direct help that birds give to farmers. One describes how red-winged blackbirds, bobolinks, meadowlarks, doves, cowbirds, and field sparrows followed a mower during operations in a field and fed on thousands of exposed alfalfa weevils. Others relate how gulls and other birds congregate and follow plowing and harvesting operations as farm machines expose insects. There was an instance of a Minnesota farmer who started plowing earlier than his neighbors in order to attract large numbers of gulls, and he obtained almost complete control of white grubs over a forty-acre tract of corn.

ATTRACTING BIRDS TO THE GARDEN

Gardeners can attract a diversity of birdlife in many ways, by offering them food, suitable nesting and roosting sites, escape cover, and protection against small pets. Bird control works best where there is a diversity of plant and insect life. Some birds will be ground-feeders, others will feed at intermediary heights in plants and shrubs, and others will work in the crowns of trees. Some will search in the soil, some through leaves and blossoms and stalks, while others are preoccupied by insect life on trunks, branches, and limbs.

Landscaping should therefore be planned with a diversity of plants, shrubs, and trees. Wildlife borders, hedges, windbreaks, plantings of odd areas to trees and shrubs, and stripcropping of sloping fields are some of the techniques to consider. In addition to curbing soil erosion, alternate contour strips of crops and grass are known to attract more songbirds. From this point of view shrub fencing is considerably more beneficial than bare fences, and living fences such as multiflora roses will eliminate fences and posts to a large extent.

Sometimes minor aides are helpful, such as saving a "den" tree in the woods. If land is extensive and such a dead tree is not unsightly, its hollow trunk or limb may be left to provide shelter for mouse-catching owls or hawks. Chickadees, bluebirds, and some of the flycatchers may also seek out these hollows. "Releasing" an old apple tree by cutting growth which surrounds it will make its fruit available to birds and small animals. Unproductive odd areas can be planted to shrubs and trees to add wildlife food and shelter, thus finding a use for gullies, fence corners, abandoned roads, sinkholes, bare knobs, small eroded areas, and old gravel pits. Birds must have close access to trees and shrubs if they are to function efficiently as insect controllers. In the interests of the winter residents, some evergreens should be mixed with the plantings whenever possible. (Shrubs, trees, and vines which are particularly attractive to birds as food or shelter are listed in Appendix B.)

The gardener will find it most desirable to have birds year round. Some birds eat insect eggs and pupae in winter, and they are followed in turn by birds that eat young and mature insects in summer. Take for example the case of the cankerworm in eastern Massachusetts. If the winter residents, such as black-capped chickadees and others, do not do the preliminary work of thinning out the egg masses, the summer species cannot, by themselves, control the pests effectively. It takes the combined efforts of both groups.

The gardener can provide birds with additional food to supplement their natural sources in the vicinity. Even though this may not be necessary for bird survival, for the purpose of insect control it does encourage the birds to come and remain. Here again, variety is the keynote, since an assortment of bird food will attract a variety of birds. (A list of suitable bird food is to be found in Appendix B.)

A multiplicity of feeding stations, as well as a variety of food, set at different locations, will help you appeal to different kinds of birds. Judicious winter feeding will help keep insect-eating and insect-egg-eating species in the vicinity. These would include woodpeckers, chickadees, titmice, and nuthatches in the north, which are attracted with small feeders and suet sticks.

In our modern manufactured landscape many natural nesting sites have disappeared. Life becomes increasingly difficult for birds as well as other small creatures when natural habitats are lost in the spread of suburban housing and highways, industrial expansion, drainage of wetlands, and others of man's changes. It is especially helpful, therefore, to provide suitable nesting boxes for such birds as bluebirds, swallows, chickadees, woodpeckers, and other prime consumers of insects. There are specific sizes and requirements for each kind of bird, and building directions for nesting and roosting boxes may be found in many books dealing with the subject of attracting birds.

Nesting material is another thing to offer. Ordinarily birds find enough supplies with which to build their nests, but in well pruned and carefully raked communities, nesting materials may be scarce. Gardeners can provide birds with a suitable variety of manufactured goods that the birds will accept as substitutes for grasses, rootlets, feathers, spiderwebs, animal hairs, and other natural sources.

The story is told of the frugal New Englander who was known to find a use for everything. But after she died her heirs found a box in her attic labeled "Strings — too short to use." With some Yankee ingenuity, she could have utilized them for the birds. String of six- to eight-inch lengths can be offered in spring for nesting material. It should be kept this short to avoid the hazards of entanglement. White or dull-colored string or yarn is safest, since bright-colored material, woven into nests, may attract unwanted attention to eggs or fledglings better left camouflaged.

Robins, mockingbirds, and Baltimore orioles will use rag, string, or twine. Goldfinches will use strips of cotton, while cardinals will use thread. Housewrens, nuthatches, brown creepers, warblers, finches, bluebirds, juncoes, Baltimore orioles, and indigo buntings will use hair. Housewrens, bluebirds, phoebes, titmice, and chickadees will use feathers. Hemp, wool, horsehair, human hair, or sphagnum moss are also suitable items to offer. Drape the nesting materials over fair-sized tree limbs, or tack them in the bird feeder. The birds can easily pull loose what they want.

Perches, dust baths, birdbaths, mud, dripping water, and brushy places for quick escape are additional attractions which bring birds to the vicinity.

CONTROL BY OTHER CREATURES

Birds are not the only small creatures that keep insect populations under control in gardens, fields, and forests. No one species by itself is adequate to the task, but all together they can usually maintain a community stability which prevents infestations.

Bats are the night patrollers of the insect world. They begin their work as soon as the birds end their exhausting daytime patrols. Bats range far and wide in their nocturnal flights and can eat half their own weight nightly. Hence bat colonies can destroy tons of insects on their nightly foraging flights. They use their radar-like sense to locate insects as well as to avoid objects.

In 1917, Charles A. R. Campbell, M.D., city bacteriologist of San Antonio, Texas, demonstrated the value of bats for malarial mosquito control. City sewage, at the rate of 15,000,000 gallons daily, was being dumped into Mitchell's Lake, an area six miles south of San Antonio, and provided a favorable breeding spot for malarial mosquitoes. Dr. Campbell had bat roosts constructed. They were lofty structures, with dark hanging spaces, maternity wards, and hibernating areas. The bats, properly housed, thrived year after year and reared their young in the same location. They were afforded protection against their enemies — snakes, cats, hawks, and wild animals which might climb the roosts. It was estimated that each bat consumed nearly 4000 mosquitoes nightly on its foraging trip, ranging within a 28- to 30-mile radius. Dr. Campbell succeeded in eradicating malarial mosquitoes, using only bats, and aided by no other methods known at the time. The experience was hailed by medical societies and public health officials, and duplicated by municipalities elsewhere. Legislation was enacted in Texas to protect bats. An unforeseen by-product of the venture was bat guano, a good quality fertilizer. Utilization of the bats proved to be not only of medical importance, but also of economic interest.

Bats have been introduced successfully for other purposes. In the Yakima Valley in 1927 an apple grower who established some five hundred bats in his orchard succeeded in controlling an infestation of codling moths. In Germany today, at a bat research center, more than twenty different species of bats have been identified which feed on night-flying insects, and roosting structures are built close to wooded areas as part of forest management. Despite the growing problem of rabies-carrying bats in some areas, the usefulness of these creatures for insect control should be studied. Even if they are not utilized directly, recordings of their ultrasonic sounds may prove useful. (This is discussed in Chapter 13.)

Both toads and frogs are good consumers of insects. It is estimated that a toad can eat up to 10,000 insects in three months' time, and about 16 percent of this prodigious number may be cutworms. It also consumes grubs, crickets, rose chafers, rose beetles, squash bugs, caterpillars, ants, tent caterpillars, armyworms, chinch bugs, gypsy moth caterpillars, sow bugs, potato beetles, moths, flies, mosquitoes, slugs, and even moles! With a lash of its long flat sticky tongue, the toad can catch a variety of insects in movement. Certainly this is a fellow to welcome in your garden, in the strawberry bed where it will eat slugs, or even in the greenhouse.

In spring you can find toads around the edges of swamps and ponds, where you can secure some for the garden. Since they seem to possess some homing instinct, it is best to keep them penned for a while to adjust them to their new surroundings. Once they are placed in the garden, field, or greenhouse, they require some shelter and a source of water. A clay flowerpot, turned upside down, with a small hole broken out of the side, is adequate housing. Bury the pot in a shady place several inches in the ground. In addition, toads welcome a shallow pan of water, and need protection from dogs and other creatures.

If you don't have the inclination to secure your own toads and frogs, probably you can engage some children to catch them unharmed. It was reported that a golf club, eager for good lawns, presented a children's Saturday moving picture show every spring for which a live toad was the price of admission. If your requirements for frogs and toads are still not filled, you can purchase them commercially.

Other reptiles will make useful protectors of your garden. Salamanders hide under plants for shelter by day and creep out at night, when it is cool and moist, to hunt insects. Turtles in the garden eat sow bugs, snails, millipedes, and other insects. Snakes are good consumers of insect as well as rodent pests which would otherwise destroy crops. The bull, racer, king, and rat snakes are especially beneficial. It is estimated that one full-grown king snake (also called bull or gopher snake) is worth at least forty dollars annually as a pest destroyer.

If you have a pool in your garden, stock it with fish. Goldfish are good consumers of mosquito larvae, and so are the small topminnows called mosquito fish, *Gambusia affinis*. In Kearny, New Jersey, a six-story building had been planned more than thirty years ago. The concrete foundation had been built, but the Depression halted further construction of the building. Goldfish were put into the excavation at the time to prevent mosquitoes from breeding in the stagnant water which would inevitably collect from rain. In 1961, the company wanted to erect a building on the site and had to remove some 3000 goldfish that were still thriving and exercising mosquito control.

Small mammals consume insects. Hedgehogs destroy earwigs, while raccoons eat a variety of grubs and larvae. Badgers and pheasants consume insect eggs and larvae, as do skunks, armadillos, and mice. Skunks in particular are reported to eat the equivalent of their own weight several times a week in harmful moths, grasshoppers, snails, slugs, grubs, gophers, and mice. This may balance the fact that they will also consume berries and vegetables, especially corn, and have been known to seize chickens. But when the stomach contents of skunks were examined by the North Dakota Agricultural Experiment Station, 64 percent consisted of insects, of which 60 percent was grasshoppers. There was an average of twenty-eight grasshoppers in each skunk. In New Mexico another experiment showed that they were giving good control of the range caterpillar, which provided 85 percent of their food.

Although forest rodents such as mice, chipmunks, and flying squirrels are thought to be primarily plant-feeders, their food is 20 percent insects, and woodland shrews and moles eat a diet of 50 to 75 percent insects. It is estimated that half the hibernating cocoons of the spruce sawfly in Canadian forests are destroyed by mice, shrews, and squirrels.

The coyote is another creature that gives a surprising amount of help to the farmer, despite current attempts to exterminate him with poisons. Twenty percent or more of his diet in normal times consists of insects, and during periods of heavy infestation of grasshoppers or similar creatures, he feeds on them almost exclusively. In a Kansas State University study he was rated as worth at least eleven dollars a year to the farmer by controlling rabbits that eat grass and hay, and an additional ten dollars for keeping down the rats and mice that raid stored feed and grain.

Small creatures beneath the soil are also busily at work. Moles feed on Japanese beetle grubs and a variety of other insects. When the upper soil freezes, the insects migrate downward, pursued by moles. Although moles are accused of root and tuber damage, actually the other intruders, such as mice in their burrows, are the real culprits. Though burrowings may be considered a nuisance, they have value in aerating the soil and moving humus-rich surface soil and water to the subsoil.

The mole can consume as many as two hundred sawfly cocoons daily. The tiny shrew has an even better record. This creature is a mass of energy with the highest metabolism rate of any animal. It can gobble its own weight in grubs of Japanese beetles and cutworms within a period of three hours, and has been observed to eat over three times its own body weight day after day.

The value of domesticated animals in insect control must not be overlooked. Traditionally, plum and apricot trees were planted near the chicken yard. The hens ate plum curculio and kept the fruit trees in good condition. In the vegetable patch, poultry were turned loose to remove asparagus beetles, gooseberry fruitworms, parsley worms, and other insects. Hens and ducks were known to dig up sow bugs, slugs, earwigs, beetles, and worms, but leave the vegetables unharmed. Turkeys were prized for eating tomato hornworms and cabbageworms, although occasionally they pecked at kale, spinach, chard, or rosebuds instead.

Sheep and hogs were placed in potato fields after the crop was gathered to root up small potatoes which still remained, as well as potato tuberworms. Hogs rooted up cutworms in early spring and also were pastured in grass- or cloverland intended for later corn planting.

Today some gardeners and farmers still recognize the value of small creatures in controlling insects. They have "orchard flocks" as part of their agricultural practice. For example, a fruit grower in Michigan moves his chickens into his orchard. In spring he places a portable chicken coop between the trees, and allows the flock free range. The chickens eat grasshoppers and other insects, and at the same time add their manure to the orchard. Every few days the chicken coop is moved to a new location.

A citrus grower in Florida keeps peacocks in his orchard because they are especially good consumers of brown and yellow caterpillars known as "orange dogs." A few of these caterpillars can defoliate a young citrus tree in a few days. The peacocks eat slugs and grasshoppers as well.

An apple orchardist in Virginia gives skunks free range among the trees, since they are especially skillful in finding many grubs of injurious insects around the base of fruit trees and, when left undisturbed, will frequent orchards continuously.

Perhaps the best example which can be given of balancing the plant-animal community is of an avocado grove in Florida. Mice are greatly attracted to this fruit. Boxes have been set out in the grove to attract owls, which prey on enough mice to keep their numbers under control, but not eradicate them. The owls continue to inhabit the orchard since their food supply continues, and the mice continue to maintain themselves on a small percentage of fruit. The owner is satisfied since damage is minimal.

The more one appreciates the manner in which different forms of life are interrelated, the less one is apt to look upon small creatures as "friend" or "foe." Such an understanding was expressed long ago by Alexander Pope:

> Nothing is foreign; parts relate to whole;
> One all-extending, all-preserving soul
> Connects each being, greatest with the least;
> Made beast in aid of Man, and Man of beast;
> All served, all serving; nothing stands alone;
> The chain holds on, and where it ends unknown.

4. FROM THE GROUND UP

With some of our most troublesome crop pests, there is a direct relation between insect numbers and soil fertility. The less fertility, the more insects. Our experience and studies over the last several years have proved this. In other words, as we over-crop, single-crop and permit the damage of soil erosion, we grow more crops of harmful troublesome pests than we need to have.

— *Missouri Experiment Station*

IT IS NO SURPRISE that a healthy plant grown on healthy soil will have better resistance to plant diseases than one grown where soil is poor or imbalanced. But it may be difficult to realize that insects sometimes will attack the weaker plant, rather than feasting on the luscious green of the healthier specimens. In both cases, there is a direct relationship. When a high state of balanced soil fertility is maintained, insect pests and plant diseases are usually low. In fact, the resistance may be so strong as to amount to virtual immunity. But when the soil lacks any necessary nutrients or is imbalanced, pests and diseases may become rampant.

This observation has been made by countless numbers of individuals who have tilled the soil — gardeners on backyard plots, large-scale truck farmers, foresters, nurserymen, soil agronomists, and ecologists. The evidence accumulates both from practical experience and from experimental testing in laboratory and field. Yet, by and large, the health of the soil as a controller of insect pests has been ignored. There has been a failure to recognize insect infestation as well as plant disease as manifestations of some basic trouble. The appearance of either insect infestation or plant disease in a crop is often the first sign of a loss of soil fertility. But all too frequently the symptom is treated, and the cause is ignored. The crop is sprayed to stop the insects or disease, but the warning sign that a fundamental condition needs to be corrected is unheeded.

Today our attitude toward insect pests and plant diseases may be compared with the physician's view of human health and disease, now becoming outmoded, which was concerned mainly with external forces such as bacteria. The medical community has begun to shift emphasis to a study of the body mechanism functioning as a whole. What makes the body resist disease? The underlying causes of disease are sought within the body chemistry of the individual, in the hereditary and environmental factors which comprise the framework of the "human ecology."

In a similar way our approach to plant health and resistance to insects and disease should be concerned with hereditary and environmental factors in the plant ecology which produce vigor or weakness. Seed and stock breeding can be equated to the hereditary factors. By and large, these are the responsibilities of the experts. The environment — the soil, water, and air — can be manipulated and controlled by the individual grower.

What is your soil like? The answer to this question will tell you what you can expect from it in terms of plant vigor or pests. In the Book of Job it is written: "Speak to the earth, and it shall teach thee." Take a handful of soil and crumble it. Is it hard-packed and heavy, or is it spongy and friable? Is it light- or dark-colored? Take a spadeful. Do you uncover humus, clay, or sand? Do you find earthworms? The physical appearance of soil will reveal to you many of its qualities. Its structure, texture, consistency, porosity, and other characteristics will tell you some of its properties.

These soil characteristics are important in the prevention of plant diseases. Some plant pathogens will not attack in soils with temperatures unfavorable to them. Others will not ravage plants when the soil is well drained. Certain disease fungus can be controlled by the pH value of the soil.

The pH of soil, literally "potential of Hydrogen," represents the acid, alkaline, or neutral conditions of soil, measured by a scale, ranging from zero for acid at one end, to fourteen for alkaline at the other end. Neutral is placed at the midway point, at 7.0. Although many plants grow quite well over a wide range of soil reactions, most plants do best within a rather narrow range, from 6.1 to 6.9, which is slightly acid.

The solubility and availability to plants of many important nutrients is closely related to the pH of the soil. Although soils may be mineral-rich, if they are excessively alkaline or acid, they may lock up nutrients and make them unavailable to plants. Humus or organic matter tends to neutralize soil.

Portable home-testing kits, pH gauges, meters, and colorimetric indicators are available to gardeners who wish to analyze major nutrient compositions from soils on various sections of their land. Such tests can be made simply, without technical skills. Or, gardeners may send soil samples to county agents, state agricultural colleges, or agricultural experimental stations, as well as to commercial soil-testing laboratories. Although results will reveal the humus content, pH, nitrogen, phosphorus, and potash present, these tests are gross screenings. The pH analysis is not an index to total soil acidity or alkalinity, or a complete guide to the acid-alkaline requirement for a neutral soil. All too frequently the measurement of soil pH is regarded as a simple and straightforward determination. Actually it is a crude tool for measurement and interpretation, since other important factors in soil composition are not revealed by such tests.

Soil varies considerably from time to time and from place to place, even from field to field. Its formation is a dynamic, living process. Despite variations, the basic components are still the same. The gardener can vary the proportions of organic and mineral matter, water and air. Even when in the beginning the soil is poor, it can be built up to become fertile.

In nature's original setting of prairie and virgin forests there was a constant replenishment of organic material supplied by the native flora and fauna which the soil supported. Soil organisms continually converted the dying substances into humus through endless work, maintaining a permanent state of soil fertility.

But in the agricultural setting, the flora and fauna which are given sustenance from the soil are continually removed from it. In order to maintain soil fertility it becomes necessary to supply raw organic materials from which humus can be made in the soil itself, or to develop humus outside the soil, and to apply it.

Whenever agriculture has been practiced so that all wastes have been returned to the land, high levels of fertility have been maintained. However, the agricultural revolution which began more than a century ago has brought radical changes. The practice of returning all wastes to the land has been disregarded. The use of soil drugs has obscured the importance of organic matter. The accelerated growth induced by chemical fertilizers has the effect of speeding up the rate at which humus is exhausted. As this depletion proceeds, parasites and diseases may appear in crops. Soils have continued to lose organic matter at a faster rate than organic matter has been replaced. It is obvious that the problem of insect pests and plant diseases cannot be divorced from these agricultural practices.

THE IMPORTANCE OF HUMUS

Humus has been defined as the *product* of living material and also as the *source* of living material. It is the product of decomposition of plant and animal residues through the action of microorganisms. Organic materials are the raw commodities from which humus can be made. They only become humus after they have been broken down by soil organisms. Humus is composed of various decaying plant materials, leaves, dead roots, stems, straw, compost, manure, bodies of microbes, bacteria, and algae living in the soil. It is a vital material which can restore and maintain the vigor of soil. Its sponginess allows good aeration through the entire profile, and improves the structure. This increases the soil's capacity for holding moisture and avoiding erosion with leaching-out of nutrients. Humus is essential for plant growth. It not only improves flavor and quality in food plants, but makes all growing things more resistant to insects and diseases.

Many people regard soil as inert, but in reality it pulsates with life. A mere teaspoonful of it may contain billions of living organisms, many in humus, upon which plants depend for growth and health. Some of these organisms break down complex compounds into simpler forms. Others synthesize available nitrates, temporarily removing surpluses. As these are released gradually, plants have a continuous supply of nitrogen, avoiding excessive concentrations which predispose them to many diseases. A soil bacterium, azotobacker, turns atmospheric nitrogen into food. Some auximones and other growth-promoting substances act like plant vitamins and hormones, while other organisms found in humus produce antibiotics.

These helpful soil organisms are stimulated by organic matter and flourish in humus, but they may be destroyed in the presence of acid in chemical fertilizers. For example, beneficial predaceous fungi have been found highly effective, in England

and elsewhere, as controllers of potato nematodes (eelworms), but can only function in the presence of organic matter. Lincolnshire, England, was an area famous for its fertile land and livestock until potatoes appeared as a lucrative cash crop. As more pasture was converted to this plant, less stable manure became available, and potato farmers resorted to chemical fertilizers. Gradually the organic content of the soil dropped. Monoculture continued, and the potato nematode problem developed.

The potato nematode cyst is a structure enclosing from fifty to six hundred eelworm eggs which, when they emerge as larvae, attack the roots of the potato plant. However, the cyst may remain dormant in soil for many years, not threatening plant life. It hatches only when it comes in contact with a root diffusate secreted by the potato plant. The diffusate is extremely potent, even if diluted enormously.

There were many frustrating attempts to deal with the potato nematode, for the cyst resists all but the strongest chemicals. At last, the prime factor was recognized: a necessity of maintaining the organic content in the soil. Stable manure, compost, and other natural sources rich in predaceous fungi which attack the potato nematode, establish an environment in which the fungi flourish and multiply. Other growers can profit from this discovery.

Organic matter is equally vital for control of other insect pests and plant diseases. Wireworm attack can be reduced by a heavy dressing of farmyard manure applied to grassland before new plowing. Root rot is controlled by organic matter, possibly from antibiotic action of bacteria in humus-rich soil. In experiments where alfalfa was planted with cotton, there was no root rot, but the cotton planted nearby without alfalfa was ravaged by the disease. Similarly, root rot fungus of squash seed was eliminated by application of humus. In studies with artificial media cultures, a root rot fungus died even at the approach of the bacterial growth.

FUNGI WHICH BENEFIT PLANTS

One important fungus which flourishes in humus is the mycorrhiza, whose functions are not yet fully appreciated. When the
appearance of this fungus on tree roots was first reported in
1885 by German botanist A. B. Frank, it was thought to be
without significance or even a harmful parasite. Many scientists
ridiculed Frank's idea that water and nutrients might be entering
the tree through the fungus. Today we are finding that the
fungus acts as a link between the soil and rootlets of the plant.
In cases where the association is present, plants are strikingly
vigorous, achieve good growth, and gain resistance to insects
and diseases.

This symbiosis, or close cooperation, between higher plants
and certain fungi is common in the plant kingdom. Botanists
estimate that up to 80 percent of plants have mutually beneficial
relationships with various fungi. Among forest trees, and other
plants including food crops, the mycorrhizal association is widespread, habitual, and at times essential. It is stimulated where
there is ample light, an adequate pH of the soil, good aeration,
humus, and moderate soil fertility. However it is inhibited in
the presence of many chemical fertilizers.

Most feeding roots of trees gradually lose root hairs and become isolated from direct contact with the soil, resulting in a
loss of ability to absorb water and nutrients directly from the
soil. However, the mycorrhizal fungus assists the tree in obtaining its nourishment by taking up both organic and inorganic
nutrients from the soil humus and translocating them into the
rootlets of the tree.

In addition to these nutrients supplied from the soil, the
fungus exudes auxin-like and other growth-promoting substances
which possibly have a beneficial effect on the entire root system
and even the aerial parts of the trees. These exudates increase
the absorbing surface of roots, and profoundly change root metabolism.

The tree, in return, assists the mycorrhizal fungus by providing root metabolites, substances vital to the fungus for the completion of its full life cycle. At least one of these metabolites greatly stimulates the growth of the fungal association.

When conditions are favorable to mycorrhizal formation, the tree roots may exude antibiotics which inhibit pathogens. For example, root exudates of a variety of flax, which is susceptible to fusarium wilt, stimulate the growth of two fungus diseases: Fusarium and Helminthosporium. But a resistant variety of flax having prussic acid in its exudates, depresses both fungi.

The beneficial effects of mycorrhiza have been demonstrated convincingly in different parts of the world. Attempts to afforest areas which failed because of a lack of mycorrhizal fungi became successful after the soil was inoculated with pure cultures of mycorrhizae-producing fungi, or with soil taken from an old forest stand. In the U.S.S.R., for instance, certain steppes have been afforested with oak after it was found that seedlings inoculated with mycorrhizal fungi were able to resist the extreme climate. The same is true in Austria where certain high mountains were successfully afforested with spruce.

In U.S. experiments on prairie soil, inoculation produced beneficial effects on poplar cuttings with better growth and higher survival rate. White pine seedlings cultivated in inoculated prairie soil contained 86 percent more nitrogen, 230 percent more phosphorus, and 75 percent more potassium than plants in untreated soil. At the Iowa Experimental Station it was demonstrated that mycorrhizal associations unlock food elements from the soil. Experiments showed that pine seedlings with the fungus had four times as much phosphorus as pine seedlings without it.

Mycorrhizal association is of prime importance in tree nurseries and plantation practices. To produce seedlings with well developed mycorrhizal fungi, nursery soil can be inoculated with the fungus with maximum benefit to trees.

Mycorrhiza has been investigated largely in trees, but it has been found to be present in a variety of other plants including many cultivated food crops such as cereal grasses, legumes, fruit trees, and berries. Yet its significance in food crops has been officially ignored.

Vigorous mycorrhizal activity depends on adequate supplies of humus. There is a marked difference in the development of mycorrhizal formation on a plant such as cotton, which is stimulated by an application of organic material but depressed by chemical fertilizer.

ROOT EXUDATES

Not only do soil microorganisms affect roots, but plants may affect the number of microorganisms near their roots by excreting a variety of organic substances into the immediate area. Roots of many crop and pasture plants excrete substances such as amino acids, vitamins, sugars, tannins, alkaloids, phosphatides, and many other unidentified organic compounds. Experiments on white pine tree seedlings revealed the presence of more than thirty-five different compounds of root exudates, including metabolites.

Each species seems to have an individual pattern of root excretion. The nature of the particular substance released by the roots determines, for the most part, the balance of various types of microorganisms, and the total amount of the excretion released influences the general level of microbial activity in the area. Some of these root exudates promote the growth of nearby microorganisms, while others influence the soil reaction. Mustard, for example, exudes an alkaline secretion which can sweeten acid soil. Mustard oil, an exudate of cruciferae such as cabbages, retards the hatching of cysts of potato nematodes in the soil.

A Dutch nurseryman sowed African marigolds (*Tagetes erecta*) before planting his narcissus bulbs. By so doing, he found that he had defeated certain nematodes which usually attack the bulbs. After he repeated this practice successfully for seven years, the phenomenon was investigated by three Dutch nematode specialists at the Wageningen Research Station in Holland. They discovered that sulphur-containing substances called thiopenes are present in root exudates of African marigolds, as well as in many plants from the Compositae and Umbelliferae. When French (*Tagetes patula*) and African marigolds were planted among crops and trees on soil known to be infested with species of nematodes which attack living plants, the scientists achieved the same striking results as the nurseryman.

When marigolds were grown as a main crop, they cleared the soil of different species of nematodes, and did it more thoroughly than any other crop tested. In the majority of cases the degree of infestation was reduced by more than 90 percent, and the effect was observed as far away as three feet.

Other nurserymen were able to apply this knowledge elsewhere. To defeat nematodes which attack narcissus, they planted African marigolds as a cover crop before planting bulbs. In order to achieve satisfactory control, they found it necessary to plant the marigolds at least three months prior to the bulb crop. Marigolds planted around apple trees or between rows of nursery stock gave good control for apple trees used in grafting and budding.

Further application of the root exudate principle has been used successfully in city parks in Holland and elsewhere. Marigolds have been planted near roses damaged by certain nematodes. The marigolds offer good control, and the roses are restored to vigor.

The Henry Doubleday Research Association, with headquarters in Great Britain, has been experimenting with the effects of root exudates of another variety of marigold, *Tagetes minuta*, which will be described in detail in Chapter 7. The Association is composed of amateur gardeners and farmers from many countries, interested in pooling their knowledge. Their research consists of testing theories in practice with the help and cooperation of many orthodox scientists. *Tagetes minuta* has been of great interest to members of the Association since this variety of marigold, known as Mexican marigold, shows great promise. South African and Rhodesian farmers discovered that this plant kills weevils that lay eggs in the ground, as well as other soil pests. The Association members are attempting to determine whether the exudates are repellants or insecticides.

Over two hundred other species belonging to the Compositae and Umbelliferae have thus far been investigated for root secretions by the Association in cooperation with a British university, and this field of research offers promise for the future.

HOW SOIL DEFICIENCIES AND IMBALANCE PRODUCE PLANT PESTS

A soil may be rich in organic matter and plentifully supplied with soil organisms, and still not be in ideal condition. Not only must all the nutrient elements be supplied, but they must be in a state of balanced fertility. Any deficiency or imbalance of the major elements impairs the plant's ability to take up trace elements from the soil, alters its vigor, and makes it susceptible to plant diseases and insect pests.

Copper, for instance, has been shown necessary to give plants resistance to certain fungus diseases. But if the soil is sufficiently unbalanced, the copper may be *present* in the soil but *unavailable* to the plant. When calcium is in balance with potassium, potatoes are grown free of scab. In this case, balanced fertility apparently produces compounds in the root hairs which move copper into the potato, making it able to resist the scab fungus. In further experiments, it was found that a high concentration of protein in soybean plants, produced by inoculation, makes it possible for them to obtain copper from the soil, which in turn gives them resistance to scab. The important point seems to be to have the major elements in the soil in balance.

In experiments, when nitrogen and calcium were in balance

with each other, spinach was protected from insects; when these two major elements were imbalanced, the crop was attacked. Similarly, studies made in the fertile soil of South Dakota showed that nitrogen and phosphorus, in balance, protected corn from insect damage. One plot was treated solely with nitrogen; the other with nitrogen and phosphorus in balance. The first plot was infested by the lesser grain borer while the second plot was not attacked. The experiment was carried one step further, showing that the vigor bestowed upon plants may be retained beyond their period of growth. Sample ears of corn from both plots were stored in contact with one another, yet the sound ears were not damaged.

The balance of nutrients may be more important than the concentration of total fertilizer, when plants are exposed to attack by parasites. A deficiency or surplus of any one element may promote plant disease. For example, an excess of nitrogen promotes wilt disease by providing better nourishment for the parasite, and a deficiency of potassium increases the severity of many plant diseases. Outstanding examples of plant diseases which can be traced directly to soil deficiencies include: takeall disease of wheat, wheat root rot, Texas root rot of cotton, sugar beet seedling diseases, fusarium wilt of cotton, wildfire disease of tobacco, clubroot of cabbage, common scab of potato, bacterial leaf spot of peach, and powdery mildew and rusts of cereal.

Some insects are known to thrive on shortages of certain minerals, while others flourish in an overabundance. There are many instances of insects choosing and breeding more abundantly on weak and undernourished plants. Greenhouse whiteflies attack tomatoes only when phosphorus or magnesium are deficient in the soil. Chinch bugs tend to collect and breed more heavily on corn or wheat grown on eroded slopes than at the foot of land where the eroded soil minerals and organic matter have accumulated. It may be the high level of nitrogen in the vigorous crop which makes them resistant to attack. Noting that legumes are not ravaged by chinch bugs, experimenters were able to protect corn by planting soybean, a legume high in nitrogen, in proximity to it. They found that the insects thrive, breed better, and live longer on a diet low in nitrogen. For over a hundred years our outbreaks of chinch bugs have always appeared during dry seasons and we have assumed that dry weather favors the insects. This may be because crops draw less heavily on soil minerals during a dry season and thus the sap has a lower nitrogen content. One of the leading experimenters, entomologist Leonard Haseman, concluded: "What then is more simple in dealing with this pest than to keep soil fertility high with plenty of nitrogen supplied with legume green manures supplemented in other ways." He believed that improved feeding of plants has possibilities as a means of reducing insect pests.

Tests show that a boost in nitrogen increases the number of two-spotted mites on cucumbers. When concentrations of all major elements are doubled, mite populations also double. Higher rates of nitrogen and potassium increase mite reproduction.

At first, it may appear that results from these various tests are contradictory, since both mineral deficiencies and mineral abundances can increase insect and mite attack and reproduction. However, in both cases there is soil imbalance. Insect feeding and reproduction are affected by the chemical composition of the plant sap, which in turn is affected by plant nutrition.

Relationships between insect feeding and reproduction and the nutrition of the plant are not yet fully understood. Haseman wrote:

> In fighting our insects through the soil, we are trying to make the crop less acceptable to them as a normal diet. The insects' ability to produce abundant offspring is known to be closely linked with the chemistry of the food they eat . . . If through the soil we can reach our insect pests with diets that tend to slow down their power of reproduction we will have won the major battle with our insect foes.

It is important to make certain that any changes in soil balance planned to make plants less attractive to insects do not at the same time destroy or lower the nutritional value for the animals and human beings who will eat it. Current fertilizing methods often produce crops which appear lush but are deficient in key nutrients. At the Agricultural Experiment Station in New Hampshire, for example, excellent yields of brome ladino or timothy hay were obtained with high-level applications of chemical fertilizers, but the crops failed to provide adequate forage for calves. The animals showed signs of nutritional deficiencies, and, upon analysis, the crop was found to be deficient in mineral composition. The proportion of potash in chemical fertilizers is high, and potash has a specific effect of reducing protein and increasing carbohydrates in plants. Through years of continued application of chemical fertilizers, the protein content of food crops has been reduced in direct proportion to the increased use of these materials. Many insect pests prefer to attack plants which produce an unbalanced amount of carbohydrate at the expense of protein and trace minerals. Thus we continue breeding more vulnerable plants. Despite increase of yields, the concentration of protein in such basic crops as corn or wheat has shown decline through the years. Not only do such practices produce an environment which encourages insect infestation, but they lower the nutritional quality of crops for animals and man.

We can regard the presence of insect infestations as nature's way of eliminating sick plants. The insect performs the office of "signalman," warning us of lowered soil fertility and urging us to correct deficiencies quickly.

In many ancient systems of agriculture, the crops had been remarkably free from pests of all kinds, yet insecticides and fungicides had no place in the agricultural practices. Sir Albert Howard, famous British agronomist, concluded from his studies in India that insects and fungi were not the real cause of plant diseases. Plants were only attacked if crops were imperfectly grown or if unsuitable varieties were used. He considered diseased crops a sign of improper nourishment, and concluded that crop protection by sprays was an unsound practice which preserved the unfit and ignored the basic problem of trying to grow healthy crops. He felt that the key to disease resistance and insect resistance was to be found in soil fertility. He was also convinced that this could *not* be obtained with artificial fertilizers, but was absolutely dependent on adequate supplies of humus composed of both vegetable and animal wastes. He found that crops grown on land properly treated with humus resisted all pests rife in the district, and that this resistance was passed on to the livestock that fed on these crops. He concluded that soil fertility was not only the basis of health for plants, but also for animals and humans.

Writing in 1919, Howard stated:

> I had learnt a great deal from my new instructors — how to grow healthy crops practically free from disease without any help from mycologists, entomologists, bacteriologists, agricultural chemists, statisticians, clearing houses of information, artificial manures, spraying machines, insecticides, fungicides, germicides and all the expensive paraphernalia of the modern Experiment Station.

The Haughley Experiment in England, a project of the Soil Association, involves the study of interrelationships of soil, crops, and grazing of animals on a fully rotational farm system. The objective is the study of relationships of soil vitality, quality food, and positive health. The project is being carried out as a long-term program on a farm scale using three different systems of land use: organic, mixed, and stockless. Among other noteworthy observations, after twenty-five years the organic section crops appear to be less susceptible to insect pests, and rarely show any deficiency symptoms.

Louis Bromfield, in his experiences at Malabar Farm, Ohio, also became convinced that plants abundantly nourished seemed little affected by various insects, thus bearing out the English claims. Bromfield not only fertilized the soil but practiced foliar feeding by adding trace elements to the water used for irrigation. The solution was sprayed on the plants from tiny holes in a series of aluminum pipes laid on the surface of the ground.

Since Bromfield's death, the eight acres of vegetable garden on Malabar Farm have been continued, but without irrigation or foliar feeding. The same kinds of vegetables have been grown in recent years, and no chemical insecticides have been used. Since 1957, the only material used to control insect pests has been 1 percent rotenone.

The August 1962 *Newsletter* of the Louis Bromfield Malabar Farm Foundation stated: "In general, it can be said that the Malabar garden has not been seriously affected in its productivity during its long history by vegetable pests. More attention to rotation of various types of plants and continued improvement of the soil structure and fertility should assure the continued productiveness . . ." During this five-year period at Malabar, beets, peas, onions, lettuce, peppers, tomatoes, watermelon, squash, and parsnip were almost pest-free; on five varieties of sweet corn, corn earworm was prevalent in the later ones, but smut affected only a very few ears; flea beetles occurred on potatoes yearly, but had no noticeable effect on the crop; Mexican bean beetles were present, but foliage was not destroyed until after the beans had matured and were harvested; cabbage worms on cabbage, cauliflower, and Brussels sprouts were easily controlled with rotenone dust, bacterial wilt killed a few cucumbers and muskmelons yearly, but was not considered serious enough to affect the crop. On the negative side, root maggots seriously affected turnips and radishes, and this pest was not controlled.

BIOCIDES AND HUMUS

Poisonous pesticides have many adverse effects on the health of the soil. These may not be immediately apparent to the gardener as cause and effect, but their ultimate damage is unfailing. Pesticides arrest the activity of certain soil microorganisms, and lower the resistance of seedlings against unfavorable environmental factors. They also decrease the availability of soil nutrients, and interfere with mycorrhizal associations. Any soil treatment which tends to inhibit fungus activities may be a cause, direct or indirect, of an increase in parasitic larvae of many kinds. When pesticides are used, the protective mechanisms of the soil are weakened, and the plants are increasingly vulnerable to insect attack and plant disease.

Humus acts as a buffering agent for soils damaged by pesticides. In experiment, soils rich in humus suffered less severely from pesticide application than those which were light and sandy with low organic content. But while humus moderates the changes in nutrient balance caused by the toxic chemicals, experiment showed that the total effects could not be overcome. The work is significant for gardeners and farmers: If soil has been exposed to poisonous sprays, some of the damage can be lessened by the presence and development of humus.

BUILDING HUMUS

In the natural state, humus formation proceeds at an unhurried pace. Through endless cycles of decay and rebirth all the life sustained upon the land is returned to it.

For the impatient gardener, the humus-forming process can be hastened. Any vegetable and animal residues will break down into the same basic constituents, which will ultimately form humus. The different ways can be learned by observing nature's own methods.

One is the use of cover crops for "green manure." In nature cover crops are seen everywhere. The trees and mosses of forests, the grasses of meadows, and the bushes of hillsides cover land masses. Lay bare the earth and nature quickly hastens to cover its rawness with some green mantle.

When the wild prairie land was first broken, the soil was mellow, rich, and moist. It produced an abundance of crops. But after a few years of continuous grain cropping and cultivation, the physical condition of the soil underwent changes. It became finer, more compact, and heavier to handle. It dried out quickly, turned over in hard clods, and lumped when it was plowed. Although the perfect tilth and freedom from clods characteristic of virgin soil would be difficult to duplicate, some of its qualities can be restored by the use of cover crops.

Cover crops for green manure are sown with the idea of returning them to the soil, rather than harvesting them. The cover crops which are turned under add organic matter and nitrogen, help prevent erosion, and increase the water-holding capacity of the soil. The roots of these plants penetrate deeply into the soil, and, as they die, they build up riches which gradually convert to humus. Thus, cover crops become soil protectors, soil renewers, and soil builders.

As a gardener, you have a wide variety of cover crops from which to choose, depending on your soil, climate, and region. Your county agricultural agent will help in advising you. Remember that it is best to rotate cover crops as well as growing crops, if you wish to minimize insect pests and plant diseases.

For cover crops, there are many leguminous plants among the clovers. You may use common ones of red or sweet clover, or bur, crimson, Egyptian, Persian, or Wood's clover. There are leguminous peas such as cow, field, and rough peas. There are beans such as soy, and velvet bean. Other leguminous plants which can be considered include beggarweed, black medic, crotalaria (except *C. spectabilis* or *C. sagittalis* which are poisonous), fenugreek, hairy indigo, the kudzu vine, lespedeza, lupine, rape, sesbania, and vetch.

In addition, there are grasses to select, such as field brome, domestic and Italian ryegrass, and Sudan grass. There are grains such as buckwheat, pearl millet, and rye. Other possibilities include cowhorn turnip, Quaker comfrey, or even weeds. The value of cowhorn turnip results from its enormous roots that die in cold weather and contribute organic matter the following spring. The rootstocks of Quaker comfrey are planted in spring or fall. The huge leaves which grow on the plant can be shredded for green manure. Weeds can be used as cover crops if they do not draw valuable plant nutrients and moisture from other crops. Some weeds produce considerable amounts of humus and benefit the soil in other ways as well.

Other crop residues can be added to the soil when a cover crop is turned under to increase its organic content. Crop residues should be broken up by passing over them several times with a rotary mower. Both the cover crop and residues can be worked into the soil with a rotary tiller. Since the advent of small garden equipment, cover crops are feasible for many gardeners as well as farmers.

Composting is used in nature to transform materials into humus. It is also a method which has been used as long as man has tilled the soil. You can sheet-compost by putting raw organic matter into the soil directly and allowing it to decay while no crops are growing. Or, you can arrange compost materials in bin, heap, or pit and allow them to go through the cycles of change into humus and then apply it to the soil. There are many techniques of compost making, but of prime concern to the gardener is the value of the end product as a preventive for insect infestations and plant diseases.

Mulching is another method of building humus and soil fertility. You can reduce coarse materials to finely ground ones with a rotary mower. The finer the mulch, the better it composts. You can place mulch around growing crops, stationary plantings such as fruit trees (at least a foot and a half away from the trunk), ornamentals, shrubs, berry bushes, roses, rhubarb and asparagus beds, perennial borders, and rock gardens.

Mulch is an effective controller of some nematodes and root knots. Experimenters at the University of Florida Agricultural

Experiment Station used mulch with okra, tomatoes, peppers, eggplant, squash, cantaloupes, watermelons, beans, celery, and lettuce. Their report stated: "Rotting vegetable matter piled around the plants have a very marked effect in checking the development of rootknot and in enabling the plants to withstand the disease."

Trenching is still another method of applying organic matter in order to build humus. Dig a trench and remove the soil. Fill it with rotted manure, compost, rock fertilizer, and other organic materials. Fill the trench to the original level with soil. This system exchanges enriched surface soil with soil from the lower depths and creates better soil structure, drainage, and root development.

THE IMPORTANCE OF EARTHWORMS

Earthworms have been called nature's fast compost-makers. Research in England revealed that earthworms may pass through their bodies more than forty tons of castings yearly on each acre. In places such as the Nile Valley the weight of the castings is up to two hundred tons per acre. Nomadic tribes in Central Africa, realizing the value of earthworm castings, have pitched their camps on ground covered with castings in order to obtain the best grazing.

The value of earthworms has been noted by many naturalists. Darwin devoted an entire book to praise of them, and declared them to be the most valuable animal on earth, not excluding humans. Gilbert White of Selborne wrote in 1777:

. . . Worms seem to be the great promoters of vegetation, which would proceed but lamely without them, by boring, perforating, and loosening the soil, and rendering it impervious to rains and the fibres of plants, by drawing straws and stalks of leaves and twigs into it; and, most of all, by throwing up such infinite number of lumps of earth called wormcasts, which, being their excrement, is a fine manure for grain and grass. Worms probably provide new soil for hills and slopes, probably to avoid being flooded. Gardeners and farmers express their detestation of worms; the former because they render their walks unsightly, and make them much work; and the latter because, as they think, worms eat their green corn. But these men would find that the earth without worms would soon become cold, hardbound, and void of fermentation, and consequently sterile . . .

Earthworms aerate the soil, turn it over, bring up additional minerals from below, and increase the depth of the soil profile. As they die they leave valuable organic matter. The soil can be inoculated with earthworm eggs or capsules every year and also can be enriched with earthworm castings. The benefits of earthworm activity may be destroyed by poisonous sprays and soil drugs. Nitrogenous fertilizers, by their tendency to create acid conditions, kill earthworms and other soil organisms. In fact, a writer for a garden magazine recommended frequent application of a certain chemical fertilizer as the quickest and easiest way to eradicate worms. In Australia a superphosphate fertilizer on pastureland almost succeeded in complete elimination of beneficial hardy nine-foot-long Gippsland earthworms. Earthworm destruction can result in the compaction of earth, followed by a lack of aeration and porosity, which leads to lowered plant resistance.

SOIL AMENDMENTS

Where can the gardener and farmer obtain adequate organic matter to put into the compost pile or trench, or to use as mulch? Are we to believe the frequently repeated statements that sufficient organic material is not available? An executive of a large manufacturer of agricultural chemicals wrote: "The only natural fertilizer not used in this country which could appreciably augment the manure supply would be human excrement."

We read grim descriptions of the cataclysmic result of a barren agriculture without agricultural chemicals. Emotionally charged statements are issued: "Without products of modern chemistry, from fertilizers to pesticides, nature could resume its centuries-old tyranny over man." "Without pesticides, food would have to be rationed." "The price of most food items would double." "Without pesticides, millions would starve." "The United States simply could not feed itself without the aid of chemicals."

We need reminding that satisfactory agriculture has been practiced for centuries before the invention of agricultural chemicals, useful as they are in their place. It is true that today there is no longer a plentiful supply of barnyard manure, the mainstay of former years. However, we should not allow our concept of organic material to be limited to barnyard manure or human excrement. There is an ample supply of alternative organic materials available which suit the needs of large-scale farming operations as well as small-scale home gardens. Some of them are available within the community, free for the hauling, or at a nominal cost, while others are available through commercial channels. Additional ones will be made available as communities are forced to turn their attention to the pressing problems of water and air pollution. (See List of Suppliers of Materials.)

Today our waterways are being defiled at an alarming rate by waste effluvia from industry and urban populations. Hundreds of items could be utilized by individuals or farmers willing to collect the materials, and by municipalities interested in large-scale composting of municipal wastes. There are many opportunities for enterprising industrialists to convert these waste makers into waste users.

In addition to industrial materials, city sewage and garbage can be handled by municipal plants and turned into useful sludge. Currently, in the United States, we must dispose yearly of over eighteen billion pounds of sewage solids. This represents an increase of 70 percent in the past two decades. Not only does utilization of converted waste materials raise the fertility of the soil, but removal of them from waterways lessens the grave problems of water pollution and water-borne diseases. Such operations also reduce air pollution which results from incineration or burning in town dumps, those unaesthetic rat-infested areas which blight the countryside.

Some urban communities have sewage treatment plants, from which activated sludge may be obtained. This is a soil conditioner, especially useful for lawns, which is gradually receiving public acceptance. The experience of the city of Milwaukee demonstrates that such an enterprise is feasible. The activated sludge processed there as "Milorganite" has an annual sales volume of $3,000,000. The entire yearly production of 70,000 tons is sold without difficulty and is available at retailers of lawn and garden supplies in all states. It is used extensively on golf courses, parks, cemeteries, lawns of public buildings and private homes, and is also popular with mushroom growers and citrus orchardists.

The Milwaukee experience in sewage treatment is only one of a number of successful projects which could be cited in the United States and throughout the world. In addition, municipal composting of garbage refuse in many communities turns waste matter into useful soil-conditioning materials.

Fallen leaves provide rich nutrients for soil enrichment, and some municipalities have begun to distribute them gratis to gardeners for composting, sometimes delivering them directly to individual homes. Certain communities forbid the burning of leaves in order to reduce air pollution. Among other irritants in burning leaves, pesticide residues have added to the general problem. In the city of Hamilton, Ontario, a public notice prohibiting the burning of leaves and garbage refuse, ended with the suggestion that "the valuable materials be used for composting to provide soil nutrients for the next growing season." Another ingenious economy is practiced by a town in New York which grinds discarded Christmas trees in brush chippers and offers the chips free of charge to residents. In Florida, the state retrieves water hyacinths from canals, heaps them on banks, and those who wish to haul away this nutrient-rich material may do so. The Florida Parks Department makes available residues from pruning operations on banyan and palm trees for gardeners to shred and compost.

AVAILABLE ORGANIC MATERIALS

For the gardener who wishes organic materials for compost, mulch, trenching, and soil conditioning, there are many available materials which vary with the location. Some which are commonly obtainable include:

> incinerator ash and wood ash
> birdcage cleanings
> shredded bush trimmings from utility companies
> corncobs and stalks
> dust from vacuum cleaner and dustpan
> earthworms and their castings
> evergreen needles
> excelsior
> grass clippings
> hardwood bark
> sweet, salt, or spoiled hay
> leafmold
> leaves
> oak tow
> pea pods and vines
> peat and sphagnum moss
> rakings from under trees and shrubs
> sawdust
> straw
> tea and coffee grounds
> vegetable parings
> rotted wood
> wood chips and shavings

Weeds, diseased plants, and insect cases can be decomposed safely in the compost pile, provided they are placed deep in the center where the high heat will destroy them. ~~Flies can be~~ prevented from breeding in compost if the pile is covered with a layer of soil or well rotted material.

Depending on the location, there are many possibilities of obtaining agricultural materials:

> winterkilled bees
> chaff
> cheese whey
> spent hops
> hulls from buckwheat, oat, or rice
> pomace from apple, grape, cranberry, or castor
> rapeseed meal, cottonseed meal, or linseed meal
> residue from banana, beet, citrus, olive, potato, sugar, or sisal
> shells from coffee, cocoa, peanut, or nuts
> tobacco stems or dust

In farm areas there may be sources for:

> animal tankage   horn and hoof meal
> bat guano   dried sheep, goat, rabbit, or
> blood meal and dried blood   cow manure
> bone meal   liquid manure and urine
> feathers

Seaport communities may offer:

> cannery wastes   greensand (marl from the sea)
> fish emulsions   kelp
> fish meal   oyster meal
> fish scraps   seaweed

Lake areas may have such items as water lily stems or water hyacinths.

Large industrial cities may present:

brewery wastes
cotton hull ashes, cotton burs, cotton gin trash
hair
leather dust
mill wastes of lignin, silk, wool, or felt
packing materials
sewage sludge
basic slag (an industrial by-product from iron ore smelting)
tanbark
tung oil pomace

Quarries in the neighborhood may offer possibilities of:

basalt rock	crushed marble
dolomite	rock phosphate
granite dust or stone meal	potash rock or dust
limestone	

By now it should be apparent that there is no shortage of organic materials, despite the replacement of many farm animals with tractors. We must not limit our concept of organic matter to animal manures. Actually our increased industrialization has created a far greater variety of organic materials than ever existed previously. Many new waste products are the direct result of a greater diversity of modern industry. It is merely a question of locating them, and selecting those which offer the best possibilities. These soil amendments are composed of minerals as well as animal and vegetable wastes. In combination, they will build soil fertility and act as beneficial conditioners. Indirectly they help control plant diseases and insects by providing vigorous health for the plants.

ORGANIC SOURCES OF MAJOR AND MINOR ELEMENTS

If your purpose is to remedy a particular soil deficiency or alter the balance with a specific element, there are many more sources available than is generally realized. The primary elements mentioned most frequently are nitrogen, phosphorus, and potassium. For sources of nitrogen, consider any of the following:

animal waste	fish meal
blood meal	horn and hoof meal
castor pomace	linseed meal
cocoa shells	natural Chilean nitrate
cottonseed meal	soybean meal
earthworm castings	tankage
feathers	tobacco dust
turkey manure	

For phosphorus sources, consider the following:

animal tankage	cotton hull ashes
animal wastes	cottonseed meal
bone meal	earthworm castings
castor pomace	oyster meal
chicken manure	rock phosphate
cocoa wastes	basic slag

Good sources of potassium (potash) are found in:

animal tankage	granite dust
bone meal	granite stone meal
castor pomace	greensand
chicken manure	kelp
cocoa shells	potash rock
cotton hull ashes	seaweed
cottonseed meal	tobacco dust
earthworm castings	wood ashes

Elements considered secondary, such as calcium, boron, silicon, and manganese, have also been shown to exert appreciable influence on plant diseases. Calcium can be supplied with ground limestone, granite rock, or basalt rock. Boron is found in basalt rock, and manganese in granite dust. The others, as well as many micronutrients, are plentiful in a variety of soil amendments. For example, certain kelps, in analysis, reveal some sixty different minerals in addition to other valuable nutrients. Granite gneiss contains many trace minerals. We have a growing appreciation of the enormous importance of micronutrients for the health of the soil, plants, animals, and humans. Although these elements may be required in what appears to be infinitesimal amounts, the influence which they may exert is out of proportion to their size.

Home remedies of experienced gardeners possibly have their foundations in mineral deficiencies of plants. Some people have thrown a handful of rusty iron nails around the roots of roses and claim that the practice has kept the plants healthy, and free of insects and mildew. Another practice is to plant nails around tomato plants for relief from cutworms. Others have inserted zinc-coated nails in citrus tree trunks. Perhaps the iron or the zinc in the nails supplied some vital element lacking in the soil.

For interested gardeners and farmers, or, for that matter, for all concerned with eating food, there must be a recognition of the prime importance of soil fertility. The prophetic warning of Haseman should give us all pause. As we further deplete our soils of their essential nutrients, we shall continue to grow crops that are less and less nutritious for man and, furthermore, such practices will result in larger and more destructive outbreaks of insect pests and plant diseases. To overcome this vicious cycle, we must rebuild our soils according to nature's pattern. By so doing, we shall obtain far more effective control of insect pests and plant diseases than with our present chemical warfare efforts that attack symptoms and ignore basic causes.

5. PLANTS OUT OF PLACE

Definition of a weed: "A plant that does more harm than good
and has the habit of intruding where not wanted."
> — *Dr. Adrian J. Pieters, U.S. Department
> of Agriculture*

What is a weed? A plant whose virtues have not yet been discovered.
> — *Ralph Waldo Emerson*

FREQUENTLY WEEDS are held in contempt. Some gardeners
view them as enemies to be eradicated on sight. Anything which
cannot be harvested profitably is viewed as worthless. At present, a wide array of chemical weedicides or herbicides are used
to suppress certain plants. These materials are not only detri-
mental, but their use is based on ignorance of the importance of
weed plants.

In truth, we need a reorientation of viewpoint which will take into consideration the positive values of weeds as well as their undesirable qualities. We need to know their contribution in the larger setting of a balanced complex of plants of animals. Our best means of controlling them comes from an understanding of their life cycle, their habits, and their relation to other living organisms in the garden, field, roadside, or waterway.

VALUES OF WEEDS

Weeds are among the most vigorous and aggressive plants that form the green cover of our world. The tenacity that is sometimes the despair of the gardener has been the saving of soil and fertility in times and places where less resistant domesticated plants perished. Weeds are plants that may have deep and nearly indestructible underground rootstocks and tubers, that will grow again from the smallest portion of severed root, that reproduce by runners and suckers and layering, as well as by seed. This quality of hardiness has enabled them to endure drought, heat, cold, fire, and wind, and to reclaim burned and eroded areas.

Some "weeds" are, of course, valuable crops in themselves. They yield oils, potherbs, salad greens, condiments, drugs, and ornaments for man, forage crops for animals, seed food for birds and small creatures, and shelter for beneficial insects. The common stinging nettle, dandelion, and thistle all have higher protein content than cultivated grassland plants. Plantains and dandelions, both relished by cows, contain protective substances as well as nutritive elements.

In the garden many weeds are valuable soil conditioners. Their vigorous roots penetrate deeply into the subsoil where nutrients and minerals may be abundant, and transport these riches to the surface. The roots break up the soil and aerate it, improving its structure. Weeds help hold soil in place and protect resting land from erosion caused by wind and water. Some deep-rooted weeds can be used in crop rotation to break up any hardpan present and allow the roots of the subsequent crop to feed deeply. Among the weeds considered good soil improvers are annual goldenrod, nightshade, ragweed, and sunflower, which have been found beneficial when allowed to grow in moderation through farm crops. Other deep-rooted beneficial weeds include sow thistle, lamb's quarter, ground-cherry, and wild lettuce. Yet many from this list are subject to eradication attempts with chemical weedicides.

Certain weeds are valuable indicators of poor soil conditions and warn the observant gardener, just as insects and plant diseases do, that some gardening practice is poor. Their presence may indicate excessive soil acidity, deficiency of minerals, unbalanced fertilization, loss of humus, or erosion. Some weeds reflect poor cultural practices such as lack of drainage, poor aeration, or lack of crop rotation. The gardener can benefit from these warning signs by correcting basic conditions.

Weeds and earthworms have a mutually beneficial relationship which aids the gardener. Nearly all weeds have root exudates which are attractive to earthworms. The weed roots make use of earthworm tunnels to penetrate to the lower depth of the soil. In turn, after weeds die their tunnels are used by earthworms.

Weeds have beneficial associations with various garden plants and bestow upon them increased vigor, improved taste, and greater resistance to disease when grown in their proximity. American Indians knew this when they grew morning glories near corn to enhance root vigor. Others have learned that the presence of nettle or yarrow gives greater aromatic quality to herb crops. Jimson weed is especially helpful to pumpkin, while lamb's quarter and sow thistle aid watermelon, muskmelon, pumpkin, and cucumber. Lupine, a legume, helps corn as well as most other cultivated crops. Small amounts of yarrow and valerian give vigor to vegetables. Wild mustard is beneficial to grapevines and fruit trees. Dandelions, in the area of fruits and flowers, stimulate them to ripen quickly.

Stinging nettle seems to have a number of helpful qualities, changing the properties of neighboring plants and making them more insect-resistant. The iron content of nettle helps plants withstand lice, slugs, and snails during wet weather. Mint and tomatoes are strengthened in the vicinity of stinging nettle, while fruit packed in nettle hay is hastened in its ripening. This weed deters fermentation, keeps fruit free of mold, and bestows upon it good keeping qualities.

Redroot pigweed also performs a number of helpful functions. It loosens soil for root crops such as carrot, radish, and beet. It helps produce an abundant yield of potatoes. It is beneficial to tomato, pepper, and eggplant, improving the biological quality of the tomatoes and making them more resistant to insect attack.

Weeds have even been found helpful in the flower bed. Lamb's quarter gives vigor to zinnias, marigolds, peonies, and pansies. A carpet of low-growing weeds from the purslane family among rosebushes improves the spongy soil around their roots.

Even the most despised of weed crops may have a place in the total scheme. In many areas which have been badly overgrazed, the cheatgrass brome has followed. This is an annual weed considered noxious, yet it has the ability to form a ground cover quickly over denuded soil and thus prevent erosion. At the same time, the cheatgrass replaces plants that are host to the beet leafhoppers. Thus this weed is of great importance to sugar beet, bean, and tomato growers.

DISADVANTAGES OF WEEDS

Helpful as some weeds may be, they are usually plants the gardener wants to control. Weeds may remove nourishment, moisture, and light from cultivated plants. They may overcrowd, which results in poor crops whether they are cultivated or wild. On the range, weeds may produce poor or even poisonous forage, or create fire hazards.

Some weeds may act as host plants to insect pests and diseases.

Those which are of great importance in this respect include weeds from the mustard family, milkweed, nightshade, motherwort, and ground-cherry. But at the same time weeds may also act as hosts for beneficial predators and parasites. The same lamb's quarters that harbor the leaf miner may also play host to the beneficial lady beetle. For this reason there are situations which call for clean cultivation and others for allowing weeds to remain.

An enlightened viewpoint for the gardener would be to aim at *controlling* weeds rather than eliminating them. Weeds should not be permitted to compete with a crop to the point of injury. It is not a question of eradicating every last one of them from cultivated land, but rather of improving methods of cultivation so that they are not troublesome.

SOIL FERTILITY AND WEED CONTROL

As soil fertility declines, a favorable environment is established for invasion by noxious weeds. This is true both of grasses and cultivated plants.

Pasture or lawn will maintain itself as long as the soil properly supports the favored grasses. But let difficulties arise with the soil, and weeds will grow more vigorously than the grasses.

This was demonstrated at the Missouri Experiment Station with two plots of timothy. Over the years one was given annual applications of barnyard manure. The other had no treatment. The manured plot always produced a fine sward of timothy and yielded good quality hay. The plot with no treatment became so rank with broom sedge and tickle grass that the timothy required plowing and reseeding every five or six years. Hay from this plot was poor much of the time.

Both plots were equally subject to invasion by wind-borne seeds of these weeds, yet the manured plot, with its dense growth, resisted them. Broom sedge appeared on the poor plot directly up to the soil line dividing it from the other plot, yet it failed to cross the border. There was a sharp line of demarcation separating the two plots. The conclusion drawn there. Fertilize the soil so that it will grow grasses and make nutritious feed and these troublesome plants of no feed value stay out.

Other experimental plots at this Missouri station were planted to six-year rotation of corn, oats, wheat, clover, timothy, and timothy once again. The results were similar: The rotated crop plot which received manure, phosphate, and lime resisted invasion of tickle grass. A sharp contrast could be seen between this plot and the neighboring one which, without soil treatment, was unable to resist the weed.

These weeds reflected soils with declining fertility and crops with lowered nutritional values. When soil fertility was restored, the spread of such weeds was checked.

Elsewhere, soil amendments rich in phosphorus and potash increased the growth of legumes and certain grasses. With the exception of cocksfoot, all species considered weeds regressed with the application of fertilizers rich in phosphorus.

Where land has become overgrazed through the years, the perennial grass cover is weakened. There is a marked increase in objectionable growth which indicates declining soil fertility. A glaring example of this malpractice was witnessed at Grand Mesa, Colorado. At an elevation of over 10,000 feet, in a superb setting sheltered by Engelmann spruce, the ground was covered with vigorous bunchgrass. For more than half a century this grassland was severely overgrazed. Gradually the bunchgrass weakened and the land was invaded by lupine, sneezeweed, and needlegrass. The area became heavily infested with pocket gophers, that riddled the region, exposing tons of bare soil. The topsoil washed away. Excessive misuse of the land by domestic herds increased susceptibility to erosion. This case reflects the close relationship of the weed problem to the larger one of ecological management.

Attacking the weed problem with chemical weedicides does not remove the *cause* of weed development. Since most weeds reflect impoverished soil which is overly acid and wet, it is important to correct these conditions rather than to suppress the symptoms. Good soil management which raises soil fertility and corrects drainage are prime factors in weed control.

Chemical eradication in grasslands is often carried out during the active growth period of desirable grasses, the very time that they are particularly sensitive to the effects of hormone weed killers. This may lead to serious malformations.

But perhaps the greatest injury resulting from continuous use of weed sprays on cultivated land is the loss of foraging by the weed roots in the lower soil. Without this activity, which improves the sponginess, the soil becomes impacted. Valuable minerals and nitrogen in the subsoil may remain locked up and unavailable if weed roots are not present to channel them to the surface.

CULTURAL PRACTICES FOR WEED CONTROL

Although good soil management is basic, changing the environment for certain weeds is sometimes helpful as a control measure. One method is to eliminate them by a smothering crop which grows faster and thicker. In the country of Hunza, a barley crop is used to choke out weeds. Elsewhere, sunflower, buckwheat, cowpea, millet, soybean, and Sudan grass have been found effective. Rye overpowers chickweed, sweet clover smothers wild carrot, and zoysia grass chokes out crabgrass.

Heavy year-round mulch will deter weed growth by precluding access to light. Gardeners have found that mulch eliminates the work of weeding and hoeing; most of the weeds do not have a start, and the few that do manage to appear can be pulled easily, since mulch keeps the soil loose.

There is a wide variety of mulching materials for successful weed control. The commonly used organic ones have been mentioned in the section on soil amendments in Chapter 4. In addition, some gardeners have used ground dolomite rock in orchards. Such inert materials as aluminum foil, glass wool, tar paper, and many thicknesses of wet newspaper have been used along garden paths or along edges of gardens to eliminate the spread of weeds. However, the organic materials offer additional value, enriching the soil as well as controlling weeds.

Certain annual weeds may be anticipated to follow tilled crops. Once land is cultivated lamb's quarters, purslane, chess, and ragweed may invade, or perennials such as bindweed, quack grass (*Agropyron repens*), or nut grass may follow.

At times a change in cultural methods has been found helpful in weed control. The moldboard plow buries weed seeds deeply, and they may remain dormant for long periods of time. Then, when the land is plowed, the seeds, exposed to sunlight and warmth, may sprout. If the chisel plow or rotary tiller is substituted for the moldboard, weed seeds are kept closer to the soil surface where they may either rot or grow. The survivors can be controlled when crop residues are chopped.

Often crop rotation will help control weeds. Cover crops rotated with grain crops will suppress weeds. A crop of rye checks weed growth, and planted twice in succession it deters quack grass.

Some weeds may be introduced inadvertently. It is wise to select clean seeds from reputable seed companies. Such weed seeds as clover dodder may be introduced with bad clover seed and remain alive in the soil several years. Weed seeds in grass seed may pass through the digestive tracts of animals and still be viable. Therefore compost thoroughly before using it. This cautious practice not only destroys weed seeds but also insect eggs and disease organisms which may be present.

On pastureland, consider crop and animal rotation. By alternating grazing and growing, the sward growth thickens and makes weed invasion more difficult.

This system, known as rational grazing, embraces the ecology of land management by grazing animals on previously cut sward. The grazing reduces bare ground and weeds in mown sward.

Studies in New Zealand, on deteriorated mown meadow, showed that weeds represented some 65 percent of the flora. This was reduced to 11 percent on the same ground after two years of rational grazing with sheep. The full animal excrement was considered a fundamental factor in the improvement of the meadow. The urine stimulated the growth of grasses, and the manure increased the clover. It is believed that excrement favors earthworms, which in turn assist rye grass. At the same time, the excrement depressed bent, and completely eliminated crested dogstail, both poor quality grasses.

As a gardener, it is helpful to know the habit of growth of a particular weed in order to cope with it. Some act as "dragon's teeth." For example, witchgrass — also called quack grass — propagates by creeping underground stems as well as by seed. Each piece of root or stem broken off can develop new plants. Hence, if you attempt to cut up witchgrass and turn it under, still more vigorous growth may result. Sweet clover also continues to grow if chopped up or turned under.

Leave wild carrot undisturbed when it first blossoms, and after seeds have matured. If you mow it at either of these stages, it will grow two to five new blossoms instead of merely one. The wiser plan is to allow this weed to grow until seed formation is ended. If you mow at this time, the plant will no longer possess the vigor to produce new blossoms.

Handle purple melic grass in just the opposite way. In spring this weed has a late growth start and is slow to accumulate its reserve in bulbs at the base of the stem. Hence cut this plant early, close to the base. Later in the season it has the vigor to withstand cutting.

Cut thistle whenever it is sufficiently developed. This weed begins to accumulate enormous quantities of reserves in its roots. But as soon as thistle begins to grow, the reserves diminish. Weaken it by cutting at the base at the onset of flowering. If you can plan to cut just before rainfall, so much the better. The cut stem is hollow, and rainwater accumulates in it. If the temperature is sufficiently high, mold may result and hasten the destruction of the plant.

It is best to control annual weeds before they have a chance to bloom and go to seed. The seed of crabgrass, an annual, does not germinate until early summer. A crop of white clover, sown in early spring, can be established before the crabgrass has a chance to develop. Other cultural practices discourage crabgrass. This low-lying plant will be prevented from reaching necessary sunlight if the grass is cut no lower than three or four inches. An occasional drenching with water and fertile topsoil will also discourage this particular weed.

You can plant crops which are weed deterrents. For example, barley prevents wild larkspur or poppy from establishing themselves. Tomatoes check quack grass. Marigolds help deter invasions of bindweed, ground ivy, and ground elder.

INSECTS FOR WEED CONTROL

When a plant has escaped into a new environment where it develops into a noxious weed, biological methods offer great possibilities for control. The natural predators of these plants may be introduced unaccompanied by their own natural parasites and diseases. The control of prickly pear in Australia is a notable example. In the late eighteenth century cactus plants were introduced into Australia for culturing cochineal insects for dye. Various species escaped from gardens, among them the prickly pears, which spread rapidly in the absence of their natural enemies. By 1925 some twenty different kinds were found growing wild, and over sixty million acres were adversely affected, half of them so densely covered that the land became useless.

Beginning in 1920 the Australian government had sent entomologists to the Americas to study insect enemies of the prickly pear. Seventeen years were spent investigating possible control insects; more than half a million insects of fifty different species

were sent to Australia for trial. Several were successfully established. A cochineal insect, a large plant insect, a moth borer,
and a spider mite began to check the new growth and reduce
the density of the plants. However, adequate control was not
realized until 1930 when a moth from Argentina was considered.
In the first trial, three billion eggs of this moth were released.
Seven years later the last dense growth of the prickly pear was
destroyed. The land was reclaimed and opened for colonization
and grazing.

The ranchers in Humboldt County, California, have erected
a monument to honor a beetle. They have done so because a
tiny creature, the Chrysolina beetle, has saved the area an estimated $21,000,000 through its control of a range weed.

The Klamath weed, also known as St. Johnswort, or goatweed
(*Hypericum perforatum*), was a native of Europe, where it was
held under control by native enemies. However, when the plant
invaded extensive temperate regions throughout the world, including our own country, it was no longer held in check by local
control. In the States it continued to move westward and gradually invaded vast areas of overgrazed rangelands, displacing
more desirable range plants. The deep root system of the Klamath weed enables it to overwhelm even the sturdiest of grass
competitors. In some sections of California, grasses dry rapidly
in the spring, but the Klamath weed remains abundantly green.
Animals that eat much of it become scabby, with sore mouths
and skin blisters.

Beginning in 1944, through the joint efforts of the United
States Department of Agriculture and the University of California, the Chrysolina beetle was imported from Australia. This
small, metal-colored beetle, which fed exclusively on Klamath
weed, was thought to hold promise as a control. Exhaustive
tests under quarantine conditions showed that the insect would
not reproduce on, or seriously damage, other plant species in
California.

The adult beetle feeds voraciously on the foliage of the flowering Klamath weed, and when it has finished feeding and sunning it retires to summer sleep. It remains inactive during the dry season stage beneath some protection of debris, small stones, or crevices in the soil. There it stays for four to six months without food or water. During the same period the weed also enters a dormant phase. It develops and ripens a seed crop, but drops most of its leaves, becoming hard and woody.

The larva feeds actively in warm periods in the winter and spring. This intensive feeding keeps the plant stripped of its leaves over a long period of time when the food reserves of the plant are low. Ultimately the root system and the plant weaken from starvation.

The rains in the fall and early winter reactivate both weed and beetle. The plant sends out vigorous leafy shoots, while the beetle mates and places eggs on the new growth. Both the larva and host weed grow during the winter in relation to temperature. The larva survives the heavy snow and cold, but the weed suffers progressive destruction of its foliage by the leaf-eating larva. Ultimately the weakened plant succumbs.

This drama is reenacted annually. After the third reproductive year the number of Chrysolina beetles may reach a level at which they can exert sufficient pressure on the Klamath weed to control it. To date, some five million acres of infested Western rangelands have been returned to profitable grazing. Half of these are in California, where the beetle has held the weed to less than 1 percent of its former level. It is desirable to maintain this minimal percentage to sustain the Chrysolina. Since releases were begun, land values have risen, there have been profitable weight gains in cattle, and weedicide expenditures have been saved.

In the case of the Klamath weed it was not essential to kill an entire stand of weeds in order to control them. It was only necessary to weaken the weeds and allow more valuable forage plants to compete and eventually to replace them. When this technique is supplemented by proper grazing management and other cultural practices, the Klamath weed will continue to be held in control.

Many more examples of weed control by insects could be given, such as control of the poisonous tansy ragwort (*Senecio jacobaeae*) in the Northwest rangelands by the cinnabar moth (*Hypocrita jacobaeae*) from France, or control of gorse (*Ulex europaeus*), Scotch broom (*Cytisus scoparius*), and puncture vine by imported insects. Workers who investigate the biological control of weeds must take extreme care that the insect being considered is highly restricted in its diet. It is necessary to screen many economic plants to make certain that the insect will affect only the weed plant against which it is to be liberated. The life cycle of the weed and that of its insect enemy must coincide in the new environment, and the influence of interrelated plants and animals must be studied. To date there have been remarkable successes achieved with this method of control, and still more show promise.

ANIMALS FOR WEED CONTROL

Animals have proven their worth not only in keeping insect populations within bounds but as controllers of weeds. Geese, for instance, have been valued by many gardeners, and have been used successfully in cotton fields for at least half a century. They thrive on many of the grasses and weeds that infest the fields, particularly Johnson grass (*Sorghum halepense*) which chokes cotton plants and resprouts even when attacked by chemicals, cultivators, and chopping hoes. In a three-year study at the University of Tennessee, not only were the expenses for weed control in cotton lower for geese than for a herbicide or hand hoeing, but the yields of cotton where the geese had been employed ran 6 to 10 percent higher than in fields weeded by chemicals or manpower. This was on land where Johnson grass infestation ran as high as 65 to 85 percent.

"Cotton goosing," as this is called, has expanded rapidly in recent years in the Southwest, where thousands of white Chinese geese are rented or sold to individual cotton planters for the weeding season. The geese are placed in cotton fields as soon as the first grass appears in spring, prior to planting time. The animals have access to the fields early and late in the day. Their needs are simple: they must be protected from predators, supplied with water, and have their weed diet supplemented with a modest amount of grain which costs approximately fifty cents annually per goose. After weeding operations are completed, the geese may be returned, if rented, or sold to processors for marketing as food, or kept for the next year's operations.

Weeding by geese has been extended recently to banana plantations in St. Lucia, British West Indies, where they were shipped as a gift to the Peace Corps unit. The geese are reported to thrive on weeds which have invaded banana plantations without damaging banana growth. Geese have also been established among ornamental evergreens in a commercial tree nursery in Pennsylvania. The owner estimates an approximate yearly saving of seventy-five dollars per planted acre, which money would otherwise have to be spent on labor or chemical weed killers.

A Connecticut nursery has achieved good weed and brush control by means of one cow pastured on each two to three acres of land planted to Christmas tree stock.

Goats are well known as eaters of poison ivy. After harvest, goats, and sometimes sheep, are often set out to graze on minor grasses in fields of grain or secondary meadows.

On the San Joaquin Experimental Range, ground squirrels were observed feeding on broadleaf filaree, brome, and fescue grasses in spring, and later on tarweed. Prairie dogs also eat some range plants such as sage, saltbush, and Russian thistle, which are less attractive to livestock than other plants.

Apparently the little European hedgehog offers some value as a controller of weeds. In a letter written in 1770, the naturalist Gilbert White wrote of them: "They bore under the plants, and so let the root off upwards, leaving the tufts of leaves untouched.

In this respect, they are serviceable as they destroy a very trouble-some weed."

OTHER BIOLOGICAL CONTROL OF WEEDS

The weed-killing action of certain plant root secretions is being studied. In Britain, the amateur gardener experimenters of the Henry Doubleday Research Association, in growing Mexican marigold (*Tagetes minuta*), discovered that it destroyed certain starchy rooted weeds. The Association enlisted the help of several thousand gardeners, and this investigation represents the first mass attempt to replace chemical weedicides with seed packets. The target weeds are all noxious perennials, including ground elder, bindweed, couch grass, and ground ivy — against which selective chemical weedicides are not considered very effective.

Best results were obtained when the *Tagetes minuta* seeds were sown in May, on ground cleared of surface weeds, and allowed to reach a height of five feet or more. In some cases, the roots of ground elder were reduced to hollow shells, with browning. Some appeared to be eaten through, as if by an acid. These effects were found even at some distance from the *Tagetes minuta*.

Witchweed seed requires a stimulant from root exudates of its host plant in order to germinate. Researchers are attempting to find a stimulant that will cause witchweed to germinate in the absence of its host plant. One has been isolated from corn, and many more may be present in other plants. If these natural stimulants can be isolated, identified, and synthesized, they may be useful in control of witchweed.

Diseases, nematodes, and other biological agents may play a future role in the control of certain weeds. Accidentally introduced plant disease organisms have devastated certain native species, indicating that highly specific fungi may be discovered which could be used to combat some weeds.

MECHANICAL CONTROL OF WEEDS

If you are a gardener, working in a small area, who prefers not to mulch but to practice clean cultivation, you can hand weed at the same time that you thin out. You start hoeing early for less weeding later. The hoe, sickle, and small spade are all useful weeding tools for the small area. If the soil is in good tilth, it is soft and crumbly. Under such conditions it is possible to pull out weeds readily. When the soil is in a high state of fertility it is not necessary to wait until after rain in order to weed.

Cultivating before rain may be wasted effort in weed control, unless you remove the weeds to the compost pile. Rain falling on uprooted weeds may give them new life and they may reroot.

For weeding larger areas, the harrow, rotary tiller, field chopper, and chisel plow are useful pieces of mechanical equipment. Use them when the soil is not too wet or dry.

On grassland swards, use rolling for weed control. It damages certain weeds that cannot tolerate compaction. Grass and clover will increase, while weeds such as cow parsley, wild chervil, and knot grass will decline.

Rolling destroys horsetail if the life cycle of this weed is understood, and the practice is well timed. The stems of horsetail are slow to develop. If rolling were practiced at the time of the first cutting of grasses, the horsetail would hardly be disturbed. However, by waiting until it has developed its coarse stems, a rolling can weaken, though not defeat it. The vigorous root system of this weed supplies an abundance of reserve substances that will help it develop new stems. These will only be destroyed by a second rolling when the reserves of the plant roots are depleted.

Wild mustard and kale in oat fields can also be controlled by rolling. The technique should be used early in the morning, when the dew is still on the plants. The flexible oats spring up again, but the mustard or kale are broken.

A similar technique, called railing, has been used widely on weeds found on grazing land. Large nonsprouting shrubby brush, which is stiff and brittle, is uprooted by a heavy implement made from a railroad rail. This instrument is dragged over the plants to break them off and mash them down. It is particularly suitable for big sagebrush, and it is an inexpensive method of dealing with this plant. The method is not adapted to herbaceous or shrubby species that sprout from roots or have flexible tops.

Plowing is also practiced on grazing land for control of annual and nonsprouting perennials on areas which are relatively free of rocks. Since plowing destroys the ground cover, it should be followed by reseeding.

ROADSIDE WEEDS AND BRUSH

Undesirable herbs and shrubs comprise the "weeds" of roadside vegetation. The problems differ somewhat from agricultural weed control. In gardening and farming, the concern over weeds is usually within the life and death of an individual crop species during one growing season or a few years. But in roadside weed and brush control a long-term view is needed. Instead of turning roadsides brown in an effort to wipe out all existing vegetation, only to have some stubborn weed take over and demand attention year after year, it is possible to plan for a self-sustaining low growth which will be in balance with the whole plant-animal community of the roadside.

Whenever possible, this is the least expensive and most effective technique. A stable community of suitable vegetation can often be established which tends to keep out undesirable weeds and brush. It can be maintained by a periodic removal of unwanted invaders, mainly trees which have encroached as seedlings on grassland. Shrub land is rarely invaded by trees.

The oldest demonstration of such stable vegetation can be found in southern New York State, in the Ten Mile River Scout reservation where work began in 1934. Today, the area still exists in stable vegetation, a treeless plant community which resists the reinvasion of unwanted tall woody plants. There has been no expenditure for brush control for more than twenty-five years, and no significant amount of unwanted brush has entered. Many of the species have high wildlife values. It might be noted that the most important species are spray-sensitive, and would be destroyed in any of the blanket spray operations which are commonly used in roadside treatment.

The study was initiated originally by the Boy Scouts of America Greater New York Council, owners of the land, in cooperation with the American Museum of Natural History. The area was studied by vegetation scientist Dr. Frank E. Egler and his associates, who examined the geological substructure, climate, major plant communities of the region, and other factors of importance for brush control by means of low relatively stable vegetation. They were able to utilize the results of previous operations by a Civilian Conservation Corps camp which had been established on the Ten Mile River tract in 1933. This group had chopped down trees, blasted stumps, and removed by means of mechanical equipment the roots of larger shrubs such as laurel and blueberry. No bulldozers had been used and the native topsoil was kept in place. The original plan was to drag spike-tooth harrows over the fire lines wherever outcropping bedrock did not interfere with the operation, so as to maintain a bare-soil firebreak, and the C.C.C. proceeded on this basis from 1934 to 1936.

Thus the initial mechanical conversion of the area had been accomplished under unusual circumstances. Although the operation had not been performed for the purpose of producing stable vegetation, some of the results were useful in the scientific study. The work was done prior to the advent of pesticides, and clearance was accomplished at a minimum cost which could not be duplicated today. The project is important nonetheless as an example of operational procedures for mechanical conversion to low vegetation types.

Fifteen years later, it was found that in one part of the fire-break the ground was covered with a stable treeless plant community, low enough to be suitable as a truck trail in emergencies. This cover was being maintained without interference from man. Since there had been no invasion by trees, thinning operations were not necessary. Tree seedlings were held in check by the extreme density of the low cover and the matting down each autumn by falling vegetation. Also the small and feeble appearance of the seedlings showed evidence of repeated cutbacks by rodents and other mammals.

The Ten Mile River area is an example of what can be achieved when ecological knowledge is utilized. The actual cover types of this study are common, widely distributed, and typical of very extensive areas of the Northeast. The botanical principles involved are to a large extent, though not completely, representative of forest regions in all temperate climates, and in many tropical ones as well.

Scientists do not believe that every roadside can be brought into such favorable balance as to require no further maintenance. Such experts as Dr. Frank Egler and organizations like the Right-ofway Resources of America believe that for long-term planning the ecological approach will be the wisest and most economical. They would hope to eliminate blanket spray operations, and apply, when necessary, a minimum of selective herbicides in spot treatment only, so as to effect root kill, not just shoot kill. Once such discriminate maintenance operations have produced a stable low vegetation, no further herbicide applications may be necessary for many years, possibly even for several decades.

Although ragweed is valuable as a soil improver, it is frequently subjected to eradication programs along roadsides. Since this weed requires open soil in order for its seedlings to become established each year, it is reduced and controlled as soon as a dense continuous cover of other species, such as perennial grasses and broadleaf flowering plants, appears. But there are sometimes areas along the shoulders of roads, inadequately scraped or strewn with too little rubble, where the weed seeds in and forms a narrow "ragweed belt." It may also occur abundantly farther from the pavement when vegetation has been "opened" by previous herbicide spraying. Ragweed can be choked out by close vegetation when highways are constructed with shoulders.

Animals such as mice, deer, and rabbits all exert pressures on plant communities which should be considered in roadside weed and brush control. Their value cannot be predicted since their populations fluctuate. But their usefulness should be appreciated. For example, deer may choose a truck trail on a wide shrub-covered transmission line and serve to keep it open, even of brambles. Rabbits will sometimes ring red maple sprouts in winter.

Whenever hedges, brush, or roadside vegetation are destroyed, we should be aware that we are destroying preserves and covers for small animals, birds, and insects. A brief may even be held for such plants as poison ivy, whose berries are of value to wildlife and which forms a ground cover resistant to tree invasion.

It is apparent that what we consider to be noxious plants, like noxious insects, can be managed by a variety of approaches which are not hazardous. These controls depend on an understanding of biological processes, a view which shows us the foolishness of some of the short-term methods in common use.

6. AN OUNCE OF PREVENTION

> Probably more pests can be controlled in an armchair in front of a February fire with a garden notebook and a seed catalog than can ever be knocked out in hand-to-hand combat in the garden.
>
> —*Neely Turner, State Entomologist of Connecticut*

SNOW BLANKETS the land, and stark branches thrust skyward. An absence of motion is sensed in the air; there is no flutter or buzzing from the insect world. Indoors, snug and pensive, your thoughts are with the next season's garden. The arrival of seed catalogs is well timed, and the pictures of luscious crops, larger than lifesize, look like dreams of the things you hope to grow. The handsome specimens are marred neither by insects nor disease, but as you continue to glance through the catalogs you are shaken from your fantasy. You encounter the listings of sprays, dusts, animal repellants — these pages have a sense of reality. What can be done against the pests?

As you ponder this problem you glance outside the window. You are not alone against the insects. Movement and sound catch your attention. It is a flock of chickadees, searching for insect cases in minute crevices of tree bark. Wind-tossed branches tap and scrape against the windowpane. Such winds will rend insect cases from their secure moorings and dash them to the ground. The cold which frosts the corner of the windowpane will seal the fate of some insects in the ground. They will not overwinter to greet the spring.

Thus, some of the insects which might have threatened your future garden have perished without your intervention. But you must plan your own stratagems. This is done best during the quiet of winter. Fortunately, there are any number of cultural practices which will afford you good protection against garden damage.

First, list those crops not usually afflicted with insect pests, those with pests which are easily controlled, and those which give you difficulty. Over the years, experience will teach you the hardy ones to select. Discard those which bring yearly trouble.

Choose a variety of plantings. This practice should be observed whether the selection is for a vegetable or a fruit crop, trees, shrubs, or flowers. The greater the diversity, the less likelihood of a buildup of insect infestation. Mixed plantings also attract a greater variety of insects which appear at different seasons, thus providing a steady supply of food for the insect predators which usually prevent any single insect species from multiplying to excess.

Next, choose resistant and disease-free seeds or stock. Varieties should be selected suitable to your particular soil and climate. Seed companies and agricultural agents can provide you with helpful sources of information.

YOUR GARDEN PLAN

It is advisable to plan the garden on paper, keeping your sketches or notes from year to year for the purpose of crop rotation. Arrange your paper plan so that you have actual space allotments for various plants. Spacing has a direct relation to insect density. In nature, survival of plants is often related to spatial patterns. For instance, many plants drop an abundance of seeds in the immediate area, as do mustard, cabbage, and cress of the cruciferae, resulting in a nearly solid mat of young plants the following spring. When these dense plant stands are attacked by insects that overwintered, only a few are destroyed. The same number of insects attacking a stand less dense would destroy a greater proportion of the plant population. Insects and other creatures, feeding on crowded plants, help to thin out the dense seedlings, enabling the survivors to make better growth.

Spatial relationships are important in orchards as well as gardens. Air circulation is vital and orchards should not be "walled in." Standing air moisture favors the development of aphids and fungus disease. Trees should have protection, but the wind should circulate freely.

CROP ROTATION AND PLANT COMBINATIONS

Crop rotation is a good weapon against garden pests. Repeated plantings of the same crop encourage insect infestation, and crops also breed their own diseases in the soil. For both reasons, do not repeat the same crop each year in the same location. In fact, do not have members of the same family follow one another. For example, do not rotate melon, cucumber, and squash with each other, since all are cucurbits; nor cabbage, cauliflower, Brussels sprout, kohlrabi, broccoli, radish, or turnip, all in the cabbage family.

In planning crop rotation against insects, remember that the tomato fruitworm is the same insect called corn earworm, cotton bollworm, and tomato budworm. To reduce the possibility of plant infestation, do not plant crops together which are attacked by the same insect. For example, do not grow tomatoes near corn or cotton, or in the same bed, or after either of these crops, or after beans or peas. Flea beetle will attack both tomato and potato; if last year's crop of potatoes was troubled with this insect, do not plant tomatoes in the same ground the following year. The rust fly will attack both celery and carrot; do not have these crops follow each other in the same bed.

In greenhouse culture crop rotation is also important. More than ten times as many two-spotted spider mites were found where two crops of hothouse tomatoes were grown annually than where one annual tomato crop was alternated with radish, cress, or lettuce.

Certain sequences are desirable. A cover crop of clover, or clover and oats, following sod before corn is planted, minimizes white grubs in the corn. A cover crop of rye following sod reduces black root on strawberries and pink root on onions. A cover crop of alfalfa, repeated yearly, gradually lowers wireworm infestation, possibly from better soil aeration and drainage. Crotalaria is a valuable legume cover crop which aids in control of soil nematodes, while other legumes may protect grain and forage crops from white grubs.

Plant combinations are important, and you, as a gardener, can be guided by some relationships found in nature. Since various plants require different elements from the soil, crops can be divided into heavy feeders, light feeders, and legumes.

The heavy feeders include cabbage, cauliflower, kohlrabi, broccoli, Brussels sprout, tomato, celeriac, leek, cucumber, squash, sweet corn, spinach, celery, and leafy vegetables such as chard, head lettuce, and endive. Plant the heavy feeders in soil newly fertilized with well rotted manure. There are other heavy feeders among perennials and not included in crop rotation, such as strawberry, raspberry, blackberry, and rhubarb.

In crop rotation, the heavy feeders should be followed by the light feeders which include root crops such as carrot, beet, radish, turnip, and rutabaga. The light-feeding vegetables favor compost, especially when mixed with finely pulverized raw rocks.

Legumes are the third group in crop rotation, including: pea, pole and bush bean, broad and lima bean, and soybean. These are soil improvers because of the nitrogen they collect on their roots. In a live humus soil they may be planted third, but in poor soil they should follow the heavy feeders and will benefit from a light application of compost.

Consider crop combinations when you make your garden plan. Certain groupings are favorable to each other because their roots occupy different levels in the soil, while others find in each other's company the light requirements which suit them best. Plant compatible crops in proximity to one another. They give mutual aid, and, in doing so, produce more vigorous growth which may help resist disease and insect infestation. Whether it is a matter of composition, exudate, or other influences as yet unexplored, there is an accumulation of practical experiences of gardeners concerning helpful and harmful combinations. Planting asparagus with parsley, for instance, gives added vigor to both. Similarly, beets with kohlrabi or onions benefit from one another, carrots with peas, onions with beans, and strawberries with bush beans.

Some plants apparently are incompatible. For example, do not plant sunflowers in proximity to pole beans, since both compete for root space and light, with resulting poor growth. Do not plant sunflowers near potatoes either, or you may grow stunted vines and undersized potatoes. (Bio-Dynamic gardeners and farmers, a group that has given careful consideration to good gardening practices, has contributed practical information on plant relationships which is detailed in Appendix C.)

As we have already observed in Chapter 4, some plants have repellent effects on garden pests. You can take advantage of this knowledge in your own garden. For example, garlic has been planted in hills of beans or among flowers for insect control, while onion skins have been placed in newly planted cucumber hills against squash bugs. (More of these practices are detailed in Appendix C.)

Certain plants have beneficial effects on the vegetable garden because of their peculiar characteristics. The aromatic oils of herbs are important in determining which insects visit the garden.

TIMING TO AVOID GARDEN PESTS

Another part of your plan which will pay big dividends in some cases is the timing of planting dates and the use of early or late maturing strains to avoid the probable peak of insect infestation or disease. Of course this varies with each region and also with each season. For specific advice, approach your local agricultural agent. Once you have the general schedules established for plant and pest, you have an additional useful tool for your stratagem.

As an example of what you can do by manipulating the calendar, plant squash as early as possible to avoid borers which lay eggs in July. By that time the early-grown plant has vines large enough to withstand damage. Melon, pumpkin, and winter squash (except butternut) are not very susceptible once they are past the seedling stage.

In the region of Connecticut, radishes planted before April 1 and after May 20 and cabbages set after June 1 usually avoid maggots. In the same area a crop of early peas planted not later than April 15 may mature before root rot and mosaic ruin the vines.

In the early days, farmers seeded winter wheat in September, and anyone not finished by September 21 was considered a laggard. But after the importation of the Hessian fly, the stems of the early sprouting wheat were attacked. Now the Agricultural Extension Service recommends that winter wheat should be sown after the first week in October, at which time the Hessian fly is no longer active.

Timing is important not only for the individual gardener or farmer, but for large-scale farming and forestry practices as well. In southern Texas, for example, the pink bollworm can frequently be controlled without insecticides if deadline dates are established both for the planting of cotton and the destruction of stalks after harvest. When both timings are observed, not only is the buildup and spread of pink bollworm prevented, but the overwintering population of boll weevil is reduced as well. Similarly, forestry researchers identify and mark individual ponderosa pine trees susceptible to the western pine beetle, so that logging operations can be timed to begin before the actual infestation occurs.

GOOD GARDEN HYGIENE

Always keep in mind that the condition of the soil is primary, and that you need to start with healthy seeds and plants. But since conditions are never perfect, remain aware of minor troubles sometimes brought about inadvertently.

As a general rule for gardening, avoid handling infested plants and then moving on to healthy ones, as you may spread the infection by contact. In working with trees, too, avoid spreading disease organisms. Clean your tools thoroughly after pruning diseased trees. Make certain that wounds are cleancut and sealed with tar or commercial materials to keep out moisture and prevent insects or pathogens from entering.

It is also a sensible practice to stay out of the garden when it is wet. At such times plants are tender and bruise or break more readily, making them vulnerable to mildew and rot. Certain fungi and bacteria that produce plant diseases thrive on moisture and move from leaf to leaf during rainy periods.

However, some diseases are more destructive in dry weather than in moist periods. In this case mulch and irrigation both help to maintain soil moisture, thus staving off wilt disease in tomatoes, cucurbits, eggplants, and cabbages, as well as pea root rot and blossom end rot on tomatoes.

In the battle against garden pests, good hygienic practices help. Keep the garden or orchard clear of rubbish, old baskets, sacks, and other debris. Such materials can harbor destructive organisms such as pea weevils, striped cucumber beetles, and squash bugs.

A knowledge of the habits of insects will help in planning useful sanitation measures. For example, codling moth larvae cocoons are often spun in protected places like apple boxes, or a packing shed. If the harvesting equipment is stored in a shed, moths will soon emerge. For this reason, these areas may be screened or equipped with electric grid traps, to prevent the moths from escaping into the orchard.

In the spring dislodge codling moth larvae which have over-wintered under loose rough bark by gently scraping off the loose bark onto a sheet or canvas placed under the tree. The debris can be buried deep in the compost pile where it will decompose safely.

Decaying dropped fruit and vegetables provide a favorable environment for disease organisms and insect larvae, and they should be picked up soon after they fall. Infestation of curculio can be reduced by raking up the small dropped fruits early and placing them in the sun where the curculio dry up, or by putting the fruit in the interior of the compost pile, where it is destroyed by fermentation. Brown rot is more readily controlled by systematic removal of infected stone fruit and removal of mummies from the trees.

EARLY SEASON PRACTICES

There are many cultural practices available to the gardener during the growing period which will offer control of garden pests. They are based on an understanding of the life cycles and the habits of the insects, as well as the environments which favor plant diseases. Such preventive work, as we have seen, over the years is far safer and more effective than the dependence on one more poisonous pesticide for each new pest.

If you have previously established lady beetles, praying mantis egg cases, or cards of trichogramma, early spring is the season when these beneficial insects begin to aid you.

In the small garden, plan to provide a few minutes of close observation each morning in early spring to destroy egg clusters. Before the sun is strong, bean beetles on cucurbits and beans are sluggish. Pick them off and destroy them. You can easily locate slugs, caterpillars, squash stinkbugs, Colorado potato beetles, harlequin bugs, tobacco hornworms, and cutworms. Hand pick these pests. Remove mealybugs on individual specimens with a toothpick, wooden matchstick, a pair of tweezers, or a cotton swab dipped in alcohol.

In some cases dust deposits on plants inhibit the activities of natural enemies such as parasites and predators, and favor the increase in pests. Dusts may be produced by numerous practices such as frequent disking of loose dry soil, ash deposits from nearby burning of rubbish, field roads, nearby building operations, or ditch digging. Whenever you can eliminate or minimize such sources of dust, you may tip the balance to favor natural enemies. Sometimes the dusty field road can be oiled. In other cases you can limit dust by using mulch rather than cultivating the soil.

PHYSICAL AIDES

Young seedlings are especially vulnerable to insects and small creatures in the garden. There are numerous aides which afford some protection, including small cheesecloth tents, temporary wire cages or screens, plastic netting, hot caps, or makeshift devices such as waxed milk containers with bottoms and tops removed. (Commercial aides may be found in the List of Suppliers of Materials.)

To protect young cabbage and similar crops against root maggot, set tar paper discs around each plant immediately after planting. Purchase the discs readymade at garden supply dealers, or make your own as follows. Cut a four-inch square or circle from tar paper, punching a hole in the center with a spike. Cut a slit from the outer edge to the center hole to fit the paper around the stem of the plant. Hold the edges of it down firmly with soil. The disc must fit the stem tightly to prevent the adult fly from laying her eggs in the soil at the base of the plant. The fly is repelled by the tar paper odor as well as the physical barrier.

To protect young plants from cutworm damage use commercial wrappers, or homemade stiff paper collars wrapped around the stems of young plants. Cut the paper three inches wide, extending one inch into the soil, two inches above it, and clearing the stems by a half inch. Hold the collar together with a paper clip or pin.

Banding of tree trunks is useful for keeping crawling insects such as cankerworms, white-fringed beetles, and climbing cutworms from ascending. Apply rings of tar or other viscous material early in spring before insects emerge. Exercise care to form a complete band around the trunk, from two to four inches wide and at least 1/16 inch thick. Apply narrower bands around the spurs and canes of vines, or stems of shrubs or plants. Commercial non-toxic compounds in can, tube, and aerosol are available.

In addition, tree bands are sold, if you prefer indirect application. Place the removable prepared banding material with the "wool" side to the bark of the tree. The paper side is coated with a compound.

TILLAGE

Plowing and cultivating can be helpful in your preventive campaign, if you know the habits of the particular pest. The western cutworm, for instance, dies quickly after it hatches in spring if all the newly sprouted vegetation is killed by thorough cultivation as soon as the worms have had a little time to feed. They will die more quickly after having begun to feed than if they have had no food at all.

In experimental plots, by plowing under and disking second-year sweet clover before it reached its full bloom in spring, 99 percent mortality was achieved with sweet clover weevils. The early plowing destroyed the food supply of the larvae.

Rotary tilling of soil in late spring brings June beetles to the surface where the birds will prey upon them. However it has been found that the multifurrow tractor plow does not allow grub-eating birds time enough to seize grubs before the freshly turned up soil is covered up once again by the next furrow.

A rotary tiller can also be used against the European corn borer. It can chop the corn stalks, shred and cover them with soil at the end of the season, thus denying both air and light to the eggs laid inside the cornstalks.

A thorough tillage of the surface of the soil during summer months kills many pupae of the curculio. In times of grasshopper infestation, post-harvest plowing discourages egg laying, while tilling the following spring before seeding prevents grasshoppers emerging from eggs which are still present.

OTHER HELPFUL PRACTICES

Heavy rolling destroys the larvae of certain pests such as white grubs. If they are to be affected by the pressure, they must have returned sufficiently near the surface after overwintering.

Summer fallowing of land is a practice which has been used primarily for the conservation of moisture. In Canada this practice of allowing land to remain untilled has been found highly effective as a means of pest regulation. Not only does it control weeds, but it prevents egg laying by grasshoppers. Since the crust is undisturbed during the flight of the moth of the pale western cutworm, this fallowing practice prevents egg laying and infestation in the succeeding year.

Sometimes the combination of a number of cultural practices is needed against a particular insect. Take the seed-corn maggot, for instance. Since it may breed in soil where raw manure is applied, the use of well rotted manure is essential. Then corn is susceptible to injury from the maggot before the seeds germinate; if the seedbed is prepared to promote rapid germination, and the seeds are planted shallow, some trouble can be avoided. Cool wet periods retard germination and tend to promote injury by maggots. Timing is also important; it is possible to delay planting until the first generation of seed-corn maggots has reached the pupal stage, but before the second generation has made enough of a start to make trouble. Seed-corn maggot damage to potato seed pieces can be prevented by allowing the cut seed pieces to form a protective layer and heal before planting. Maggots are known to attack the sound pieces only when the skin is broken or the surface is injured.

Infestations by the white-fringed beetle may be kept low by a similar campaign, using a multiplicity of practices. Since this pest prefers legumes, oats or other small grains should be planted instead, in potentially infested fields. No more than one fourth of the cropland should be planted in annual legumes, and the same land should be planted with these crops not more than once in every three or four years. Corn should not be intercropped with leguminous crops of peanut, soybean, crotalaria, or velvet bean.

Infestations of the chinch bug may also be kept low by a variety of cultural practices. When legumes are grown among small grains and corn, the legumes may produce conditions favorable to chinch bugs; hence non-grass crops should be grown adjacent to fields of small grain. Whatever promotes thick vigorous growth of small grains, such as thorough tillage, ample fertilization, and timely seeding, helps reduce injury from chinch bugs.

White grubs are reduced by rotating deep-rooted legumes unfavorable to them. Such legumes as alfalfa, sweet clover and other clovers can be planted with crops which are susceptible, such as timothy and small grains. Legumes are most effective when planted in years of anticipated major beetle flights.

LATE SEASON PRACTICES

It is important to dispose of pest-laden crop residues *properly* rather than to destroy them. For many years it was recommended practice to burn infested stalks and vines. However it is now recognized that by so doing the natural enemies which attack the pests may also be destroyed. For example, in Louisiana it was an old custom to burn remaining stubble and debris after sugarcane was cut. But it was discovered that this practice actually favored the sugarcane borer because most of its natural enemies hibernating in the debris were also destroyed.

Proper disposal is based on a knowledge of the particular insect, and the case of the pink bollworm serves as a good example. When operations are begun early and the stalks of cotton are cut with a stalk cutter and crushed to the ground, the insects are exposed to the heat of the sun, and many perish. Following this, the roots are plowed out and the crop debris plowed under. This destroys any seedlings or sprouted cotton plants which may have developed, and allows a long pest-free period between crops.

Plowing under refuse as soon as a crop is harvested is helpful in regulating many insect pests, including the harlequin bug, corn borer, sugarcane borer, sweet pea weevil, and pea weevil. Trash shields, wires, and chains simplify this practice. Many insects which infest wheat, such as Hessian fly, stem sawfly, midge, and joinworm, can be eliminated by burying refuse deep in the compost pile.

Late season sanitation is helpful in the garden. Seek out egg masses laid by the tent caterpillar, tussock moth, brown-tail moth, fall webworm, bagworm, and others to reduce the overwintering population for the following season. After removing the egg cases, destroy them.

In the town of Wilton, Connecticut, five hundred boy scouts undertook as a service project the collection of tent caterpillar egg masses found mostly on the twigs of black cherry trees. Total removal would be undesirable by reducing normal food sources for birds, but it would be nearly impossible to achieve complete eradication from any area.

Pruning and applying dormant oil sprays (see Chapter 7) are activities in the late season of the garden. In putting the garden to rest for the following year, the gardener appreciates that "a strong man armed keepeth his palace in peace."

7. EMERGENCY MEASURES:
SIMPLE SPRAYS AND OTHER MATERIALS

The proposed decoctions and washes we are well satisfied, in the majority of instances, are as useless in application as they are ridiculous in composition, and if the work of destroying insects is to be accomplished satisfactorily, we feel confident that it will have to be the result of no chemical preparations, but of simple means, directed by a knowledge of the history and habits of the depredators.
— *Editorial in the first number*
of The Practical Entomologist, 1865

REGARDLESS of how carefully the gardener plans and carries out good practices, there may be times when insect pests or plant diseases threaten to get out of control. The gardener must distinguish between a moderate amount of insect life, and the buildup of an insect pest to the proportions of an infestation. In the former case, there are probably enough natural controls at work in the garden to maintain balance. In the latter case, however, the gardener must decide upon a course of action. Emergency situations may arise from conditions outside the gardener's province: unusual drought or excessive rain, pesticidal drift from a neighboring property, diseased stock or poor seed.

There are emergency measures which are not toxic or self-defeating, but offer relief. Many of the materials are simple, readily available, and inexpensive. They should be given first consideration in meeting emergencies. All soil amendments which provide vigorous health for plants indirectly aid in controlling diseases and insect pests. Gardeners have found certain amendments, especially those rich in minerals, useful for direct control in emergencies. For instance, kelp is highly prized as the best single soil additive, both as a preventative and for emergencies. Ground rock phosphate is used against flea beetles and striped cucumber beetles, as well as against flies in the stable. Granite meal or dust is helpful in preventing attack by insects, mites, and fungi.

Dry powdery materials, including lime, tobacco, and road dust, have been used by gardeners to combat striped cucumber beetles. Every few days these materials are dusted on leaves wet with dew, covering not only the top surfaces but the undersides as well. Very fine road dust has been sprinkled over cabbage heads against cabbageworms, and on cucurbits against striped cucumber beetles.

Wood ashes are a versatile material, used around the base of cauliflower and onion plants to control maggots, against club root, red spiders, bean beetles, and scab on beets and turnips, aphids on peas and lettuce, and around plants such as corn which need strong stalks. To control tree borers, some gardeners make a thin paste of wood ashes and water, painting this mixture on the trunks of trees. To control cucumber beetles, a handful each of wood ashes and hydrated lime are diluted in two gallons of water and this mixture is sprayed on the upper and lower sides of cucurbit leaves.

Several sources of calcium have been used for insect control. William Bartram, the eighteenth-century American naturalist, observed that ground oystershell was placed around roots of apple, peach, and plum trees to reduce insect damage. Crushed eggshell has been strewn around plants and covered with soil to control cutworms. Steamed bone meal repels ants and prevents them from spreading aphids, and it keeps leaf rollers away from strawberry plants.

Various tobacco wastes are helpful in small amounts. Tobacco stem meal discourages slugs, aphids, and other insect pests. Tobacco dust serves as insecticide and fungicide against root maggots and wireworms. It protects radish and cabbage seedlings from flea beetles, and, added to mulch, it controls wilt on tomatoes.

SIMPLE SPRAYS

Water. The simplest and least toxic spray of all consists of water. Confine its use to plants not damaged by frequent watering. For example, wash off young cabbageworms from plants. Dislodge mealybugs from infested plants by a forcible stream. Eliminate red spider mites by persistent syringing of the undersurface of leaves. Use force but little water to avoid drenching the bed or washing away soil from the plant. Use an ordinary sprayer or a pressure tank.

Aphids dislodged with water generally fail to return. Alder blight aphids and other aphids as well as flea beetles can be removed with a stiff stream of water. This treatment is especially good during a dry season when these insects are apt to be numerous.

If a small plant is infected with aphids, submerge it briefly in water which is 125°F. Use the same treatment for rose bugs, having the water between 125° and 135°F. The plants will not suffer injury.

Apple growers were advised to use water spray in spring, in conjunction with other measures, for effective control of codling moth. Dwight Powell, of the University of Illinois, recommended spraying of loose bark to dislodge the larvae. He suggested using a standard orchard sprayer, with a pressure stream of water, held two to four feet away from the tree, directed against the trunk, large branches where bark is loose or rough, the crotch, and punky areas. He also advised directing the water stream downward at a 45° angle at the bottom of the trunk.

Whitewash. Whitewash, a solution of lime in water, is an oldtime material thought to be of some value to fruit trees by reducing insects and disease organisms that burrow in the bark tissues, possibly killing insect eggs. It has been found helpful against peach tree bark beetles, and may prevent some scald and heat injury in bark tissues of very young trees, especially in hot sunny regions of the country. Whitewash is applied three times a season to the trunk and main branches, beginning in early spring. It is brushed on the base of the tree, three feet up the body.

Diatomaceous earth. Diatomaceous earth originates from ancient deposits of many tiny marine creatures and is a valuable source of minerals and trace elements. It can be mixed with water and sprayed on both sides of leaves of roses, citrus plants and others against aphids, red spiders, and on tomatoes to combat mildew. When the spray dries a harmless white dust remains which may be hosed off, if desired. Although diatomaceous earth is non-toxic, it is an extremely fine dust which may be irritating if inhaled. Take precautions against breathing it in while preparing a spray.

Mineral oil. Despite the old adage, oil *can* be made to mix with water, in the form of emulsions, by dispersing the oil as tiny droplets through the water. Usually miscible oil is applied to fruit trees as an emulsion with about 3 percent oil.

Water-borne oil sprays are used as preventives to control chewing and sucking insects, such as aphids, red spiders, thrips, mealybugs, whiteflies, psyllids, all kinds of scale insects, mites, eggs of codling moths, Oriental fruit moths, various leaf rollers and cankerworms.

Oil sprays, intended for use on hardy fruit trees during the wintertime or early spring while the trees are leafless, are known as dormant sprays. Those applied to trees in foliage are the summer oils, or "white oils." The two differ chiefly in the degree of refinement of the oil and in its heaviness, with summer oils being more highly refined and lighter in weight than the dormant ones. (Consult Appendix D for miscible dormant oil spray recipe.)

An oil spray apparently kills insects and mites by enveloping them in a continuous film of oil, thus smothering and ultimately killing them. The oil interferes with the successful establishment of the young that may emerge for some days following treatment and prevents some eggs from hatching. Such a residual effect is important in the total action achieved in the control of mites and scale insects.

In the amounts used, oil sprays do not harm the soil, plants, warm-blooded animals, or man. "Oils are less toxic than many other insecticidal materials to man," stated P. J. Chapman, a professor of entomology. "Their relative safety in that respect recommends them for wider use. Insects have shown a disturbing ability to develop resistance to some insecticides, but so far not to oils. The way oils kill insects and mites, apparently through physical means, merits attention; it may prove to be a valuable quality in the future use of chemical treatments for the control of pests."

Mineral oil has been useful in controlling corn earworms. After the silks wilt and begin to brown at the ends, gardeners inject one fourth of a teaspoon of refined white mineral oil into the tip of each ear. Earlier treatment is inadvisable because it may interfere with the pollination and result in poorly filled ears.

Salt solution. Salt and saline solutions have been used for many years to control insect pests by disturbing their body chemistry. Gardeners have sprayed weak solutions consisting of an ounce of common table salt to a gallon of water to control spider mites in greenhouses, while others have used solutions of

a tablespoon of salt to two gallons of water to control cabbageworms.

In the eighteenth century, as the naturalist William Bartram
traveled through America, he observed that fruit trees grown
along the seacoast region were free of curculio. He reasoned
that a weak solution of brine water sprayed on fruit trees might
offer similar protection from curculio.

Salt has been used for weed control in soils which are not intended for gardening. These include areas such as tennis courts,
paths, surfaces to be asphalted, and land along railroad ties. The
action of the salt depends on the withdrawal and retention of
the moisture from plants. The salt is applied either in a strong
solution, or in a dry state. It is most effective in hot dry weather.

Milk. Skim milk has been used as a spray against mosaic
virus, a disease which affects tobacco and other plants. It works
not only on tobacco in the field, but on tobacco, peppers, and
tomatoes in the greenhouse. Tomato and pepper pickers have
been urged to dip their hands in skim milk to avoid transmitting
mosaic virus. Tests with skim milk gave nearly 100 percent inhibition of disease symptoms. Whey proteins were also effective.
It is not yet fully known which constituent of milk is the effective one; possibly the thus far unknown globulins in milk are the
inhibiting agents. Experiments are currently being conducted to
learn whether skim milk may also check virus diseases of animals.

A spray consisting of milk and blood has been used in orchards, and found effective in controlling fungi.

A spray of milk and coal tar has been used by some gardeners
against chinch bugs. Variations of this spray are: one part each
of coal oil and soapsuds, diluted in nineteen parts of water; or
an emulsion of one pound of soap to ten gallons of water.

Sour milk, or buttermilk, sprinkled over cabbages, has been
used against cabbageworms.

Liquid manure. Liquid manure, known to gardeners as "manure tea" or "Russian tea," is valued as a preventive against
potato blight, yellowing of tomato leaves in time of drought,
and black spot on roses. Make an infusion by soaking one part

of dry animal manure in ten parts of water by volume at least twenty-four hours. Strain and use it as a spray.

B.D. tree spray. Bio-Dynamic gardeners and farmers have developed a spray for use on trees which consists basically of a specially prepared clay, with extracts of powdered material and botanical insecticides such as ryania. This mixture, diluted in water, is applied to the entire tree as a preventive of insect pests and diseases. It may be used on shrubs and berry bushes as well.

The clay is so fine that it can flow into all small cracks, and leaves a colloidal film on bark, twigs, and leaves. This seals any wounds on the bark, offering a protection against invasion by pests and fungi.

Used before the buds of blossoms and leaves open in the spring, it protects against aphids, borers, and other insects which hibernate on twigs. Used as a foliage spray after blossoms have dropped and the fruit has set, it is applied mainly to the leaves and fruit. Although the leaves are thoroughly covered with the film, they will not stop breathing; yet scaling, sucking, and egg-laying insects will perish. In cases of heavy infestation, this spray may be repeated at intervals of two to four weeks throughout the summer. After the fruit has been harvested and the leaves have dropped, a third spraying is suggested for fall and winter protection. This can be a heavier application, covering the trunk, branches, and twigs of the entire tree, sealing off hibernating eggs and larvae. The material will adhere to the tree bark many months after application. It does not contain any lasting poison which leaves residue on fruit, and it is harmless to beneficial insects, birds, and mammals.

Essential oils as insecticides. Essential oils are also known to have insect-killing properties. In experiments for control of cotton pests, using 2 percent emulsion sprays against red spiders and cotton aphids, within a period of twenty-four hours, more than 90 percent of the insects were killed with oil of lemon grass, *Lippia triphylla,* and *Dracocephalum moldavica* from the mint family; from 51 to 80 percent were killed within the same period of time with oil of coriander, geranium, lavender, and sage. The essential oil from both summer savory and *Mentha longifolia*, from the mint family, showed increasing toxicity as the concentration of the emulsion was stepped up and they controlled the aphids.

A number of oils have been effective against mosquitoes and mosquito larvae, yet, by and large, they are ignored in mosquito control programs. (See Appendix D for a listing of them.)

A number of common oils have been used as insecticides or ingredients in insecticides. Oil of cottonseed, linseed, olive, peanut, soybean, and thyme have been used. Soybean oil is not poisonous; its action is chiefly mechanical. Oil of thyme contains thymol which is an active principle. Corn oil, raw linseed oil, and seal oil emulsions were tested in South Africa against various insects and mites on fruit trees. Corn oil emulsions have been used on the foliage of young peach and apple trees. The oils of corn and peanuts were found to be the least injurious of all vegetable oils tested. Mustard oil, derived from the seeds of different species of brassicae, Chinese colza oil, and rape oil are often used in emulsions as insecticides and, occasionally, as repellants.

THE GARDENER'S HERITAGE
OF TRADITIONAL BOTANICALS

Through the centuries, at various places, gardeners have resorted to botanicals as emergency materials. The effectiveness may vary, but their usefulness has been attested in a long tradition evolved through the experiences of many gardeners. Among them are many parts of plants with lesser-known insecticidal properties, such as: corm of Indian turnip (*Arisaema dracontium*); root of fetid bugbane (*Cimicifuga foetida*); foliage and rootstock from some members of the lily family; leaf and stem of canna; flower head of common camomile and camphor yarrow; the cockroach plant (*Haplophyton cimicidum*) from Mexico; leaf of sugar apple (*Annona squamosa*); leaf and twig of crystal tea (*Ledum palustre*); Labrador tea (*Ledum groenlandicum*); bark of common oleander; seed and root extract of the fish poison climber (*Millettia pachycarpa*); oil from croton plant; *Tournefortia hirsutissima* from Haiti; and *Lantana camara*, similar to verbena.

Many decoctions have been valued by gardeners, especially against aphids. Trees were washed with nasturtium juice, primarily at internodes of twigs; eucalyptus oil was painted on infested parts of trees; leaves from the Virginia creeper were rubbed on apple trees; and a tincture of colocynth (*Citrullus colocyntis*), a plant from the gourd family, was applied with a stiff brush against red spiders and cactus aphids.

Cyclamen elegans, in the primrose family, was esteemed in killing parasites on fruit trees. Now we know that saponin, a principle found in its bulbs, is effective fresh or dried. Bags of sumac leaves were buried around the base of apple trees infested with wooly aphids. Tannin has been discovered as an active principle in sumac leaves.

In *Lady's Annual Register* of 1840, farmers were advised to save the water in which potatoes were boiled, and to sprinkle it over garden plants or grain. Supposedly the liquid destroyed all insects in every stage from egg to grown fly. This claim appears to be a gross exaggeration, but it may contain an element of plausibility. Possibly the potato flour in the water acted mechanically as an adhesive.

The same periodical recommended an infusion of elderberry leaves in warm water. This elixir, sprinkled over roses and flowers, was recommended for blight and also to control caterpillar damage.

Crushed elderberry leaves have also been placed over the rows of plants to repel flea beetles.

Tomato leaves. Researchers and gardeners from many places report insecticidal value in tomato leaves which have been found to contain an alkaloid similar to digitalin and more active than nicotine. An alcoholic extract of this substance was highly effective against aphids on roses, pears, beans, and other vegetables. Elsewhere, a spray of macerated tomato leaves, soaked in water, freed peach and orange trees as well as rosebushes of aphids, and water extracts have been used against grasshoppers, flies, and caterpillars on eggplant.

Onions. Onion spray has been effective against red spiders and various aphids, especially those attacking roses, in the greenhouse and in the orchard. Some gardeners grind up onions in a food chopper or an electric blender, add an equal amount of water, strain the mixture and use it as a spray.

Hot peppers. Pods of hot peppers, ground and mixed with an equal amount of water and a little soap powder to make the materials adhere, seem to be effective against cabbageworms, ants, spiders, caterpillars, and tomato worms. Ground dry hot pepper dusted on tomato plants offers protection against insects. Dry cayenne pepper sprinkled over plants wet with dew repels caterpillars. A water spray of cayenne pepper has been used successfully against both caterpillars and fleas.

Some gardeners have used combinations of several materials as an all-purpose spray. One is made of three hot peppers, three large onions, and one whole bulb of garlic, ground together. The mash is covered with water, placed in a covered container, and allowed to stand overnight. The following day the mixture is strained through a fine sieve or cheesecloth. Enough water is added to make a gallon of spray which is used on roses, azaleas, chrysanthemums, beans, and other crops three times daily for one or two days during a heavy infestation. If necessary, the spray is repeated, especially after a heavy rain. The mash can be buried among rosebushes.

Rhubarb. A spray consisting of rhubarb leaves, boiled in water, has been watered into drillings before sowing brassicae, wallflowers, and other seeds, as a preventive against clubroot, and has been used on roses against greenfly and black spot.

Seaweed. Gardeners who live near the seacoast can take advantage of certain seaweeds for pest control. In Germany, a mucilage from *Chondus crispus*, a variety of Irish moss, has been used to control insects in orchards and vineyards. A pound of it is boiled in five gallons of water for an hour. When the mixture thickens it is sprayed on infested plants. As the spray dries, pieces flake off, taking with them eggs and larvae of injurious insects. For large-scale operations, more effective results were obtained by adding a pound of ethereal oil of mustard dissolved in ten pounds of methylated spirit to every ton or two of Irish moss.

A water spray of Iceland moss, a lichen (*Cetraria islandica*), has been used to destroy eggs of leaf-eating caterpillars on trees. A pound of Iceland moss is boiled for an hour in five gallons of water, and more water is added as needed to maintain a constant volume.

Herbal Tea. Many herbs, through their essential oils, have natural fungicidal and bactericidal properties. Sprays containing them are used by gardeners and farmers at regular intervals as preventives and for control. For the Bio-Dynamic group, these sprays are not isolated measures, but an integral part of an entire method.

Methods of preparation vary. The herbs can be steeped in boiling water, or soaked in cold water for a day, or allowed to ferment in water until a "liquid manure" is formed. This last mentioned product is useful but not generally favored because of its odor. (For details, see Appendix D.)

COMBATTING PLANT DISEASES WITH OTHER PLANTS

Scientists are now discovering that many plants produce actual plant medicines which are natural bactericides and fungicides. For instance, a few drops of an extract from cauliflower seeds has been found to inactivate the bacteria causing black rot, and radish seeds also contain an antibacterial substance. In Helsinki, Professor A. I. Virtanen, testing nearly 1300 plants, found that

105 of them contained antibiotic substances which were especially high in the cruciferae (*mustard family*).

Folklore has credited garlic and onions with medicinal properties which are now being established experimentally. Researchers, using garlic juice or commercial liquid and powdered extracts, and disguising the odor with a deodorizing agent, found it to contain a powerful antibacterial agent. It is an effective destroyer of diseases that damage stone fruits, cucumbers, radishes, spinach, beans, tomatoes, and nuts.

T. A. Tovstoles, a Russian biologist, experimented with a water solution of onion skin. Used as a spray three times daily at five-day intervals, the solution gave an almost complete kill of hemiptera, a parasite which attacks more than a hundred different species of plants.

Onion spray will also serve as a nontoxic fumigant. In one experiment, a water solution of onion skin and crushed onion was sprayed on apples as they were packed in boxes. Within two to three weeks, the onion odor had disappeared and the damage to fruit in treated boxes was significantly lower than in untreated boxes.

A chemical from asparagus juice has been found an effective killer of nematodes, including root-knot sting, stubby root, and meadow nematodes. When the diluted juice of this chemical was poured around the roots of tomato plants and others, it offered considerable protection against the nematodes. Spraying the leaves was even more effective, which may indicate that the juice offers possibilities as a systemic insecticide.

At Stanford Research Institute, work is being done with chemical compounds occurring naturally in many plants which may in some way prevent the spread of virus diseases. Twenty-three out of seventy species were found to have such inhibitors. One compound, when used as a spray to protect other plants, reduced lesions on tobacco plants from the mosaic virus 99 percent or more. These inhibitory compounds do not kill the viruses, but seem to change the plant so that it is no longer susceptible to infection.

Unlike anti-metabolites and other anti-viral chemicals that have been used, these natural inhibitors are not toxic to plants. Since they occur in edible portions of plants, most probably they are nontoxic to animals and humans.

Other experiments in this field have made use of harmless tree fungi and bacteria called saprophytes, which provide an unknown factor helpful to trees in resisting a broad range of tree diseases such as bark canker, decay fungi, and a leaf rust fungus. Water solutions made from the saprophytes not only gave trees better vigor and prevented infection, but, when tested on roots, increased the production of secondary roots. These useful growths are destroyed when toxic chemicals are applied to trees.

BOTANICAL ATTRACTANTS

Insects have highly specialized smelling apparatus, and they may concentrate on detecting only one or a few odors, like a radio set permanently tuned to a certain wavelength. Scents are vital to them, luring them to their mates and other members of their kind, leading them to their egg-laying sites, and guiding them to their food through their keen and discriminative senses of smell and taste. Insects recognize many essential oils, gums, resins, and the less pungent salts, acids, alkaloids, tannins, and other substances in specific plants. These odors may be extremely complex blends, but usually one chemical gives an identifying characteristic to a particular plant. At times this element can be isolated and synthesized for use as bait in traps or to lure insects away from a main crop. But the manmade mixture does not always have the same appeal to the discerning insect as the natural scent.

Insects follow the commands of instinct, which may be triggered by the proper scent. Larvae of cabbage butterflies, for instance, will eat abnormal fare such as leaves of wheat and maize, as well as starch and filter paper, when these materials are treated with mustard oil, a strong attractant for these insects.

Larvae of milkweed butterflies seek out and eat bizarre items, inappropriate as food, but which smell of milkweed latex. Experimentally, these butterflies devoured milkweed offered to them even when the leaves were coated with disagreeably tasting solutions.

Gardeners and farmers do not need to work with highly refined plant extracts to make use of this principle. Trap crops which attract by means of scent may be planted to protect the main crop. This practice has been in use many years and several examples may be given. Squash, cull onions, peas, or asparagus have been planted as trap crops to attract egg-laying insects. Later the trap crop is removed and destroyed before the insects can hatch and damage the main crop. Sometimes a belt of hemp seed is placed around a cabbage field or soybeans around a cornfield to serve as trap crops. Both nasturtium and mustard contain mustard oil, attractive to several groups of insects. These plants help protect the garden members of the mustard family: cabbage, cauliflower, radish, kohlrabi, Brussels sprout, turnip, and collard.

Japanese beetles can be lured to feed on a variety of plants as trap crops. They are attracted to African marigold, evening primrose, and woodbine, and are lured to, but poisoned by leaves of castor bean and blossoms of white geranium. Smartweed tempts them, but if used as a trap crop it is wise to cut the flowers of this noxious weed before mature seeds can propagate. Catawba grapes attract Japanese beetles and are used in vineyards to protect other varieties of grapes.

Attractants such as essential oils, fermentation products, protein and fat are useful substances for baiting insect traps. Eugenol, a chief constituent of oil of cloves, pimento, star anise, citronella grass, and other plants, as well as geraniol, a chief constituent in sassafras, apple, and other plants, are two commonly used attractants.

Current experiments give promise of an attractant for termites, developed from a material found in a water extract of decaying wood. The wood is inoculated with fungi, and temperature and humidity are controlled to promote decay. Although the substance has not yet been identified chemically, it has been patented by the Wisconsin Alumni Research Foundation. More benefits will accrue from the use of attractants as this field is further explored.

BOTANICAL REPELLANTS

Repellants and attractants are intimately related. One seems to be the antithesis of the other, yet a single substance may produce both effects. An odor which attracts in a small amount, may repel in a large quantity. Some repellants have efficient knockdown quality and become effective insecticides. In most instances, a repellant must compete with an attractant. Actually, many of the so-called repellants are really deodorizers that counteract the effect of more inviting odors.

Through the centuries many repellants have been used to ward off insects. Pliny recommended a mixture of red earth and tar against ants. Bedouins used camel urine on their faces, and others used smoke from wood fires, burning hemp, punk, and joss sticks to drive away insects. A mixture of equal parts of old soot and agricultural lime, having a strongly repulsive smell, was placed in small containers set on the ground to keep flea beetles from crops.

Insect repellants have been prepared from crushed leaves, infusions, or essential oils from such botanicals as citronella, eucalyptus, pennyroyal, rose geranium, cedarwood, thyme, wintergreen, clove, lavender, cassia, anise, bergamot, pine tar, bay laurel, and sassafras.

Teakwood, quassia, and cedar are woods which have long been valued as being immune to insects. Elder and ginkgo are noted for repelling certain insects. Few ticks are found where sage or pyrethrum forms a ground cover, and this is equally true of lavender plantations, although neighboring stands of elm, oak, and shrub may harbor high densities of the pest. Spurge laurel may be free of insects, and frequently dead beetles, flies, and wasps are found beneath it. In Africa, lemon grass (*Cymbopogon citratus*), repellent to the tsetse fly, has been planted as a control measure. The field of repellants awaits future expansion for insect control.

Botanicals are helpful for safe storage of crops. The soapberry tree (*Sapindus marginatus*), native to Florida, bears berries which are both repellent and insecticidal to weevils and other insects. Experimentally, only three berries from this tree were sufficient to protect a whole bushel of wheat. Some plants used to ward off weevils in grain include hemp, coumarin, *Clematis vitalba*, *Atractylis ovata*, and a decoction of persicary. Stored grain has been protected when coated with oil such as coconut, lemon, or mohwa, and when kept moist.

Ground black pepper, stored with dry beans, repels weevils. A water spray of wormwood keeps beetles and weevils out of granaries. Stalks of Jerusalem oak, also known as feather ceramium, preserve dried fruit and corn, while a handful of sassafras bark mixed with each bushel of dried fruit wards off insects. A few sound apples stored with potatoes give good keeping qualities to the potatoes and retard their sprouting.

Botanicals have been used to control household pests, to protect garments from the ravages of insects, and to relieve domesticated animals from insect attack. (For more information, see Appendix D.)

Before the meteoric rise of chemical insecticides in the 1940's, there were concerted efforts to study the repellent qualities of various plants for practical application in pest control. For example, the Japanese beetle, which was widespread in the 1930's, came under intensive scrutiny, with examination of extracts from plants immune to its attack. In one study alone, some fifty-six plant species showed good repellent qualities. Research on other insect pests revealed a similar multiplicity of botanical repellants.

Despite these findings, the use of these materials has largely been ignored, and the more hazardous chemicals have been favored. With current concern over pesticides, the time is ripe to exploit the botanicals.

At present, there is renewed interest in attractants and repellants for insect control. Three substances which may prove useful against the boll weevil have been isolated from cotton flower buds: a repellant, an attractant, and a feeding stimulant that makes plants appetizing to insects. These materials could be turned against the boll weevil in different ways. For instance, plant breeders might develop cotton varieties containing a high content of the repellant or a low content of the attractant; conceivably, the repellant could be used to starve the boll weevil by driving it away from the food it needs; or the attractant might be used to lure the insect into a trap, or to an area away from the cotton crop. In laboratory tests the repellant kept boll weevils away from cotton squares, bolls, and seedlings for from five to twelve hours, even when the insects had no other food. The weevils left the treated plant parts untouched for the thirty-six hours of the experiment when food was available. Although the feeding stimulant does not attract weevils from a distance, it offers the possibility of forcing them to starve on the wrong type of diet.

BOTANICAL INSECTICIDES

Hidden away in the life processes of plants are many chemicals, proteins, activators, hormones, and other substances which may be present in minute quantities but which have remarkable powers. The lore of the herbwoman, the medicines of the ancient world, and fish poisons of primitive tribes are frequently plant extracts whose action is scarcely understood today.

If we wish to avoid having to use some of the too-powerful creations of the test tube and the laboratory, there is a great range of partly explored plant chemicals available. The attractants, repellants, and insecticides derived from plants offer us effective but less menacing control of agricultural pests. The chlorinated hydrocarbons and organophosphates, so popular today, strike at the basic cellular processes of all life, and their effects may persist for an unknown length of time. Every person living in the civilized world now has them stored in his body, and Eskimos who have had limited contact with white men, as well as fish far out at sea have measurable amounts of chemical pesticides in their fat. Botanicals, closer to their plant sources, share the universal law of change and decay. After their usefulness is past, they break down readily and dissipate. Therefore, even those materials which are strong poisons do not persist in the soil, in crops, or in the tissues of man and animal. We may yet need that margin of safety.

There are more than three thousand known species of plants which have insecticidal properties. Some are from the higher order of plants and others from lower orders such as algae, fungi, mosses, ferns, and horsetails. Perhaps not all of them warrant further investigation, but some are sufficiently deserving of intensive chemical analysis and toxiocological studies for practical use. A few are available commercially, and more show promise.

Even though these materials are found in nature, it does not follow that they are harmless. Botanical insecticides are toxic and must be handled with caution. They are toxic to insects, and, in many cases, to fish and other cold-blooded creatures, but generally their toxicity is low for warm-blooded animals. There have been rare cases when these materials have produced acute toxicity and adverse effects on certain individuals who are highly sensitive or allergic, but damage is not lasting.

Usually botanical insecticides are not stable, and they break down readily in the soil. Since there is no evidence that they are stored in either plant or animal tissue, they do not produce lasting residues.

Since 1927, chemists in the Bureau of Entomology and Plant Quarantine have engaged in some research on principal insecticides of plant origins. However the number of people working in this field is limited. As is true with attractants and repellants, research has been stymied by the overwhelming predominance of the chemical approach. The field of botanical insecticides still needs to be explored and exploited.

Louis Feinstein, research chemist of the U.S. Department of Agriculture, said recently:

> Plant insecticides are only a small fraction of the insecticidal material used each year. Yet in the development of new insecticides, they deserve careful consideration. Often they are highly effective against many insect enemies that are not successfully controlled by inorganic insecticides. The plant insecticides often are relatively nontoxic to man and other plants. Poisonous residues on fruits and vegetables may menace public health. The relative safety of plant insecticides to man helps to maintain their continued use.

The subject requires the knowledge and experience of botanist, chemist, entomologist, plant pathologist, and toxicologist. A team approach is needed like that used in importation work in biological control. First a particular plant with satisfactory qualities must be found and identified by a botanist, and studied for its characteristics, habitat, and effective parts. The available natural supply must be sufficient to warrant the effort, and means must be devised to collect, ship, and deliver it to processors at a reasonable cost.

Many tests of botanical insecticides in the past were inadequate. Not all parts of the plants were examined, proper solvents were not used for extraction, and the material was not tried against the proper insects. In the light of past experiences, modern testing methods have been improved. Several species of insects, representative of different orders, are used as targets. It is now appreciated that many active principles deteriorate when dried plants are stored. Present trials are conducted shortly after plants are collected. Materials are tried as contact poison, stomach poison, and fumigant, using fine powders as well as extracts made with different classes of solvents. With present practices, it is possible that many plants formerly discarded as worthless, if retested, would actually have value.

From the time of the early Romans to the twentieth century, there were three outstanding botanical insecticides in widespread use: hellebore, pyrethrum, and nicotine. More recent large-scale investigations were made of other botanicals such as derris and lonchocarpus, prior to the appearance of chemical pesticides.

White hellebore. White hellebore (*Veratrum album*) has been used since ancient times as an insecticide. Greeks mixed it with milk to kill flies, and Romans used it against mice and rats. The plant is a hardy herbaceous perennial of the lily family, and the powder from the rhizomes and rootlets contains its insecticidal materials. Since it loses its toxicity when exposed to light and air, it is less poisonous than other oldtime materials, such as arsenic.

White hellebore controls a number of leaf-eating insects which attack ripening fruit, such as sawflies on raspberry, currant, gooseberry, strawberry and sweet potato; currant spanworm and currantworm; slugs on grape and cherry; onion maggot; and cabbageworm.

Although white hellebore grows in Europe, at present it is not produced in the United States. However, it can be obtained from specialty companies.

Pyrethrum. If historical records are interpreted correctly, pyrethrum may have been used nearly two thousand years ago in China. In modern times, pyrethrum was grown in the nineteenth century and was the secret basis of Persian insect powder. In 1828, it was produced on a commercial scale and introduced into Europe by an Armenian trader. By 1860, it had reached the United States and become popular.

Pyrethrum is an herbaceous perennial chrysanthemum called "the bug-killing daisy." The ground-up flowers of certain species contain substances which are toxic to many insects by acting directly on their nervous systems. When pyrethrum is applied to plant foliage, it breaks down rapidly in sunlight or strong artificial light, having a very short-term residual action. For this reason it can be used as a pre-harvest spray. The United States Department of Agriculture terms pyrethrum "probably the safest of all insecticides for use in a food plant." In the amounts used, its toxicity is low for mammals. Even if ingested, there is no evidence that it is stored in tissues, and it breaks down into simple harmless compounds rapidly eliminated from the body. In addition to these assets of lack of residue and low toxicity, pyrethrum has rapid knockdown power and it is a material to which insects do not develop resistant strains.

Chemists attempted to find the active principles in pyrethrum, and succeeded in isolating four esters. Pyrethrin i and ii, and cinerin i and ii are the main toxic principles, but possibly additional active ingredients are present in the flowers. Attempts have been made to reproduce the unique properties synthetically but the process is expensive and the product not as effective as the natural material.

Before the First World War, most pyrethrum was grown in Dalmatia. Then Japan developed as a major producer. Beginning in 1928, under British supervision, experimental culture was undertaken successfully in Kenya. Other producers were in the Belgian Congo, Tanganyika, Yugoslavia, and Brazil. Our own demands became so extensive that by 1945 we imported yearly over 18 million pounds of pyrethrum flowers. Its popularity continues, and at present there are American-owned plantations in Ecuador.

When world supplies became relatively limited in relation to growing demands, it was discovered that non-toxic substances could be added which would not only make it possible to use less pyrethrum, but would strengthen its effect. These agents, called synergists, are partly derived from plant products such as asarinin from bark of Southern prickly ash, sesamin from sesame oil, and peperine from black pepper.

Pyrethrum has been used to control a variety of insects, including pickleworm, aphid, leafhopper, spider mite, harlequin bug, and imported cabbageworm on a growing plant. It is useful on agricultural crops which require control up to the very time of harvest, and for stored plant products such as wheat, cocoa, tobacco, and dried fruit which need protection for considerable time after harvest. In addition, it is widely used against household insect pests, and as a spray or dip for animals.

New Jersey Mosquito Larvicide. New Jersey Mosquito Larvicide was developed by Rutgers Endowment Foundation, which now licenses a commercial company to produce the concentration. The solution is effective in controlling larvae, pupae, and adult mosquitoes, and has been widely used by individuals as well as mosquito control commissions. The larvicide contains pyrethrum and used in recommended dosages will not harm fish, waterfowl, plants, or mammals. It is compatible with all types of water and can be used during spring, summer, or early autumn.

Nicotine. Tobacco, and its main alkaloid, nicotine, have been used for insecticidal purposes since the late seventeenth century. In a pure state, nicotine is a colorless fluid with little odor, but it is a virulent poison for insects and is highly toxic to mammals. However, it is volatile and dissipates rapidly from products on which it is sprayed or dusted. It is useful against small soft-bodied insects such as aphid, whitefly, leafhopper, psyllid, thrip, and spider mite.

Nicotine sulfate, an extract treated with sulfuric acid, is less toxic than free nicotine, and is an oldtime material still available. When used, it is highly diluted in water, and soap solution may be added to make the mixture spread and adhere better. Nicotine fumigators are available for greenhouse use. These too are toxic and must be handled carefully.

Dried, ground nicotine, added to a suspension of bentonite in water, has been sprayed on apple trees to control codling moths. Experimentally, a water spray from an extract of wild tobacco, used on apple trees, successfully controlled certain psyllids, young caterpillars, Tortricidae, and related pests. Similar sprays had some effect on cabbageworms and flea beetles.

The alkaloid nornicotine is more effective than nicotine against aphids attacking nasturtiums, and peas. Nornicotine and nicotine are equally toxic to cabbage aphids, citrus red mites, and other spider mites.

The alkaloid anabasine, which closely resembles nicotine in insecticidal properties, has been reported four or five times as toxic to certain aphids of economic importance. In the U.S.S.R. it has been produced commercially and used extensively as a dust.

Coiine, another alkaloid related to nicotine and found in poison hemlock (*Conium maculatum*), used experimentally was an effective insecticide against blowflies and bean aphids.

Quassia. The quassia tree, native to South America and the West Indies, has no odor, but contains a peculiar bitterness more intense and lasting than that of any other known substance. The bitterness, especially concentrated in the bark, extends to the roots, wood, leaves, and even to the flowers. This quality makes it effective as an insecticide. Articles made from the wood of the tree are impervious to insect attack, and the lumber, including the inner bark, is made into chips and sold. In water solution, the spray is applied on a wide variety of insects, including greenfly, leafhopper, slug, mealybug, and thrip.

Derris. Long ago the Chinese discovered the insecticidal value in derris or tuba root. It is one of several plants known as fish poisons because of their ability to stupefy fish. When the crushed roots, stems, and leaves are thrown into lagoons and streams, fish float to the surface, insensible. Despite the extreme sensitivity of fish to this material, in normal concentrations derris is considered harmless to domestic animals and man. It is eliminated rapidly from the body and there is no evidence that it is stored in animal tissue. Derris is used both on plants and animals for insect control.

To date, a number of species of derris have been tested and found effective, notably against leaf-eating caterpillars, mosquito larvae, and aphids. The addition of oil of teaseed as a synergist increases its toxicity to squash bugs. Derris is widely used on farms as animal dips, controlling lice and ticks.

Experiments demonstrated that when derris was applied to young bean plants, leaf growth was less palatable to Mexican bean beetles than similar new growth on untreated plants. Later trials showed that the active principles in derris translocated from the outer surfaces of the treated leaves to ones which developed after application. Distribution of insecticides to inaccessible parts of plants has been a major obstacle, and derris became recognized as a systematic insecticide. However, the amounts translocated were too low to be of great practical value.

Rotenone. Rotenone has long been used as a fish poison in Asia, Africa, and South America; in China it was used for many years as an insecticide in vegetable gardens. Currently, Cynthia Westcott, a garden expert, refers to it as "probably the gardener's best chemical friend."

Rotenone comes from the roots of different species of trees, especially the lonchocarpus from Latin America, the cube from Peru, and the timbó from Brazil. Percentages vary from plant to plant. Roots containing at least 5 percent rotenone are finely ground, and the powder is used against a wide variety of insect pests including the spittlebug, potato and tobacco flea beetle, aphid, spider mite, chinch bug, harlequin bug, imported cabbageworm, carpenter ant, pea weevil, mosquito, and housefly.

The effect of rotenone on insects is to slow down the rate of their heart action and breathing. Little is known of the fundamental basis for its effectiveness. It can cause paralysis of the breathing mechanism in mammals, possibly acting on the bronchial tissues. However, it is eliminated rapidly from the body and there is no evidence that it is stored in animals. Used in normal concentrations, it is not considered harmful.

Rotenone was first used as a spray against pea aphids in the early 1920's in Maryland. Its value in dusts and sprays was shown experimentally in Wisconsin in 1935, where the materials did not kill aphids as rapidly as nicotine, but had good residual effect. Under favorable weather conditions, rotenone continued its knockdown power for several days. Many tests were made with different diluents and, by adding oils and conditioning agents, performance was improved. Rarely did rotenone give a high degree of control by itself, but in combination it gave satisfactory commercial control, especially in humid areas.

In the 1930's, the Pan American Society of Tropical Research brought to the United States nearly three million seeds of yerba de la pulga (*Helenium*) a plant possessing rotenone. After extensive experimentation, scientists concluded that the plant possessed excellent insect-repelling qualities. It not only contained, but actually exuded sufficient quantities of rotenone to make a single growing specimen of the plant virtually repellent to all forms of insect life within an area of some fifteen to twenty square feet.

Ryania. Ryania is a Latin American shrub, native to Trinidad, which is a relative newcomer among botanical insecticides. During an extensive testing program of plant materials conducted cooperatively by the New Jersey Agricultural Experiment Station and a pharmaceutical company, ryanodine, an alkaloid with insecticidal properties was discovered in ryania. Although the active principle occurs in greatest concentration in the roots, the wood stem is used commercially since it is the part of the plant available in large quantities. The roots are left undisturbed to permit further production of the stem wood.

Ryania does not always kill insects outright, but rather puts them in a state of "flaccid paralysis." The appetites of the insects wane, they become incapable of normal activity and stop feeding. Although ryania may not actually reduce population densities, it offers crop protection. In the amounts used it does not injure plant tissues, and it has low toxicity for mammals. It presents no residue hazard and is exempt from tolerance on growing crops.

D. W. Clancy of the United States Department of Agriculture, working in West Virginia, was the first to field test ryania against codling moth. It has been used against this apple pest by A. D. Pickett and associates in commercial orchards in Nova Scotia. By using this botanical in conjunction with biological measures, and at the same time sharply curtailing the use of chemical pesticides, the growers achieved 90 percent control of the codling moth without inciting population rises of other insect pests or spider mites. Although ryania is not entirely innocuous to beneficial insects, it remains at present the most selective insecticide known against codling moth. In Nova Scotia, ryania gave good control of the eye-spotted bud moth and other tortricoid species, apple-infesting aphids, leafhoppers, and spider mites. All these orchard pests became less injurious than at any time in the past three decades. Ryania offered such benefits in Nova Scotian apple orchards that since 1954 it has been the most widely used insecticide in that region.

Of many species of ryania tested, *Ryania speciosa* is the most effective. Various portions of the plant have been used, in different types of extracts. The powdered stems and roots, for instance, used against larvae of Oriental fruit moths, were as effective as DDT. Ryania dust applied to a field of soybeans not only controlled caterpillars, but increased the yield of the crop. Extracts from the stems proved 700 times more potent than from the stem wood.

Ryania has been found useful against a wide variety of pests, including the European corn borer, sugarcane borer, cranberry fruit worm, cotton bollworm, apple aphid, potato aphid, squash bug, milkweed bug, onion thrip, Japanese beetle, elm leaf beetle, asparagus beetle, yellow mealworm, imported cabbageworm, cabbage looper, diamondback moth, corn earworm and silkworm. Gardeners can obtain ryania which may be used as a dust or spray.

Sabadilla. Sabadilla has been used as an insecticide since the sixteenth century. It contains several active alkaloids, including veratrine, veratridine, and cevadine. Sabadilla has curious characteristics. All extracts of the plant are non-toxic, except its mature seeds. When heated or treated with alkali, they become toxic to many insects. Contrary to the behavior of most botanical insecticides, the toxicity of powdered sabadilla seeds increases with age during storage.

A number of tests with sabadilla reveal its versatility as a dust or extract. It is effective with a large group of insects of economic importance, including the grasshopper, European corn borer, codling moth larva, armyworm, webworm, silkworm, aphid, cabbage looper, melonworm, squash bug, blister beetle, and greenhouse leaf tier, as well as household pests. Sabadilla dust is available commercially. Exercise care in handling it and avoid breathing it in, since it can irritate mucous membranes and cause sneezing if inhaled.

OTHER PROMISING BOTANICAL INSECTICIDES

The Mexican marigold, *Tagetes minuta*, is a plant that deserves intensive investigation. This is an unusual half-hardy annual which has traveled all over the world. Originally it was a native of Latin America, but later was introduced into Europe. In the 1900's a packet of seeds was shipped from England, where it had failed to set seed, to an Australian gardener named Roger. Instead of becoming a good garden plant, it promptly became a fast-spreading weed. It was dubbed "Stinking Roger" as an everlasting tribute to its perpetrator. During the war, in 1915, it was inadvertently sent to South Africa in hay used as fodder for horses of the Australian cavalry known as "Kharkibos." It spread rapidly as far as Rhodesia where it became known as Mexican marigold.

The greatest handicap of *Tagetes minuta* is its name. It was christened by Linnaeus for the minute size of its pale yellow star flowers, from a dried specimen of the top of the plant. Gardeners in Britain and United States who have grown this variety of marigold to a height of twelve feet feel that *Tagetes gigantea* might be more appropriate.

Currently, *Tagetes minuta* is being studied by members of the Henry Doubleday Research Association for possible use as repellant, insecticide, nematocide, fungicide, and selective weedicide, since the plant displays a wide range of talents. Investigators are testing the plant grown from seeds. To date, results are variable but promising.

Oil glands in the leaves of this marigold give the plant an aromatic scent. In Rhodesia it is used as a repellant of flies, fleas, and lice. Bunches of leaves are hung in dog kennels and in cowsheds to keep flies out.

Also present in the plant are principles, similar to the alkaloids in pyrethrum, which have knockdown power as an insecticide. European fruit farmers in Rhodesia gather wild Mexican marigolds, boil them in water, allow the mixture to soak overnight, and strain it. Used as a spray, this solution is reported effective against codling moths, aphids, and weevil eggs in the ground.

In Britain, results of experimentation with extracts of this material were inconclusive. Apparently, whatever active principles are present in the leaves and stems are not in the proper stage of development to synchronize with the spray schedule for fruit trees.

It is estimated that a successful extract of *Tagetes minuta* would be far cheaper than pyrethrum, and yield about twenty tons for each acre of foliage. Mexican marigolds have the favorable feature of remaining stable in water, which pyrethrum does not do. However, to date, no effective extraction process has been developed for *Tagetes minuta*.

In addition to the insecticidal principles in the leaves of this plant, there are separate principles in the root exudates which are effective nematocides and fungicides. The exudates show promise against certain nematodes that attack potatoes and strawberries as well as against wilts of potatoes and tomatoes.

The root exudates seem to inhibit underground slugs, and act either as insectifuge or insecticide against wireworms, the larvae of the click beetle. When Mexican marigolds were planted near rows of potatoes, wireworms were absent for a distance of three feet. In 1962 experiments, Mexican marigolds planted in May between rows of potatoes depressed the potato yields by six ounces per foot of row. It was estimated that, on a garden scale, it would be possible to grow the Mexican marigolds to control wireworms and nematodes without lower yields than would be caused by pests.

In a large garden it appears to be possible to use Mexican marigolds in rotation to clear plots of weeds and pests. Mexican marigolds do not harm trees or shrubs having woody roots. The effect on weeds is limited to those with starchy roots, with no effect on weed seeds already present in the soil. Although *Tagetes minuta* has escaped as a weed in tropical countries, there appears to be little danger of it doing so in the United States. Thirty-two species of *Tagetes* already grow wild in Mexico and Central America and none have established themselves in California or Florida. Out of many species collected by Mexican members of the Henry Doubleday Research Association, *Tagetes minuta* appears to be the most effective. As a botanical, it has possibilities worth exploring to the fullest.

Various other plants are being tested today, some of them with surprisingly strong effects. Extracts of chinaberry, for instance, have killed 97 to 98 percent of cabbage aphids, as well as proving useful against locusts, grasshoppers, cockroaches, and termites. Tests of devil's shoestring (*Tephrosia virginiana*), a native North American weed, show that nineteen species of this plant have valuable insecticidal properties, yet it has low toxicity to mammals. Common field larkspur (*Delphinium consolida*) yields the alkaloids delcosine and delsoline, found effective against aphids and thrips. A naturally occurring chemical compound has been identified in turnips which is deadly to aphids, spider mites, houseflies, German cockroaches, and bean beetles. Myristicin, a compound in parsnips which has been synthesized, has been found to be a selective insecticide for fruit flies, Mexican bean beetles, pea aphids, and mosquito larvae, a repellant for other insects, and an effective synergist.

The Amur corktree (*Phellodendron amurense*) from Asia, the thundergod vine (*Tripterygium wilfordii*), a common insecticidal plant of southern China, the mamey tree (*Mammea americana*) from the West Indies, the seeds of tropical yam beans, all are yielding their secrets to investigators to provide safer and more specific weapons against pests.

The systematized and empirical knowledge of botanical insecticides should be used to fuller advantage. Plant products can control many insect pests without danger of residues on crops. Their toxicity to warm-blooded animals is usually low. Some of the plants could be grown in the United States and offer possibilities as new crops for cultivation. The use of by-products as insecticidal diluents could utilize materials which, at present, are all too frequently wasted or pollute waterways by careless disposal. An examination of the rich varieties of emergency controls made possible by botanical insecticides recalls the phrase of Emerson: "Everything in nature contains all the powers of nature."

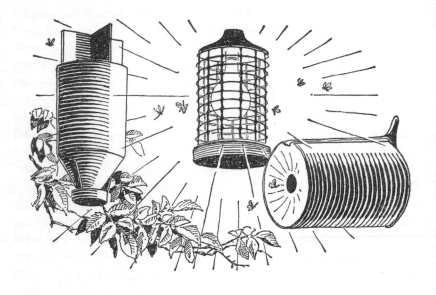

8. EMERGENCY MEASURES: TRAPS

The interest in traps remains at a high level and efforts to improve their effectiveness and extend their range of usefulness continue. The day may come when traps will be devised that are greatly superior to those we now have; the efforts to develop them will be worth while.

—*Howard Baker and T. E. Hienton,*
U.S. Department of Agriculture

TRAPS LEAVE no poisonous residues on crops, nor do they develop resistant strains of insects. Their use will not create problems in your water supply a year later, or kill off the natural enemies of the insect you wish to control. Our present tendency to look for the *one* answer to any insect problem makes us forget that traps may be a useful addition to other controls, particularly in emergency situations.

Useful traps may be made of extremely simple materials such

as chips, blocks, stones, boards, butterfly nets, or they may be complicated devices using lures, baits, sounds, colors, lights, or electrical equipment. They all serve one purpose: to catch insects unaware and hold them long enough to permit destruction.

Simple Traps. In the small home garden, many insects can be trapped using materials commonly found at hand. As early as 1840, the plum curculio was trapped under bark chips or stone placed in a cleared area under the tree. This material provided a hiding place for the adult curculio which were later collected and destroyed at regular intervals. This simple trap was superseded by other methods, but the principle is still in use today.

Flat boards, stones, blocks, or a handful of broadleafed weeds placed directly on the ground near plants will succeed in trapping insects such as the squash bug, snail, wireworm, beetle, and harlequin bug, which crawl under them to hide. You can enhance the value of these traps by coating them with a suitable bait like molasses. Examine the traps early in the morning, and destroy any insects that have collected.

Trenches, Furrows, and Ditches. Many insects can be stopped by digging a deep, dusty-sided trench ten feet wide as a barrier to the field or garden. The corn chinch bug, armyworm, and wingless May beetle can be stopped in their migrations. These insects fall into the trench and are prevented from escape by the loose dirt.

Furrows, and postholes dug at intervals along the bottom of them, trap many insects which can be crushed with a heavy stick. Tar barriers can supplement the furrows. In the West, irrigation ditches serve this same purpose. They keep the Mormon cricket, for instance, from migrating out of rangelands to irrigated fields.

Sheet Traps. Sheets or large canvases, spread beneath fruit and nut trees, act as traps for the plum curculio and pecan weevil. Both species of insect fold up and drop to the ground to "play possum" when disturbed. By jarring the trunks and larger branches of infested trees you can dislodge many adult insects which will fall into the sheet and may then be destroyed.

Crop Traps. Use plants as bait for insects that hide during the day but feast in the garden at night: the snail, slug, grub, cutworm, and earwig. Strew leaves of lettuce, spinach, cabbage, slices of raw potato, or used halves of grapefruit or orange rind turned upside down. The night feeders will collect beneath these materials, and you can dispose of them in the morning.

A method of trapping cutworms, used more than a century ago, consisted of placing compact handfuls of elder sprouts, milkweed, clover, mullein, or green vegetables in every fifth row or hill of cultivation and tamping them down. Cutworms gathered in this trap material, where they could be regularly collected.

Wireworms, especially, are attracted to raw potato or carrot. If a stick is passed through the bait, it will later serve as a handle.

To control sow bugs, also known as pill bugs, save used corncobs. Place them under pans or flowerpots which are tipped slightly. Early in the morning, carefully lift the pans or pots and tap the sow bugs off the corncobs into a deep pan, then destroy them.

Earwigs may be trapped by simple devices. They are attracted to hay, paper, or moss stuffed into inverted pots set on top of sticks or stakes. Or rags and paper can be placed under bushes where earwigs are apt to be found. Earwigs crawl into cooler earth in the heat of the day. Therefore check the trap materials early in the morning.

Another effective trap for earwigs is based on the knowledge that they favor small dry places in which to lay their eggs. They breed in April and are active at night. Tie together four pieces of one-foot lengths of bamboo, open at both ends. Place several such bundles under bushes and against fences. Early each morning tap the bundles over a pail of hot water, dislodging the earwigs.

In former years, logs were felled or fallen trees allowed to remain as trap crops to attract certain injurious bark beetles. After the tree or log was thoroughly infested, it was removed and destroyed.

Banding traps. As early as 1840 a banding trap was used to catch codling moth larvae. Material was wound around the trunks of apple trees, or the larvae were trapped in cloth placed in tree crotches, and then destroyed in a hot oven. Farmers learned that more larvae could be trapped by scraping the rough bark from trees and clearing the ground of weeds and trash. This practice of sanitation forced more insects to go up into the bands. By the 1860's a hay rope was used as banding, followed by a variety of papers, flannel, canvas, and burlap. At present, banding traps are improved with the use of commercial adhesives and readymade banding strips containing adhesives.

Baited traps. There is no universal agreement on the value of baited traps in reducing pest numbers. For experimental purposes, obviously, such devices have definite value for sampling insect populations and determining the presence of suspected new invaders in an area. But for the individual gardener, additional insects may, in some cases, be attracted to the area by the baited trap.

For instance, the value of individual Japanese beetle traps is questionable since these insects are vigorous travelers. Within a heavily infested area, even when as many as a hundred traps per mile were erected, the local population of Japanese beetles was reduced only slightly. There was evidence that in the presence of large numbers of traps, invading beetles increased. It is conceded, however, that over a period of years, sufficiently large-scale trapping operations on a community basis may reduce or retard a general infestation of this insect. Meanwhile, the individual gardener can use milky spore disease and other biological agents, as well as make use of good cultural practices and repellent plants.

Codling moths, on the other hand, serve as an example of insects for which baited traps are of value. Apparently these moths do not migrate very far, so that traps capture those in the vicinity without at the same time encouraging invasion. A large number of females may be captured, of which as many as 95 percent may be ready to deposit eggs. In one experiment, codling moth traps, used as a supplement to other control measures, gave 12 to 15 percent more clean fruit. Therefore codling moth traps should be considered as a valuable aid to the orchardist.

For the home gardener, simple and inexpensive materials for both traps and bait have been known for centuries. A trap can be made from many handy items such as a glass jar, stew pan, pail, tin can, or sticky coated baffle. The old phrase "you can catch more flies with honey than with vinegar" tells what to use for bait. Fermenting carbohydrates, sugars, molasses, beer, and yeast are some ingredients which attract the codling moth, Oriental fruit moth, fruit fly, and borer. Sometimes bait becomes more attractive after a few days of fermentation.

Aromatic essential oils such as sassafras, anise, or pine tar oil attract some insects. Protein materials such as powdered egg albumen, dried yeast powder, or casein, linseed oil, or soap are also used. Certain chemicals which, to our knowledge, do not exist in nature have been potent insect attractants. Auto lacquer lures the palmetto weevil, while dry-cleaning fluid, as well as wood and cigarette smoke, attract others. (For specific bait, see Appendix E.)

Sometimes poison is used with bait. There is less objection to its use in this manner than in using toxic material in any other present method of insect control. In bait, it does not contaminate, nor does it offer hazards to other forms of life. Non-toxic materials are useful diluents for poisoned bait, many of which are inexpensive wastes. (For details, see Appendix E.)

Many factors affect the efficiency of traps, including the activity of the insect, the weather, location of the trap in relation to the source of infestation, presence of preferred food plants, and obstructions such as buildings. Insects follow odors upwind and are attracted from the lee. Therefore, place traps on the windward side of the tree.

Specialized bait: sex attractants. Secretions given off by certain female insects are so highly attractive to the male that these substances have been called the most fantastically potent biologically active materials ever discovered. Odorless to humans, they attract male insects from great distances. The highly sensitive smelling apparatus with which the insect is endowed to survive or thrive in a hostile environment proves to be its weakness as we take advantage of this trait to hoist the insect on its own petard.

Fabre, the celebrated French naturalist described with great astonishment the power of this sex scent. The female of the great peacock moth had emerged in his laboratory and he had cloistered her under a wire-gauze bell jar. The window of his study was open, and during the evening some forty male moths entered and fluttered around the bell jar. They had found their way through the darkness of an overcast night to a house quite hidden in shrubbery and trees, yet they had directed their flight skillfully. Even after Fabre removed the female to other parts of the house, the males unfailingly were able to locate her. Fabre surmised that the moths had traveled great distances, since he had never encountered them in any numbers during his concentrated studies of the neighborhood.

Japanese investigators placed infinitesimal quantities of sex attractants, taken from the silkworm moth, on a particular spot on a paper strip. Approaching it, male moths became excited and shook their wings violently.

During the Second World War a crash program was launched to find sex attractants of insects, particularly those of medical importance. At first, screening tests were made completely at random, but as structural leads were uncovered, related compounds were synthesized. Up to the present, more than 16,000 compounds have been tested, including a large number of extracts of plants, animals, essential oils, food, waste products, synthetics, and other materials of indefinite composition. Of all the items tested to date, a few proved practical.

An outstanding example is the gypsy moth. A very potent extract is prepared from the last two abdominal segments of the virgin female, which contain her scent glands. If the extract is made of the entire moth, it is not an attractant. Some five hundred tips are required to produce one drop of the liquid. Yet the material, when accumulated, is so potent that 1/10,000 of a billionth of a gram is effective. Male gypsy moths have been lured to the substance from more than two miles downwind. The extract can be stabilized by hydrogenation, and will keep its potency for ten years or more.

Recently this gypsy moth attractant has been partially identified and synthesized under the names of gyplure and gyptol. An ounce of it, equivalent to the amount of natural attractant gathered from some 300 million female moths, appears attractive to the males. Its manufacture will make the material standardized, cheaper, more readily available, and easier for baiting.

The gypsy moth trap is a simple metal cylinder, inside of which a screen cone has a hole for moths to enter and sticky paper to prevent their escape. They are lured into the cone by the sex attractant placed on a corrugated paper roll.

Attractants of other insects of economic importance are being studied, and, if successful, our dependence on pesticides may be reduced. For example, a new attractant bait for the imported fire ant requires only one-seventh of an ounce of insecticide per acre, and to date has presented no problem of residue on food crops, nor hazard to bees, fish, wildlife, domestic animals, or humans.

Recently the natural attractant from the female American cockroach has been isolated by means of a painstaking technique, but the studies may be useful for other insects. Air circulating around the insects picks up the volatile attractant which is trapped and chilled. Moisture is drained off, and the attractant becomes concentrated in a crude substance which contains only

about ½ of 1 percent of it. By using some eight thousand female cockroaches, about three drops of crude attractant are obtained weekly. The insects need to be replaced approximately
every three months.

Highly specific chemical substances have been isolated in such
insects as female houseflies, cabbage loopers, and others, and
they are currently being investigated. The value of such attractants is that they may be used in traps, combined with poisoned
bait, or chemosterilant, without contamination of crops.

At present, the U.S. Department of Agriculture is conducting
tests against the Oriental fruit fly, using a combination of synthetic sex attractant and toxicant, with which small squares of
fibreboard are impregnated. The sex attractant, methyleugenol,
is sought greedily by the males, and, if permitted to, they will
engorge themselves until they die. The attractant is potent
enough to lure them from a distance of one half mile. Airplanes
have dropped treated fibreboard wafers over several western
Pacific islands. Tests were judged highly successful on the
island of Rota, with a complete temporary decimation of the
insect. During a month of trials, not a single male Oriental fruit
fly was recovered in a hundred traps scattered through the island.
The same technique may offer possibilities for detection and
control of the Oriental fruit fly if it should ever threaten the
continental United States.

Another possibility is the use of a sex attractant without a
toxicant, by spraying the attractant over a wide area. Such a
spraying might possibly confuse male insects in their attempt to
locate females of their species.

The value of sex attractants is that they are highly specific for
their kind. As far as we know, they offer no hazards to beneficial
insects or other forms of life.

Electric light traps. The lure of the flame for the moth is
proverbial. It is equally true that other night-flying insects are
attracted to light, and this knowledge has been put to use in
capturing noxious night-flying insects.

Years ago, lights were hung over pails of water. Both lanterns and fires were used at night to attract and trap boll weevils. Edison's early carbon filament electric lamp furnished more visible light than other lamps, but the yellow color was only slightly more attractive to insects than the weak yellow light of the candle or kerosene lantern. The tungsten filament lamp was a stronger attractant. Farmers sometimes strung a few low wattage bulbs one to two feet above ground inside the duck pen, so that ducks would eat the night-flying insects which flew around the lights.

The ordinary incandescent lamp will lure some insects. An ordinary seventy-five to two hundred watt bulb will attract the European corn borer moth, an Argon lamp, with only three two-watt lights per trap, the pink bollworm moth, and a pink or green fluorescent lamp the striped and spotted cucumber beetle.

Blacklights. It remained however for work with "blacklights" to give even greater control of noxious night-flying insects. Blacklight is radiated energy in the near ultraviolet region. Although not seen by humans, it is most suitable for insect attraction. Wavelengths and intensity of radiation affect the responses of insects, with increased intensities enhancing the attractiveness.

Generally, ultraviolet blue and green are more attractive than yellow, red, or infrared, while ultraviolet or blacklight is particularly effective for the European corn borer and tomato hornworm moth.

Just as certain lights attract night-flying insects, there are others which repel them. Yellow and red lights often keep night-flying insects away, and are used in insect-repelling lights for porch and patio.

Electric traps using blacklights are varied. Some are mechanical devices, while others utilize suction, with or without bait, and a collection or killing chamber. Still others depend on grids, which electrocute insects and allow them to fall into collection trays. All are available commercially.

Electric light traps have several advantages. Once installed they work automatically, therefore no strict time schedule for application of controls is needed. They can be used when the soil is wet, a condition which limits the use of many other insect controls. The traps leave no poisonous residue, nor do they develop resistant strains of insects. They are not injurious to wildlife, nor do they kill bats. Since beneficial insects such as bees and wasps do not fly at night, these creatures will not be attracted to the light.

Electric light traps attract several hundred kinds of noxious night-flying insects, including many insects of economic importance such as moths, many beetles, the European corn borer, pink bollworm, armyworm, European chafer, gnat, mosquito, and others.

Recent field studies at Geneva, New York, with lamps of varying visible light and blacklights, have been used to detect infestations of the European chafer. The larvae feed on the roots of plants, damaging and destroying meadows, pastures, lawns, turf, winter grains, and legumes. Tests in 1958 showed that adults of this insect were highly responsive to blacklight, and efficient levels of light were found to attract and catch them.

A simple, home-constructed device has been designed to control the codling moth in apple trees. (See Appendix E for a description.)

Timing is important for efficient operation of electric light traps, which must be started early in spring in order to kill moths before they lay eggs from which insects later emerge to ravage crops.

Despite the values of these traps in regulating certain insect pests, there are disadvantages, vehemently expressed by Dr. Frank E. Lutz, past curator of insects at the American Museum of Natural History:

Many people kill hundreds of Chrysopa in those damnable traps that electrocute insects that come to lights. These people, misled into thinking that the traps are efficient mosquito-killers (although practically all of the mosquitolike insects that they see killed are non-biting midges and other harmless or even beneficial things), wonder why they then have epidemics of plant lice. When used near streams or lakes, such traps destroy large quantities of the natural food of fish.

Suction electric light traps. The suction electric light trap is especially useful with certain moths that are attracted to light but continue to fly around it in circles. This device creates an air current that draws insects into a fan and forces them into a container where they are destroyed or collected. This type of trap may be combined with bait.

In one night, a suction-type trap caught approximately eighty-five pounds of Clear Lake gnats, representing about one million insects per pound. Such traps have been useful in collecting cigarette beetles in open tobacco warehouses.

Electric insect traps are being used for survey purposes, to detect existing and new insects.

Although not obvious, the ultraviolet output of the blacklight may decrease with time. It is advisable to replace the lamps before they actually burn out, or at least to replace them each season.

At Purdue University, an experiment was designed to determine just how effectively a trap could control garden insects in a fifty- by sixty-foot plot. Three different fifteen watt fluorescent light traps were used: one equipped with a single blacklight, another with a black and green light, and the third with three blacklights.

The most effective of these was the three blacklight trap which protected corn, potatoes, tomatoes, and cucumbers from insect damage. The traps effectively controlled striped and spotted cucumber beetles and prevented bacterial wilt of the cucurbits, a disease transmitted by these insects. In addition, the corn earworm, European corn borer, potato leafhopper, and tomato and tobacco hornworm were adequately controlled.

A drawing of the standard survey trap used at Purdue University is available, although investigators are improving its design from season to season. The trap is simple to make and operate, and it can be adapted to home use.

In addition to the experiments on the home vegetable garden plot, investigators also worked on larger fields of cotton and tobacco. One electric trap, equipped with a single fifteen watt blacklight fluorescent lamp, protected an acre of tobacco from the hornworm.

Recent tests using light traps to reduce tobacco hornworm indicate that the device may be a means of reducing populations of these pests to levels below those at which chemical insecticide treatment is necessary on tobacco crops. The light traps were able to reduce tobacco hornworm populations by 50 percent, and may be even more efficient in combination with other techniques, such as sterilizing males, or cutting tobacco stalks in autumn to reduce overwintering populations. Trapping over countrywide areas would be necessary, since this insect, being highly mobile, is capable of moving into fields from adjacent areas.

There are various electric blacklight suction machines. Some collect insects in permanent bags which must be emptied every morning, while other have disposable, replaceable bags. Some kill the insects and allow them to fall to the ground where they may be eaten by birds or small creatures. This type of machine has an unlimited capacity, and may be installed over ponds to provide food for fish.

Dead flies, in sufficient quantities, may be utilized as compost material. A woman, who in a flower show won first prize for zinnias, admitted that the soil in which the flowers had grown was enriched by many dead flies!

Some of these electric blacklight suction machines are mounted permanently, while others are portable and can be set up at different sites. A few have automatic timers which can be attached, while others are equipped with an electric eye which automatically lights at dusk and turns off at dawn, yet is not affected by lights from passing cars, and does not flicker.

Some of the machines are small and intended primarily for garden, porch, or patio; others are large enough to control approximately five acres of field, providing no trees or shrubs obstruct the light.

Electrocuting light traps with grids. Electrocuting light traps are made as lamp, lantern, or panel, consisting of parallel wires, connected alternately to terminals of high-voltage, low-amperage circuit. The insect is lured either by blacklight or bait, and, passing between any pair of wires, it completes the circuit and is electrocuted. This device is not harmful to humans.

These traps can be used indoors or outdoors. They have been useful in many field tests to check the time of emergence of insects and the density of their flight.

The same principle is used with an electrocuting screen over a baited box which must be emptied each morning. This device is effective in attracting house and stable flies, and can destroy up to a hundred thousand of them daily.

A home-constructed electrocuting trap has been devised to catch pests of fruit trees. (For a description see Appendix E.)

Trapping with suction. Resourceful gardeners have been known to capture garden pests by suction. One ingenious woman used a vacuum cleaner to remove whiteflies from berry bushes, and the insects were killed as they were drawn into the hose. Another unorthodox gardener used a vacuum cleaner on the front lawn to suck in dandelion heads gone to seed and threatening to spread.

Although these instances were on small home garden plots, the same principle has been applied to large-scale farming practices. A company in Texas developed a machine which, in essence, is a large vacuum cleaner, used to suck off noxious insects from cotton plants. The insects are collected in large bags and dumped into irrigation ditches. Similar devices are used successfully on potato plants.

The supplier of trichogramma, the microscopic parasite, uses vacuum sweepings in cotton fields to sample the presence of noxious insects, which helps to determine if liberations of the parasites are justified, and if so, the quantities needed.

For research purposes, vacuum samplings are taken in fields to determine the presence and possible densities of certain pests or beneficial insects. It is conceivable that insects may be gathered alive from certain areas by suction, and liberated elsewhere.

Recently a suction machine, similar to a vacuum cleaner, has been used experimentally by the United States Department of Agriculture to control the boll weevil. The machine has several flails that rotate at 1800 revolutions per minute. The suction lifts from the ground the weevil-infested cotton flower buds that have fallen from the plants. The buds are beaten to pulp and blown back onto the ground. In laboratory tests, only 1 percent of the weevils in the chopped material survived. It is believed that the survival rate under field conditions should be even lower because of heat, dry weather, insect parasites, and birds, all of which will destroy some eggs or larvae that may survive the flail. The machine is now ready for field testing.

While the technique of suction may have limited application, it is one which has not been explored fully. With the technological knowhow of which we boast, such practical devices need to be developed to meet special needs.

Natural insect traps. The leaves of molasses grass, *Mellimus minutiflora,* are covered with glandular hairs which exude viscous oil. The grass possesses marked adhesive properties capable of trapping small insects. The sticky secretions do not kill young ticks, but simply deter them from crawling upward to come in contact with an animal. Cattle pastured exclusively on this grass in Guatemala were reported to be entirely free from ticks within a year. Molasses grass has been planted in Florida and Puerto Rico to prevent the propagation of animal ticks. In addition to its property of trapping ticks, it also repels mosquitoes and tsetse flies, although cattle like to graze on it.

Although insect-eating plants may not contribute a very significant means of pest control, they should be mentioned for their minor contribution. If one were to plant a number of them near a patio, or indoors, conceivably a certain amount of control could be achieved.

There are some 450 known species of plants, belonging to several distinct families, which are wholly or partly insectivorous. They have probably adapted themselves to this mode of life by the dearth of nitrates in the soil or water where they grow.

The venus flytrap, pitcher plant, sundew, butterwort, and cobra lily are all well known insectivores. Their functions reveal a variety of cunning devices, with honey glands to attract, leaves that snap shut, downward-pointing hairs, and viscous secretions which entrap. Some of these plants may be found in their native habitats of swampy, humid bogs. You can transplant them successfully if you maintain similar conditions. The common varieties can be purchased.

In examining the various lures, snares, and traps found in nature, plants that are insectivores, weeds that are adhesive, and the lowly nematodes that trap, we realize that many manmade techniques are merely borrowed from nature. Gilbert White, in a letter of 1768, wrote, "It is, I find, in zoology as it is in botany: all nature is so full, that that district produces the greatest variety which is the most examined."

9 CONTROLLING UNWELCOME
BIRDS AND ANIMALS

There is no human being who is not directly or indirectly influenced by animal populations, although intricate chains of connection often obscure the fact . . . not only do animals have this influence on man, but man has an increasing power over the fate of the animal populations that still throng the world. It seems that considerable caution should be exercised before ordering the destruction of a species on the chance that it may be doing harm to human interests.

—*Bureau of Animal Populations, University of Oxford, Animal Report 1930–1937*

IN THE NORMAL COURSE of affairs, when there is predation it is probably prudent to let well enough alone. It is only when an abnormal amount of damage is anticipated or experienced that it seems necessary to interfere with wildlife.

Since man began to till the land, he has had to defend his fields against depredation by birds and mammals. To a great extent he has been forced to depend upon his own ingenuity for the development of procedures and devices that would be effective. Flails, brushes, brooms, swatters, nets, scarecrows have all been used. At one time the occasional firing of a shotgun, or sending a young boy into the field with a rattle to scare off crows from seeds seemed sufficient. Furthermore, oldtime farmers planted more than they needed and had a philosophy of sharing some of their bounties with the creatures of the field, sky, and soil.

Today crop damage to garden and orchard from birds and small creatures seems to have become more critical. There are various attempts to repel or decimate these predators, but there is little understanding of *why* these creatures plunder more than in the past. When the basic question is asked, the solution will be forthcoming.

Is it possible, for example, that our present farming and gardening practices force birds and small creatures into our gardens and orchards? Predation in recent years has been aggravated by agricultural specialization in certain areas. Monoculture in corn or other crops produces the possibility of a buildup of pests, whether they be insects, birds, or small animals. Diversity and rotation of crops reduce this hazard.

There have been vast changes of landscape. As the land becomes more urbanized, with more concrete surfaces and fewer natural habitats, the predators of small creatures are themselves reduced in numbers. Conversions, such as turning wetlands into rice fields, for example, produce vast changes, disturbing the customary habitat of many birds.

As areas are sprayed regularly with poisons for insect, weed, and brush control, are we denying the birds their normal foods? As a result of "clean cultivation" are we driving them into gardens and orchards?

Given a choice, birds and other creatures usually will prefer their natural wild food to our cultivated crops. It is observed,

for example, that birds will eat tart wild berries before coming
to the milder domesticated ones. Robins and catbirds will go
to the fruits of the shadbush and Russian mulberry before all
others, so these wild fruits can be used as a lure to protect
cherries and strawberries. Later in the season, mulberries, choke-
cherries, and elderberries can be used for cultivated raspberries
and blackberries, while wild black cherries, elderberries, and
Virginia creeper help protect cultivated grapes.

Planting a substitute crop appears less of a hardship when
it is balanced against the more dangerous and expensive methods of trying to eradicate the birds. During the time when
redwing blackbirds consume grain, damage can be minimized
by offering crops of sunflowers, oats, or barley grown at a fair
distance from the birds' roosting places. A sunflower crop has
been found effective as an attractant to birds at a time when
peaches are ripening.

Corn is one of the crops subject to bird depredations, and
there are many ingenious methods of protection which have
been worked out through the years. The oldtime farmer learned
that a bucketful of shelled corn, soaked overnight and scattered
in the field where corn is just beginning to come up through
the ground, will induce crows to leave the growing stand alone.
Other helpful techniques are to scatter grains of corn within
plain sight of crows, and to keep bird feeders full when the
crop is coming up.

There are cultural practices of great importance to commercial corn growers. For instance, the farmer can take advantage
of the fact that blackbirds stop to roost in woodlots and bushy
hedgerows before entering a field, and then eat as close to
safety as they can. Planting strips of buffer crops such as millet
or grain sorghum along the woods' edge or between hedges and
crop fields will divert the birds from the corn, if the buffer crop
ripens when the corn is at the milk stage. At times it is helpful
to cut back the roosting places. Bird activity is lively near
watercourses, and whenever possible crops not subject to bird
damage should be grown in such fields.

Other methods have been worked out, such as planting when winter flocks of birds have disbanded, scheduling the maturing date so that such plants as wild rice attract the birds, and planting seed more deeply.

Plant breeders have developed varieties of corn — with long tight husks and deepset ears — that are less subject to bird predation and which have demonstrated considerable effectiveness. In one test, the least resistant variety received 185 times the damage of the most resistant one. Production and growing qualities of the varieties have not yet been widely tested, but the six most resistant varieties tested over a three-year period, were:

(Most resistant)	Pioneer 302 A
	Pioneer 312 A
	De Kalb 837
	New Jersey 7
	Connecticut 870
(Least resistant)	De Kalb 950

One New Jersey corn farmer completely eliminated his losses due to blackbirds by using Pioneer 302 A.

Some individuals, seeing a flock of crows, starlings, or blackbirds swoop down on a crop, feel that such birds should be exterminated. The Federal Migratory Bird Treaty Act, which protects blackbirds, cowbirds, and grackles, allows these birds to be killed when they are found committing, or about to commit, serious depredations upon any agricultural crop, ornamental or shade trees, unless state law prohibits killing. Crows and starlings are not yet protected. There have been numerous articles in agricultural magazines calling for wholesale slaughter of starlings and blackbirds. In some fruit-growing regions bounties are offered. This is on a par with the hunting of eagles and hawks by professional hunters from airplanes, or the suggestion that the federal government embark upon a wholesale campaign of bird destruction.

Even when such birds are predators or mere nuisances, extermination is not only repugnant to many individuals, but fails as a biological solution. Usually, severe depression in bird populations is followed by increased breeding success of the survivors. Large-scale reduction of blackbirds and starlings may actually increase insect damage to crops. There is not yet enough research to assess the problem completely, but the evidence points to no simple solution.

The U.S. Fish and Wildlife Service has found that only 5 to 10 percent of the entire diet of redwinged blackbirds consists of corn, and what damage the birds do may be caused by their search for corn earworms. Another report, from the Canadian Department of Agriculture, claims that blackbirds save more grain than they eat, and are not as predaceous as many people believe. After examining the stomachs of some 500 blackbirds, mostly redwings, researcher Dr. R. D. Bird concluded that the birds in spring eat many insects which harm grain crops, including grasshoppers, beet webworms, pea and grain aphids. In the relatively short period when blackbirds do consume grain, they also eat troublesome foxtails and wild buckwheat seeds, and can be attracted to trap crops. A redwing fledgling can consume cutworms, cabbageworms, and grasshoppers in quantities equal to its own body weight. These findings were confirmed by another scientific report from Ohio, which stated: "The redwing is beneficial to the farmer during all periods that it occurs on the northern breeding range with the exception of about three weeks while corn is in the most susceptible stage."

Bluejays, too, are held in contempt by some persons. Yet over 80 percent of their food is estimated to come from weed seeds, grasshoppers, beetles, and other insects.

In urban and suburban communities, there have been many projects for repelling or exterminating "nuisance birds." Shotguns, giant searchlights, fire hoses, noisy recordings, shell crackers, and chemical warfare have been used. In some cases roosts have been dynamited at night to kill blackbirds in large numbers. This may kill other kinds of birds, including waterfowl. It is especially objectionable because many of the birds are not killed outright, but maimed.

Such widespread destruction is to be condemned. It is ineffective, and makes no real assessment of the role of birds. It disregards biological facts and substitutes brute force.

We need to reexamine our own attitudes toward these predaceous birds and small creatures. Through the years there has been a change in outlook. When the farmer was formerly content to plant a little extra, growers now are imbued with the business-like attitude that they must harvest as close as possible to 100 percent of their crop. It is considered wasteful and uneconomical to share any portion of the crop with other creatures. There are great pressures to destroy not only every last insect, but anything which interferes with a complete harvest.

But crops as well as wild growing things are dependent upon the complex interactions of multitudes of living things, in which nothing ever works out 100%. Until we grasp these basic tenets of cultural practice, we will continue to thrash about wildly for solutions. Instead we must seek underlying causes and controls which are biologically sound. We need to develop a willingness to share a portion of our harvest with other living organisms who also inhabit our community.

MINIMIZING BIRD PREDATION

Although we must have a full appreciation of the value of birds as insect controllers (discussed in Chapter 3), at the same time we must recognize that during limited periods, especially when crops are ripening, certain birds may be predaceous in garden and field. If we act wisely, damage can be minimized. We must understand that at most times and seasons bird operations are not too severe. During the periods when birds may become nuisances, there are certain practices which are not toxic and which give relief Emergency measures against birds, if we are not to harm them, consist mainly in covering the crop or in repelling the birds.

Netting seems to offer one of the best safeguards in the home garden to protect berries or small seedlings. You can use discarded thin curtain material, cheesecloth, or some of the newer coated materials or plastics.

Some gardeners have found it feasible to tie up individual clusters of grapes or fruits, such as figs, in cellophane or polyethylene bags before the crop ripens. A tubular plastic is now available which may be slipped over grape clusters or ears of corn while the crop is growing. While such devices may be useful in a small home garden, the amount of hand labor makes it impractical for large-scale operations.

Newly planted seeds can be covered with a homemade portable screen. Old door or window screening will do very well. Cut it into 18-inch strips and nail it to old lath for a framework. Placed over newly planted seeds of lettuce, chard, and beets, it will prevent the birds from picking out the seeds, and it can be kept over the bed until the plants have had a good start. "Hotcaps," obtainable at most seed supply companies, will protect young seedlings from birds and insects.

Fruit cages are useful over fruits and vegetables where the crop is valuable and the birds a nuisance. A simple device will accomplish the same thing with birds which fly straight up when startled. It is a network of very fine galvanized iron wires, only 22 gauge or 0.028 inches thick, stretched a foot apart, six feet above the crop, and invisible to the birds. This has been used successfully in England to keep wood pigeons out of Brussels sprouts. The birds enter the garden from the sides, but, when alarmed, fly up vertically and catch against the wire with their wings. They are not harmed, but gardeners note that, once having experienced the wire, the birds do not attempt to return. The effect on new arrivals who see the crop but not the wire is to touch a wingtip, flutter and recover, and then avoid the bed.

The wire lasts at least three years, and appears less obtrusive than fruit cages commonly used.

Frequently gardeners have used noise and motion to scare away birds and small animals. Devices may be simply constructed of materials at hand. The discarded round tops and bottoms from empty tin cans can be strung together to move, clatter, and shine. Thin sheets of aluminum foil can be crumpled into balls and suspended. Strips of cloth have been used to keep birds away from newly planted seeds. There are a number of commercial devices such as spirolum twirlers, plastic flags, pennants, shiny propellers, and pinwheels that rustle, rattle, and whirr in the breeze and flash in the sunlight.

Some gardeners leave small mirrors on the ground to discourage crows. Others have left empty glass jugs, placed on their sides, so that the wind can whistle into the containers and repel small creatures. In suburban areas, brightly colored celluloid pinwheels were planted around several homes to prevent persistent downy woodpeckers from pecking at shingles. Another version of the pinwheel is the addition of revolving cowbells, used to keep birds out of cultivated berry bushes.

There are various nontoxic materials available which discourage roosting birds. These include adhesives, projectors, and electric devices. (For useful physical aides to curb "nuisance birds," see List of Suppliers of Materials)

Several companies manufacture traps which capture birds and other small creatures alive. The traps are designed specifically for sparrows, starlings, hawks, owls, pigeons, and animals. But such devices may catch various creatures, and ultimately there still remains the problem of disposal.

Effigies have long been used to scare away predaceous birds. Years ago, a scarecrow, dead crow, the decaying body of a bird of some species, or a salt herring hung from a pole, were some of the materials used. When fruit was ripening, a stuffed hawk was set out in the orchard. A potato, stuck with many feathers and slung high, simulated a hawk. English gardeners used brown-paper effigies of a death's-head moth to repel bullfinches.

Currently, plastic silhouettes of hawks are weighted and mounted so as to move about in the wind. A hawk effigy suspended in air by hydrogen-filled balloons, which permit the figure to hang high and move, is being tested over orchards.

A foot-high replica of an owl is available which can be hung or mounted in a garden, with the figure visible from any angle. Presumably it has the same effect on birds and small creatures as a scarecrow. Although owl effigies were used successfully at the Busch-Reisinger Museum at Harvard University, they offered no relief from New York City pigeons in the sculpture garden of the Museum of Modern Art.

Today, simple effigies are considered limited in their effectiveness. More elaborate, lifelike creations with moving parts improve their value, especially when combined with noise, and when moved about frequently to new locations in the garden.

In addition to effigies, there are sophisticated bird-scaring devices, some of which are more appropriate for commercial growers than for home gardeners. But in all cases, the techniques will be most effective when operations are begun early in the season, as soon as birds begin to show an interest in crops. Once birds have become accustomed to feeding regularly in a particular field, it is difficult to get rid of them.

Birds become accustomed to most scaring devices which are used constantly. Different approaches used on alternate days have proved more successful than a single method used day after day.

Noisemakers must be used at daybreak during the first hours of bird activity after their arrival from the night roosts. It is far easier to keep them out of a field than to frighten them away once they have begun to feed. Once they have settled down they often stay in the vicinity for the rest of the day.

There are carbide cannons or exploders available which give a blast comparable to that of a 12-gauge shotgun. They are designed to detonate automatically at frequencies from four times per minute to once every ten seconds. The initial expense of these exploders is high, but operating costs are low. They often require attention several times a day. Mechanical difficulties have been reported common in some models. However, when they work well they are effective, and will last for many years. They have been found useful in small fields, and where other devices are undesirable.

Rope firecrackers, salutes, two-shot repeating bombs, and roman candles offer hazards, and are not to be recommended. Some commercial growers have tried using light airplanes, often equipped with sirens or horns, flown slightly above the tassel height of the corn. Pilots attempt to work a field systematically so that the birds are gradually herded to one edge of the field and finally chased out. This technique was attempted in Florida and not considered very effective, since, at the approach of the plane, the birds often dropped farther down into the corn instead of being flushed out. The method is further limited because airplane operation is restricted to favorable conditions. The most important time for operating scare devices is at dawn, and this is apt to be a time of day when flying conditions are unfavorable.

Other scare devices using noise offer promise. Call notes, alarm, distress, and food-finding sounds can be used to attract or repel birds. Their language is so specific that a certain species can be affected while other birds in the vicinity remain undisturbed. Selective alarm calls of various birds have been recorded and broadcast over an area. Recorded distress calls of starlings have made them fly off in great disorder, have flushed them out of fields, and kept them away from tree roosts and airports. The same technique has given some degree of relief from species which at certain seasons may be considered pests, such as various blackbirds, house sparrows, robins, and gulls. For effective results, there must be a knowledge of the bird's habits, and proper timing and placement of the recording. Dialects vary for gulls and crows in different parts of the world, and the correct one must be chosen for effective response. Records have been used in large-scale operations, by industry and municipalities, but the technique is expensive. If left outdoors, the equipment must be protected. It is costly to broadcast sound over large distances. However, a home gardener can have a simplified version of a sound-scaring device by placing a radio near the garden and tuning it to voices, music or mere static sounds. Many families now own tape recorders, which opens a field for amateur research in recording and broadcasting bird sounds.

Birds learn that broadcast noises are synthetic and gradually ignore them. To increase the effectiveness of recorded calls, other devices are used as supplements. Scientists at federal wildlife centers at Laurel, Maryland, and Denver, Colorado, are testing combinations of noisemakers, calls, and visual scare devices. A composite contrivance may consist of a mounted bird effigy in a position of anguish, armed with speaker, amplifier, and tape recorder to broadcast distress calls.

The use of sonic, ultrasonic, and electronic devices holds promise for future application. Scare devices operating on a dog-whistle principle are not feasible since the range of hearing for birds is approximately the same as for humans. However, it may be possible to use a sound which causes irritation, pain, or confusion in birds. At the Salt Lake City Airport, powerful radar confused flocks of geese so badly that they had to reorganize several times and detour the airport.

Light beacons have been used successfully to discourage night-feeding ducks in grain fields. Bulbs from 500 to 2000 watts can protect up to 640 acres. Such beacons are attached to turntables, and either revolve or flash.

Federal biologists have embarked on a program to develop methods of controlling predaceous birds or the damage they cause. "Nuisance" birds are marked, banded, and released to secure information on their habits in relation to crop damage. Materials are being tested in hopes of finding substances which will permit birds to live normal lives with the exception of raising young. In time this would reduce the number of offending species without actually killing any individuals. Some compounds are being tested which temporarily "knock out" the birds so that the offending individuals can be picked up, and any innocent victims left to "sleep it off," awaken, and fly away after an unusual daytime slumber. Experimentally, X ray and radioactive materials are used, since these materials repel birds or reduce their fertility.

Other means of selectively reducing bird productivity are being studied. One promising material reduces gonadal activity. Bird population may be controlled through biological agents such as diseases, viruses, or parasites which are specific to certain predaceous species, while not affecting other species.

Basic research on bird behavior may lead to future practical application for control of predation. Scientists in the United States Fish and Wildlife Service are attempting to learn if starlings have any behavioral quirks which could be turned against them. For instance, gooney birds or albatrosses on Midway Islands engage in soaring by using updrafts created by winds in sand dunes. When the dunes are leveled, the birds stop soaring. Similar environmental manipulations may be possible to control predaceous birds.

MINIMIZING ANIMAL PREDATION

A family dog frequently safeguards the home garden against small unwelcome invading creatures. A living fence such as multiflora roses may also act as a deterrent.

Non-toxic materials are available which aid in keeping small creatures out of the home garden. A repellent substance, available in aerosol as well as saturated in a length of rope, irritates the animal's nostrils without poisoning it.

Sound can be used advantageously to deter small animals from entering the garden. Some of the devices mentioned for discouraging predaceous birds are equally useful against small animals.

In India, farmers use a noisemaking machine which scares away wild elephants, jackals, snails, flying foxes, and monkeys.

In Vermont, a man troubled with rats succeeded in capturing the king rat and placed it in an empty milk can. The squeals scared away the remainder of the pack. The man made a recording of the distress call and played it to keep the rats away.

Numerous commercial traps are available for rats, rabbits, skunks, minks, raccoons, and others, which capture without injury to the animals. However, as with bird traps, there is no assurance that the desired species will be caught, and, once captured, the problem remains of removing the animal to a sufficient distance from the site of capture so that it does not return.

Ordinarily moles and shrews feed on soil organisms, which unfortunately include earthworms and other beneficial creatures. For this reason, moles and shrews are sometimes found where soil is rich in organic matter. But the gardener should appreciate that their presence in unusually large numbers may be due to a high population of soil pests, and serve as a warning that all is not well with the soil life. It is wise to investigate the reason for a greatly increased population of moles and shrews.

For gardeners overrun with these creatures there are certain useful aides. Daffodil, spurge, and castor bean plants act as repellants. A few plants of caper spurge (*Euphorbia lathyrus*), strategically placed, deter moles. However, if you introduce this plant into the garden, remember that it produces an abundance of seeds as well as vigorous, deep roots. The effect of the castor bean plant may be indirect; its large root system reduces water in the soil, which in turn may decrease the insects on which moles depend. Some gardeners place castor bean seeds in mole burrows. Although these creatures are not seed eaters, the odor from the seeds may be repellent. Mothballs placed in the burrows also act as a repellant. This aide may be useful on lawns, but should not be used where food is grown.

Sometimes moles can be induced to leave a vicinity by thrusting into the ground numerous tin windmills, similar to children's toy pinwheels. Apparently the vibrations from the rotary motion act as a deterrent.

Since the blood of moles does not clot, they bleed to death even from slight wounds, and avoid being scratched. The gardener can discourage moles from entering their burrows by pushing down small twigs such as raspberry, rose, hawthorn, blackberry, barberry, ocotillo, mesquite, or other thorny cane into the openings. The moles may abandon such places.

Being carnivorous, moles can be caught by baiting traps with fresh, raw meat. Ordinary flat mouse traps can be set at entrance runways, but should be hidden from the view of birds. In addition, there are special commercial mole traps designed with choker loops. Wear gloves when setting and handle them as little as possible, since human scent may keep moles away. After one mole is trapped successfully, its body placed in the burrow may lead to a general exodus.

Shrews can be repelled by sprinkling dried blood around the roots of vegetables.

Wire or plastic fencing is a good defense against rabbits nibbling in the garden. Over seedlings use portable frames made of chicken wire or waste lumber. As a temporary measure to protect young cabbage, tomato, and pepper seedlings from rabbits, cut out tops and bottoms of waxed quart-size milk containers, and put them over the seedlings when they are first set out.

Encircle young fruit trees with wire mesh to keep rabbits away from tender bark. Extend the mesh two feet above the ground and six inches below, away from the bark of the tree.

Certain materials are repellent to rabbits. Some gardeners have painted young fruit trees with animal fat in the fall. Rabbits, being vegetarians, will not touch this material, but it may attract rodents. Apply a commercial repellant of resin and alcohol or grafting wax around the tree trunks. Rabbits shy away from the odor of dried blood or blood meal, and you can sprinkle a thin line of this material around the edges of the garden. Dust powdered aloes on young plants, repeating the application after rain. Shake raw ground limestone, wood ashes, or cayenne pepper on plants when they are wet, applying evenly and lightly with a discarded kitchen flour sifter. Equal parts of fresh cow dung and water, mixed and sprinkled with a broom on rows of young vegetables, repels rabbits, but this material must be applied cautiously so that the fresh dung does not burn plants. Although tobacco dust is effective, it must be applied sparingly.

Certain planting practices minimize rabbit damage. Mulch is used as a physical aide to keep rabbits away from plants. Soybean is an attractant crop to lure rabbits from the main one. This practice assumes that the soybeans mature at the same time as the more valued plant, and that enough soybeans are planted to satisfy the rabbits. Onions, repellent to rabbits, can be interplanted with lettuce, peas, beans, or other favorite fare of rabbits.

An ingenious device was used by a gardener who cut up an old garden hose to represent snake effigies. The pieces were placed at strategic areas in the garden to keep out rabbits.

A variety of materials repel rodents. Both mice and rats are repelled by fresh or dried leaves of mints or their oils, pitch pine, and camphor. In order to avoid contamination, mothballs should not be used where food crops are grown. Sea onions (*Urginea maritima*) deter rats, while lavender, wormwood, corn camomile (*Anthemis arvensis*), and spurge repel mice; everlasting pea is used against field mice, Mayweed (*Anthemis cotula*) and leaves of dwarf elder against mice in granaries.

Traps for mice and rats are useful, and many gardeners place a number of them around flower beds or among growing vegetables. Bait the traps with nuts or a mixture of coarsely ground wheat or oats and peanut butter. Fasten rat traps to large blocks of wood so that the rats cannot shake free. Make certain that the traps are hidden from the view of birds. Remember, there is always a risk that small creatures such as chipmunks or ground squirrels may become caught.

When young fruit trees are first planted you may guard them against rodent damage in the soil. Make wire guards from 6- or 8-mesh hardware cloth. Cut a three-foot-wide wire cloth into two 18 x 24-inch pieces to serve as cylinders. Embed the bottom of the guard firmly in the soil around the ball of a young tree, check and reset it each fall.

Mice in the fruit orchard in wintertime may girdle young fruit trees, but some practices will minimize damage. Young orchards that are thoroughly fall-cultivated are relatively free of mice except where borders are grassy or weedy. In older sod orchards, repeated mowing during the growing season removes both food and cover, and exposes mice to such natural enemies as hawks, owls, and weasels.

Clear the vegetation at the base of the fruit tree by removing all compost and sod from the area around the trunk. Instead, place ½- to ¾-inch crushed stone, gravel, sand, or cinders within this circle, six inches deep. Compost can be placed up to the edge of this circle.

Beginning in mid-September use mousetraps in the runways or entrances to the holes. Then give fruit trees additional protection by wrapping a layer of 15-pound roofing paper or ⅜-inch square mesh hardware cloth around the tree trunk. Tie it with a cord or light wire. The paper or mesh must extend several inches under the ground, and sufficiently up the trunk so that it will be higher than the snow level. In spring, remove the paper or mesh.

Some orchardists place bales of straw or mulching hay between rows of trees as winter shelter for mice, hoping to lure them from nearby trees. However, this practice may only succeed in attracting more rodents to the area.

Squirrels can be discouraged from the garden by bending the wire fencing so that an "outrigger" is formed at the top—protruding outward at an angle. Tree squirrels are repelled by mothballs, and red squirrels by onions, interplanted with other crops.

Trees can best be protected from squirrels by having a squirrel guard on the trunk. This may consist of some slippery smooth metal, encircling the trunk in the form of a downward cone. Make certain that it is wide enough to prevent squirrels from jumping over it. Tree trunks can be encircled with wire mesh guards. Some gardeners have found smooth-surfaced materials, such as plastics, placed around tree trunks make effective barriers against squirrels. Wide bands of viscous materials, also used for tree banding against insects, may be used.

Many clever repellent devices have been used to keep raccoons out of corn. An electric wire fence approximately one foot from the ground is run between corn rows. Old screens and bushel baskets are propped up against cornstalks, to act as booby traps. Crumpled newspapers, placed between rows of corn and held down with stones, make crackling noises as raccoons step upon them. This material must be renewed after rain. Red pepper sprinkled in the silks of corn, or a small dab of hydrated lime painted on the cornstalk, repel raccoon. A string of electric Christmas lights has been draped on cornstalks, and the blinking lights deterred raccoons in their nightly foraging expeditions. Out of sheer desperation, one gardener had a corn cage constructed for the sole purpose of growing corn and keeping raccoons out. The cage was made of 14-gauge galvanized wire mesh with steel posts set in concrete. The obvious drawbacks of such a structure are the prohibitive cost and the lack of crop rotation.

Fencing has been used to keep deer out of gardens, but it must be at least seven feet high. At times electric fencing is used. Soybeans and corn have been planted as trap crops at the edge of a garden to lure deer to them. Foxglove and castor bean plants are repellent. A few pails of human urine, placed at the corners of the garden, as well as in the middle, deter deer.

The woodchuck is one of the most destructive and unwelcome of all small creatures in the vegetable or flower garden. In the absence of a dog, fencing seems to be the best protection. It should extend a foot below the soil line, and bend out at a 45° angle outside the garden to discourage burrowings underneath the fence. Also sheets of metal or cinder blocks placed in the ground under the fencing will prevent their digging. Some gardeners have found that mulched plants are not damaged by woodchucks, while others have used a soybean crop as a lure. However, the voracious appetite of this creature generally is not confined to any one crop.

Gophers are decimated by such natural enemies as gopher snakes, king snakes, skunks, and barn owls. In addition, some gardeners place a water hose in gopher holes to flood them. Others have set wooden box traps at the entrances. Gophers are repelled by fish heads placed in their burrows.

Before embarking on any campaign of eradication, it is well to heed the words expressed by Jacks and Whyte in *The Rape of the Earth*:

> We cannot condemn the prairie gopher, the Australian rabbit, the African termite, or the locust, without first discovering to what extent, if any, some action of man has upset an equilibrium in animal ecology, and therefore indirectly on plant ecology, and so affected the conservation of vegetation, soil and water.

The same holds true of creatures in our gardens, whether they walk, crawl, or fly.

10. BIOLOGICAL CONTROL

Biological control is largely applied ecology.
> — *Bryan P. Beirne, Director, Entomology*
> *Research Institute for Biological Control,*
> *Canada Department of Agriculture*

THE IDEA of using living natural enemies of a pest organism
to reduce its population is older than recorded history. For centuries the Chinese colonized ants to use them advantageously in
orchards, and the same method is still in use. The Yemenites
brought down beneficial species of ants from the mountains
each year, and placed them in date palms to prey on destructive
ants.

In the early eighteenth century, experiments were made using
parasitic insects against pest organisms. A century later, Erasmus
Darwin suggested syrphid flies to regulate aphids, while others
tried lady beetles. In 1873, beneficial mites were shipped from

the United States to France against pests on grapes, and the following year lady beetles were sent from England to New Zealand against aphids. Similar attempts were continued which gave relief, but none achieved complete economic control.

The year 1888 marks the true beginning of organized work in biological control when the vedalia lady beetle was introduced against cottony cushion scale and achieved spectacular success. In the 1880's the citrus industry of California was alarmed when its crop was threatened with destruction by a scale. No method of control was known, and many growers in despair destroyed their trees. The scale, known as cottony cushion scale because of its appearance, was caused by a small inactive insect that feeds on the sap of citrus leaves and twigs. The scale was known in Australia, where it was believed to have originated. The U.S. Department of Agriculture tried to get funds to send an entomologist to Australia in hopes of discovering a parasitic fly which would control the scale. Although no funds were available for foreign travel, the department managed to send Albert Koebele to Australia in 1888 under the pretext that he was a representative of the State Department to the Melbourne Exposition.

Koebele's study of the problem led him not to a parasitic fly but to the predaceous vedalia lady beetle. He shipped back 514 of the creatures, which thrived in California. Less than two years after introduction of the vedalia, the scale was completely under control throughout the citrus-growing regions of California. The vedalia has remained successful ever since, except for its decimation in 1945 by chemical insecticides used to control citricola scale in the California orchards. These sprayings resulted in widespread outbreaks of cottony cushion scale—the first since 1890.

After the vedalia's worth was proven in the citrus orchards of California, certain citrus growers' cooperatives established their own insectaries to promote biological control. In the past thirty years, in some 18,000 acres under biological agents, spot chemical treatment has been required only rarely. The annual cost of controlling particular pests, such as mealybugs and black scale, by biological means is estimated to be between $8 and $10 per acre. In the same growers' cooperatives, chemical control for five other pests under partial or noncommercial biological control averages approximately $40 per acre annually. Koebele's success was a dramatic example of what biological controls could accomplish. His trip had cost less than five thousand dollars and it had saved the citrus industry millions. His pioneering efforts led to an expanded program to find other beneficial predators and parasites. George Compere searched the Far East and Australia for insects to parasitize fruit flies. Frederick Muir went to the South Sea Islands to assist against Hawaiian sugarcane leafhoppers. In rapid succession, there were worldwide efforts to regulate the coconut moth in Fiji, the eucalyptus snout beetle in South Africa, and many others.

For several years biological control was regarded as a panacea for all problems of pest organisms, with the oversimplified idea that for every insect pest there must exist somewhere in the world a living organism to control it. Money and effort were wasted in ill-conceived projects to find natural enemies for all insect pests. It was a period fraught with potential dangers. A large number of insects were collected from everywhere and released, sometimes without adequate screening or quarantine measures. In retrospect it appears miraculous that these vast releases did not result in disasters. Of this era, Charles Elton commented: "Mass destruction and the casual releasing of predators and parasites may some day be looked back upon as we do upon the mistakes of the industrial age, the excesses of colonial exploitation or the indiscriminate felling of climax forests." Eventually the repeated failures brought about a return to reason. To date, some 650 species of insect predators and parasites have been imported into the United States, and at least 100 of them have become successfully established.

STANDARDS OF BIOLOGICAL CONTROL

Although early biological control work was confined to population reduction of certain living organisms by other living organisms, later it was extended to include the results of antibiotic action, plant breeding of resistant strains, the use of genetic strains of insects, nonpest species that drive out pest species by competition, and other biological agents. Some define the term as the action of predators, parasites, and pathogens operating in nature, whether or not man deliberately introduces, manipulates, or modifies the biological control agents. As it has evolved, and is used in this book, biological control is governed by ecological principles. It is an attempt to modify the environment in such a way as to favor existing natural enemies, without at the same time favoring the pests. This approach makes use of the relationships of insects, plants, and animals to their environment and to each other.

It is difficult to judge the success of biological control methods. A newly introduced biological agent is only one of many natural factors regulating an insect population. In general, an attempt is called successful or unsuccessful according to whether or not an insect species ceases to be a pest. Even though less than perfect control is achieved by any single natural enemy, the part it plays may be of distinct economic value, and there may be different degrees of control obtained.

The problem in comparing chemical and biological measures arises from this difficulty in evaluation, the chemical methods being measured by clearcut standards, and the biological ones being part of the complex of natural forces acting throughout the life cycle of a pest.

In the past, biological control work was pressured to obtain practical results quickly. With random trial and error, failures outnumbered successes. Ecological research was neglected. Today the trend is to harmonize both theory and practice. There is a continuous search for underlying principles, combined with an application of practical control measures. An expansion of basic research should allow opportunities to reexamine past failures. Some past projects may be reopened on the basis of knowledge rather than guesswork, and future ones should have increased chances for success.

The term "control" needs clarification. Workers in the field prefer to limit the term to the economic control of insect damage, and use "regulate" to mean depressing populations.

Control standards vary according to the amount of crop damage that can be tolerated, which is demonstrated in the contrast between the spruce sawfly and the codling moth. The sawfly is an important pest of forests, causing loss of growth and vigor, and even the death of trees. But the wood, which is the principal economic product, is not injured. Extensive damage to the foliage may be continued for a considerable length of time without causing intolerable economic loss. In this case, the biological control agents are able to reduce the population of the spruce sawfly to levels where damage to the foliage is considered of little economic importance.

On the other hand, present market standards of the apple crop demand virtually perfect fruit. The codling moth is an almost universal pest of apples, and, when uncontrolled, often destroys the crop completely. Conceivably biological agents could reduce the damage to fractional levels and ensure production of a crop. But a single moth larva attacking an apple will make that apple valueless by present standards. A loss of only 4 to 5 percent of apples in a crop often eliminates the grower's present-day margin of profit. Therefore, to achieve a satisfactory control in this case, codling moth numbers must be reduced to fewer than one larva for each twenty apples per tree. It is doubtful whether the most efficient of biological control agents alone could maintain the population at this low level.

These contrasting cases illustrate an important feature of control. Certain insects which cause economically significant damage only by intensive or extended infestation are considered *indirect* pests; moderately high populations can be tolerated and they are suitable subjects for biological control. Other pests, which although relatively small in population do damage by attacking produce immediately and destroying a significant part of its value, need reduction to the verge of extinction. They are considered *direct* pests, and, despite individual successes, they are not usually suitable subjects for biological control. Forest pests are indirect ones and we may expect expansion of biological control work in this area. Notable work has already been achieved in Canada and parts of Europe. Many agricultural pests are direct ones, and biological control as the sole agent is more circumscribed. Yet within the limitations, there is still much to be explored.

THE USEFULNESS OF BIOLOGICAL CONTROL

Many of our major insect pests are foreign in origin. Usually they are more destructive in new surroundings than they were in their old settings because their natural enemies do not enter with them. The objective of importation is to seek out these natural enemies. At times, such introductions are helpful but inadequate in eliminating economic damage to crops, and in these cases, other methods of control, on a reduced scale, may supplement them.

There are limiting features with all methods of pest control. With biological agents, a lack of synchronization of the life cycle of the parasite and the pest may occur, especially if the introduced insect is from another hemisphere. Or the imported natural enemy may enter a period of dormancy just when it should be active for control work. There may be no suitable alternate host to carry the beneficial insect through periods of scarcity of the pest. It may take time, even several seasons, to establish or reestablish a satisfactory balance between the pest and its enemy. During this period the damage from the pest may reach serious proportions and it is impractical for growers to wait until a balance is achieved. However, in many cases, biological control proved to be economical as well as effective. Outstanding success has been achieved in several instances with citrus crops.

The Citrus Experiment Station in California imported two parasites from Australia to control the citrus mealybug. Within three years the pest was under control. The search, importation, and establishment had cost no more than $10,000 and the citrus growers' yearly savings were estimated at more than a million dollars.

The practical value of controlling red scale with biological controls was also demonstrated for the first time by the Citrus Experiment Station in California. In 1948, parasitic wasps called golden chalcids were imported from South China, India, and Pakistan, and established successfully in citrus orchards of southern California where red scale was a particular problem.

By 1962, the red scale population was at its lowest ebb since the early 1900's. According to the Agricultural Commissioner, the cost of treatment for red scale in relation to the crop value, in Los Angeles County, has dropped nearly 50 percent during the three years 1958–1961.

The present control of red scale in California appears to be the result of the accumulation of many factors, including increasingly effective parasites, particularly the golden chalcids.

As biological control developed into an organized method, techniques were developed for mass rearing of beneficial insects for colonization. The economical propagation of imported insects was important in order to achieve control in a shorter time with a small number of importations. A number of mass rearing programs were successful, and after a half century of development biological control appeared to be on the threshold of fruitful advances when new developments syphoned away interest and research funds.

CHEMICALS IMPEDE BIOLOGICALS

The insecticidal properties of the chlorinated hydrocarbons (DDT and others) and the organophosphates were discovered in the late 1930's. The war years gave impetus to the use of emergency measures. In the 1940's, the introduction and rapid expansion of these materials in all aspects of agriculture greatly hampered and interfered with the functioning of biological control.

When broad-spectrum chemicals were used, many of the beneficial insects in the environment were eliminated along with the pests. Sometimes the result was a flare-up of certain insects, previously considered as minor pests held in check by their natural enemies. The application of chemical insecticides on vegetable and fruit crops, for instance, produced a heavy infestation of aphids and spider mites. At times these pests became more destructive than the ones against which the insecticides had been applied. There were buildups of mite scale insects and red-banded leaf rollers after chemicals were used against codling moth. Oriental fruit moths increased, and mite scale and red-banded leaf rollers developed as pests in peach orchards after chemicals were used against plum curculio. A widespread outbreak of cottony cushion scale followed the use of chemicals against citricola scale.

Economic entomologists became concerned with the problem and discussed it within the scientific community. At a meeting in 1950, Dr. George C. Decker, economic entomologist, Illinois Natural History Survey, addressed his colleagues:

> Chemical control of insects is only one phase of insect control; yet it appears that the urgent demand for information on new insecticides has led all of us into a large-scale, fadistic swing to insecticidal investigation at the expense of our other research. Insecticides are very valuable tools, and they should by all means be used where practical and advantageous, but we should not abandon other avenues of approach and thus become a group of

chemical testers and salesmen. We should, as a group, I believe, return to the conception of entomology that was held by some of our illustrious predecessors who believed that man, as a rational and intelligent being, should be able to outwit insects and not rely entirely upon chemical warfare.

The following year, G. C. Ullyett of the Commonwealth Bureau of Biological Control, then at Ottawa, wrote:

. . . The economic entomologist should be thoroughly conversant with the principles, methods and aims of ecology. Unfortunately, he is often lacking in the essential groundwork of this subject; or, if he has received adequate training, his professional career encourages him to ignore it in his daily work. He ceases to be a biologist and, in the majority of cases, becomes in effect, a mere tester of poisons or an insecticide salesman.

With the increasing use of chemical control through the 1950's and 1960's, the role of biological control was denigrated. Although official statements from agricultural circles in America have given token praise to biological agents, the work has been oriented mainly to a chemical approach. As recently as 1960 there were not more than forty academically trained entomologists in the United States who were devoting full time to biological methods of insect control. This represents approximately 2 percent of American economic entomologists.

Much of the remaining talent is directed toward the development and testing of chemical insecticides. Such imbalance, it has been suggested, is due in large measure to the generous contributions from the chemical industries to entomological research in our universities and land grant colleges. Funds for basic ecological studies and development of biological control are derived largely from state and federal funds with very little private endowment. Furthermore, new graduates are attracted to industry by higher salaries than are usually offered by public institutions.

Canada has pioneered in biological control from the earliest days. The Entomology Research Institute for Biological Control at Belleville, Ontario, maintained by the Department of Agriculture, and the Insect Pathology Research Institute at Sault Ste. Marie, Ontario, maintained by the Department of Forestry, are both world-famous for their research programs. The percentage of Canadian entomologists devoting their efforts to biological control is many times higher than in the United States. A sampling for five consecutive years in the 1950's revealed that *The Canadian Entomologist* devoted about ten times as much of its space to biological control as did *The Journal of Economic Entomology* in the United States.

The paucity of biological control work in the United States becomes clearer as more facts are examined. The state of California has always been outstanding in its enthusiasm for biological control, compared to other areas in the country. At a very early stage, it began importation of beneficial insects on an independent basis. In 1923, biological control work of the state was transferred to the University of California, and a three-way cooperation was established with the Federal Bureau of Entomology and Plant Quarantine of the United States Department of Agriculture. *At one point, the work in California was about equal to the efforts of the entire federal government in this direction.* About one third of all the species of parasites and predators established in the entire continental United States were imported by the California group.

However, there are hopeful signs that a favorable climate is being established for the future expansion of biological control, which admittedly has not been fully utilized. As many of the unfavorable features of the chemical approach come under serious scrutiny, their use may cease to be the chief or only weapon, and ultimately some sensible balance may be established.

At present, the chemical approach is vulnerable in many ways. There is grave concern about broad and long-range effects of continued use of chemical insecticides. The problem of insect resistance grows more serious and there is a recognition that many insecticides are antagonistic to biological agents. Overemphasis on chemical control has retarded progress in ecological studies. Those which have been made reveal that application of chemical control rarely produces more than a transient reduction of pest populations. On the contrary, used over a period of time, insecticides may *increase* pest densities. By changing the physiology of the insect pest or its host, the possibility is created of increasing the rate of survival or reproduction. Chemicals may reduce competition within the species or from other species, thus allowing pests to compensate for any initial population losses which result from spraying.

Manufacturers of pesticides are aware of the problems, and some are attempting to cope with them. They are considering materials in relation to side effects, residues, resistance, and incompatibility. Although the majority of manufacturers still produce broad-spectrum materials, a few are exploring more specific ones. "The fact that chemical control tends to magnify the problems it copes with and to create fresh problems in the process has convinced many entomologists of the need to base pest control so far as possible upon natural controls, and to employ chemical controls in such a manner that they supplement rather than replace these natural controls," said entomologist M. E. Solomon, in 1960.

In the report, *Use of Pesticides,* issued in May 1963 by President Kennedy's Advisory Committee, the panel recommended that government-sponsored programs continue to shift their emphasis from research on broad-spectrum chemicals to non-chemical control methods, as well as chemicals which are selectively toxic and non-persistent.

At the dedication of a new laboratory for research on Insects Affecting Man and Animals, in 1963, Dr. Byron T. Shaw of USDA said, "We could utilize biological agents to a far greater advantage if we had pesticides that would kill harmful insects without harming their parasites and predators." He expressed the belief that future insect control will combine physical, biological, and improved chemical methods.

THE INTEGRATED CONTROL PROGRAM

An approach to insect control which is favored by workers in applied ecology is "integrated control." This combines biological and chemical controls in such manner as to exploit the desirable features of both, while minimizing their limitations. In an ideally integrated program pests are first attacked by a combination of biological agents. After all possibilities have been exhausted, limited use is made of chemical control timed to inflict the least amount of damage to beneficial organisms, soil, and plant life. We must learn to make use of chemical measures, remarked Roland Clement, "as a surgeon's tool instead of as a bludgeon."

The control of the spotted alfalfa aphid exemplifies the success possible with an integrated control program. This aphid was introduced into the United States in 1954, and within two years it had spread into alfalfa hay districts of California, where it caused great concern. Chemical controls proved too costly, and left residues at cutting time which exceeded the allowable tolerance.

Experts from the University of California and Departments of Entomology and Biological Control studied the problem. To preserve the seedling plants which were easily killed by the aphids, a very light dosage of a short-lived insecticide was applied. Then beneficial insects were introduced to protect the growing plants — these included native predators such as lady beetles, green lacewings, and big-eyed bugs, and three imported species of parasitic wasps. In addition, a rust-colored fungus disease, fatal to alfalfa aphids, was introduced, and in some areas this pathogen proved to be a major controlling factor.

Results of this integrated program were excellent. The alfalfa growers have saved an estimated eight million dollars in one year alone. The program not only kept hay growers in business, but provided fodder free of insecticidal residue.

In some cases, the integrated control program has been developed successfully by modifying an existing program based largely on chemical controls. This is exemplified by the experience of the apple orchards of Annapolis Valley in Nova Scotia, long famous for its fruit. Through the years, insect pests had increased. The main difficulty was the extensive use of chemical sprays which interfered with the natural enemies of the pests.

A modified control program was devised, planned to harmonize with biological controls. General purpose insecticides and fungicides were abandoned, and those used were more specific in action and relatively innocuous to natural enemies. The timing, frequency, and strength of applications were planned to minimize damage.

Dr. A. D. Pickett and his associates discovered that oystershell scale could be controlled by its natural enemies if apple growers avoided the use of sulphur sprays. By using ryania, a selective temporary botanical insecticide, to control the codling moth, there was no interference with the more than forty natural enemies found in the area which controlled the red mite.

After this program had been operating more than a decade, outlays for insecticides in Nova Scotia apple orchards had been reduced to only 10 to 20 percent of those in most other comparable apple-growing areas. Orchardists following the modified spray program are producing as high a proportion of first-grade fruit, and are getting as good production as those growers who follow an intensive chemical program. The immediate risks of crop damage are probably no greater; the long-term risks far less. With prospects of commercial developments such as more selective pesticides, a number of insect pathogens, and other materials, as well as a better understanding of complex factors in environmental resistance, modified spray programs may become more simplified.

Following the development of the integrated program in the Nova Scotia orchards, researchers in the Province of Quebec yielded useful information on the rise and fall of insect populations which had practical application for commercial orchardists, in some cases eliminating or drastically reducing the need for insecticides.

Although more than a hundred insects are considered economic pests in the Quebec apple orchards, very few are important at any given time, and they may not be the same ones from year to year. One, or possibly two, appear to be the major pests for a time, reach their peak, and decline. Meanwhile, one or two others are ascending. The researchers were able to determine by statistical measure which pests are likely to be dominant during a particular season, as well as the key mortality factors which are apt to depress their populations. Although predators and parasites may be mortality factors, at times they are not the prime agents. Frost, for example, was found to be the chief factor with the bud moth, a pest of apple orchards. Customarily, growers in the Province of Quebec had sprayed against this insect twice during the growing season. But when it was discovered that bud moth larvae perish whenever temperatures go down to −21°F, even if only for a single winter evening, orchardists could eliminate their spray against this insect during the following season.

It is important for the commercial grower to know how many insects can be tolerated on a crop before actual economic damage is inflicted, but this type of information is generally lacking. It was found that when three to five bud moth larvae per hundred clusters are present in orchards, their population is not high enough to inflict economic damage. If the orchardist takes random samplings from his trees and finds fewer than three to four larvae per hundred clusters, it is not necessary for him to spray against the bud moth.

The modified control program has been extended to the sugar beet areas of Alberta. Elsewhere, reports from the thirty-seven year experience of the Zebediela Estate in South Africa, show an increasing reliance on biological control in producing over 35 million standard cases of oranges.

Despite these examples, there has been more talk of integrated control than action. Development of such programs must face economic pressure for the use of chemicals alone; it is obvious that an integrated control program is not in the best interests of the pesticide manufacturers. And it is difficult to work out biological control measures to be integrated with existing chemical controls.

Most biotic agents of possible value have not yet been studied and tested sufficiently for their full potential to be evaluated. There is difficulty in integrating an often slow-acting and not infrequently unsuccessful method that produces variable, though permanent results, with a fast-acting method that is usually temporarily effective and whose results are more or less predictable. In addition, there is difficulty in coordinating a method that is easily and readily applied by an individual for his personal benefit with one that must, of necessity, be applied by a government agency for the commonweal. This is a problem, but it is not insoluble, as has been demonstrated in California, Nova Scotia, South Africa, and elsewhere.

CONSERVING NATURAL ENEMIES OF INSECT PESTS

A phase of biological control neglected in the past is the protection and encouragement of natural enemies of insect pests. Ecologists are now studying the use of refuges to increase their populations and effectiveness by providing sites which offer food, nesting, and hibernating shelter, and meet other basic requirements. Such areas can help build populations of beneficial insects when they are most needed. In California, for instance, English ivy can be planted as a cover crop for a red scale parasite, and the ivy can be inoculated with scale to insure a continuous food supply when it is needed. In the same manner, newly planted strawberries can be inoculated with cyclamen mites in order to increase populations of mite predators.

Plants especially attractive to beneficial parasites can be intercropped in order to lure these insects to the vicinity. In the Soviet Union pumpkin is interplanted in corn fields to attract a parasite of the European corn borer. In Peru, early corn is planted within rows of cotton fields so that the moth *Heliothis virescens*, present early in the growing season, deposits its eggs on the corn in preference to the cotton. This results in a large population of predators on the eggs deposited on the corn. As the season progresses, the natural enemies move from the corn to the cotton and keep the moth population within bounds.

CURRENT EXPANSION OF BIOLOGICAL CONTROL

At the present time there is a favorable atmosphere for further development of biological control. On a worldwide scale, there are major expansions of staffs and facilities, with increased emphasis on basic research and the acceptance of long-term plans by government agencies in the United States, Canada, U.S.S.R., West Germany, France, Czechoslovakia, and an increasing number of other countries. The oldest international procurement agency, the Commonwealth Institute of Biological Control, has now been followed by a second organization, La Commission Internationale de Lutte Biologique, for cooperative work of countries in Western Europe. Similar organizations are being established for Eastern Europe, and possibly for Asiatic countries. Such groups promote and facilitate international cooperation in biological control, with exchange of information through periodicals, textbooks, symposia, and conferences.

The work of the United States Department of Agriculture in biological control is expanding, but at a pace too slow to meet current and future needs. A laboratory was opened in Fargo, North Dakota, in 1960 to study new insect control methods that are non-poisonous, and, more recently, another center was established in Columbia, Missouri. Research laboratories have been built for the North Central states in Brookings, South Dakota, and for the Southern states at Tifton, Georgia, to develop better methods of controlling grain insects. Insects Affecting Man and Animals Research Laboratory was opened at Gainesville, Florida, in 1963, with major emphasis on the biology of insect pests, and various methods, including biological and nonchemical methods for their control.

The United States Department of Agriculture has engaged in biological control in such places as France, Italy, Morocco, and Argentina. It has given grants to support foreign research, and has sent teams for insect survey and detection programs to the Middle East, South Asia, and Africa.

All of these efforts are commendable and deserve further encouragement, but they are inadequate and piecemeal. These activities represent a very small percentage of the total effort for insect control, and the dominant reliance is still on chemicals. In an interview on a CBS television program on April 3, 1963, Orville Freeman, Secretary of Agriculture, admitted that *the present budget of his department allots less money for biological control than the pesticide industry spends to develop one new pesticide.*

It is obvious that greatly increased budget provisions should be made to develop the full potentialities of biological control. Useful as this approach may be to farmers and gardeners, by its very nature it is one which must be developed and controlled by governmental agencies. A federal division for biological control should be established within the Department of Agriculture, and similar branches should be organized at other levels. Provision must be made to train personnel. There must be a close liaison with other governmental agencies such as the United States Fish and Wildlife Service, for example, to pool information. Greater use must be made of existing facilities such as agricultural experiment stations at home, and biological control agencies abroad.

After its establishment, the work of the division of biological control must be coordinated with, and not subjugated to chemical control. Methods must be devised for transition to "modified" control measures. Broad, long-range programs must be established which encompass basic research as well as attempts to find solutions to current problems.

11. THE USE OF INSECT DISEASES

The exploitation of insect disease organisms for commercial purposes has barely begun. One has only to observe field populations of insects devastated by disease to realize what a potent tool we may have to protect our crops from insect attack.

— *Freeman L. McEwen, Entomologist, Cornell University and New York State Agricultural Experiment Station, Geneva, New York*

THERE ARE MANY devices for insect control in nature's armory. Some are subtle, others are spectacular. Among them exists a group, unseen and unheralded, yet which perform their work with quiet drama. It is only with the help of microscopic magnification that we can appreciate the world of helpful bacteria, molds, viruses, protozoa, nematodes, and spirochetes. Slowly we begin to acquaint ourselves with these materials, learn their functions in nature, and apply them to our problems.

Diseases of insects are caused by the same type of organisms that cause diseases in other animals. But as far as we can judge, none of the organisms which cause disease in insects are harmful to other forms of life. Apparently there is a wide gap which bars cross infection. By the same token, insects generally are not susceptible to the classic diseases of man or animal.

Thousands of pounds of bacterial preparations have already been used in the laboratory and in the field on a wide variety of crops and forest stands. To date, no case of damage to plants has been reported, nor to any animal life from earthworm up to man. Studies of bees foraging within areas sprayed with these insect pathogens show that they are not likely to be harmed. Even after the laboratory specialist demonstrates that such a material offers no hazards, additional tests are conducted which attempt to infect other forms of life.

Although insect pathogens have been recognized for some two thousand years, no attempt was made to use them to regulate insect pests until the nineteenth century. In 1834, an Italian, Bassi, proved that a microbe could cause an infectious disease in silkworm. By 1873, Le Conte, in the United States, recommended the study of insect diseases for pest control. At the turn of the twentieth century, a fungus disease was used to control chinch bugs in the Central states. However it was not until the mid-twentieth century that the use of microbial pathogens opened up as a new frontier.

Early attempts with microbial diseases were not notably successful. These materials need skill, knowledge, and accurate timing of application. This is particularly true in dealing with foliage-feeding insects as compared to those inhabiting the soil. If fungi are used they need to be distributed when both moisture and temperature are high. Under some circumstances, the pathogenic organisms may have an adverse effect on insect parasites and predators of the pest. Microbial control, even if fully effective, may not be as lasting as that achieved with insect predators and parasites.

Despite these limitations, microbial diseases as regulating agents have achieved a high kill of some serious pests and they offer many advantages. Sometimes a microbial material needs only one application to protect an agricultural or woodland location for years, even spreading its beneficial effect beyond the area treated. Unlike chemicals, microbial diseases leave no objectionable residue. Certain insect diseases that do not kill outright, but are chronic, are useful if well-timed.

Many insect pathogens can be cultured and produced successfully at lower costs than predators and parasites, and some can be processed quickly for mass production without elaborate equipment. These are assets for commercial development.

When we speak of insecticide, usually we mean an insect poison. But the mode of operation of a microbial insecticide differs from that of a chemical. The poisonous substance is produced by a microbe. The toxins are the metabolic by-products of the bacteria's growth, like the toxin of botulism in human beings.

There are two different types of pathogenic bacteria. One produces insecticidal poison when grown outside the insect, and the toxins must blanket the crop which is to be protected. Application is made as often as necessary to maintain an effective concentration. With a true disease pathogen, however, it may be necessary only to introduce the bacterium into the insect population at carefully selected points to have it spread naturally through a large area. In this case, the bacteria grow inside the insect, multiplying and producing their toxic materials. The most effective of these pathogens are fastidious and are difficult to culture on artificial media.

Not only are these microbial materials free of harmful side effects, but the carriers are usually nontoxic. The most common diluent is water, sometimes with an ingredient such as corn syrup added as an adhesive. For solid or dry application, the microbial materials may be mixed with clay or talc, or combined with an insect bait such as cornmeal. Such harmless carriers offer an added safety factor, contrasting with the carriers for chemical pesticides, fuel oil, or kerosene, which compound hazards already present.

Bacillus Thuringiensis. One of the earliest and most successful of the insect-killing microbes is an aerobic spore-forming bacterium first isolated from dying silkworm larvae in 1902. When spore cultures of it were fed to larvae, they became paralyzed within sixty to eighty minutes.

The next development came in 1911, when some diseased Mediterranean flour moths were sent for study from a flour mill in Thuringia to a scientist in Germany. He found the same spore-forming bacterium which he named *Bacillus Thuringiensis.* It was used experimentally in Europe from 1920 to 1929 against the European corn borer, the gypsy moth, and the pink bollworm. But without a basic knowledge of its mode of action, scientists had poor results in field tests. No practical method was developed to produce the material, and experiments were dropped.

Later Edward A. Steinhaus, head of the Laboratory of Insect Pathology at the University of California, became interested in the potentialities of microbial controls. He believed that these agents contribute far more to natural controls than is generally recognized, operating with or without man's help. *Bacillus Thuringiensis,* occurring naturally, gives good control in some forests against western pine beetles and Engelmann spruce beetles.

Steinhaus began a thorough analysis of all past attempts to use *Bacillus Thuringiensis,* and in 1950, assisted by I. M. Hall of the Citrus Experiment Station at Riverside, California, he ran highly successful field tests in controlling the alfalfa caterpillar.

Next, the bacillus was used successfully against the cabbageworm in Hawaii and against the European corn borer in Illinois.

After the usefulness of the material was established, attempts were made to mass-produce it, but this proved to be another hurdle. Standardization was difficult since there are many varieties of susceptible species, with individual reactions to the multiple toxins. It was necessary to learn more about the nature of the bacillus and how it affected the insects.

Investigations revealed that this bacillus produced at least four distinct agents toxic to insects. When their growth is completed the organisms have a unique ability to develop into a resistant stage, known as a spore, with one formed for each bacterium. The spore is one of the most tenacious of living organisms. It can withstand boiling for several hours, heating in ovens up to 300°F., drying, or freezing.

At present, the operation of *Bacillus Thuringiensis* is not yet fully understood, but the following has been established. The spores, by themselves, may not be pathogenic to insects. To be effective, a protein-like crystalline substance must be present with the spores. These crystals, usually rhomboid or diamond-shaped when viewed microscopically, are toxic when eaten by larvae of certain insects. Possibly the crystals and toxins produced in the growth of the bacillus give the organism its unique insect-killing properties. In the early work with the bacillus, there was no knowledge of this crystalline inclusion. For this reason there were failures in fieldwork. At the time, spore count alone was considered a good measure for potency, and companies producing the bacillus competed for high spore count. But when mass production was begun, it became apparent that spore count alone was not an accurate measure of the virulence. Further studies showed the presence of other toxic substances, unrelated to the spores and crystals, which may be equally important. Apparently the spores must germinate in the presence of the crystalline toxin and grow in the midgut of the larva. Any reduction of either spores or toxin decreases the mortality. In some manner, the crystals are necessary for the successful germination of the spores and growth of the vegetative cell. Once these facts were appreciated, there was renewed interest in manufacturing the material.

How does the bacillus act? It invades the gut of the larva, at a time when the insect must eat almost continuously, and paralyzes the digestive process. The larva is basically a digestive tube with a body wall around it. It has an open blood cavity filled with fluid that performs most of the functions found in the blood of vertebrates. The gut of a healthy larva is highly alkaline, due to the production of a buffer which keeps the pH constant. But when the larva is under stress from disease and/or starvation, the buffer secretion slows down and the pH in the gut falls steadily. Only if food is reintroduced does the pH return to the strong alkalinity which permits the larva to continue in a state of health and growth.

Among the many moths and butterflies whose larvae are subject to the attack of *Bacillus Thuringiensis,* some can resist the disease because of the high pH of their midguts. Others develop general paralysis. But most of them, after eating a sufficient quantity of the spore-crystal toxins, are afflicted with gut paralysis within a few minutes and stop feeding. The pH of the gut falls slowly, as it does in a starved insect. This favors germination and multiplication of the bacteria, resulting in starvation and death of the larva within two to four days.

Bacillus Thuringiensis demonstrates the classical advantages of an effective control organism. It is highly selective in its destruction only of the order of insects classified as Lepidoptera. It does not harm lady beetles, honeybees, parasitic wasps, or other beneficial insects. It is nontoxic to humans and other warm-blooded animals if touched or eaten. Foodstuffs dusted or sprayed with it are free of toxic residues. Economic control can be obtained at both high and low population densities of insect pests. The material is being mass-produced in standard fermentation equipment, and a stable uniform product results which can be used at any time up to and through harvest.

Dr. Steinhaus has listed some sixty insect pests which may be controlled by *Bacillus Thuringiensis,* many of which are highly destructive in their larval stage. (For a partial listing, see Appendix F.)

Proposed additional uses include control of fly larvae in cattle feces by supplementing animal food with this material, for use with stored grain, and in the control of poultry mites, lice, and mosquito larvae.

The Food and Drug Administration declared *Bacillus Thuringiensis* exempt from tolerance, which means there is no poisonous residue for which tolerance levels are set. It is cleared for use on alfalfa, apple, artichoke, bean, broccoli, cabbage, cauliflower, celery, cotton, lettuce, potato, and spinach. This tolerance exemption may be extended to other crops.

Bacillus Thuringiensis is being produced in the United States and in several European countries. European formulations are prepared by governmental agencies, whereas in the United States there are commercial ones, with limited sales to the public. The material is produced as dust, as wettable powder, and recently in liquid form. The spores are durable and remain viable under normal storage conditions for several years.

For effective control, thorough coverage is necessary. However, the home gardener should apply the bacteria judiciously to avoid serious losses of caterpillars which later form butterflies as well as moths. These leaf-eating insects also serve as food supplies for birds.

Bacillus Thuringiensis can be applied as a preventive by treating foliage as soon as it appears in spring. There is no evidence that the effects are carried over from one season to the next, so that it must be reapplied. In using the material and observing results, remember that although the larvae may die slowly, their destruction of foliage stops almost immediately. Residual action continues for days, and sometimes weeks. Susceptible insects do not develop resistance.

Milky spore disease. In 1933, men conducting field surveys in central New Jersey found a few abnormally white Japanese beetle grubs. Their curiosity aroused, they took the specimens to the Bureau of Entomology and Plant Quarantine at Moorestown for microscopic examination. The grubs were teeming with bacterial spores. The disease, identified as *Bacillus popil-*

liae, was studied intensively by S. R. Dutky at the Bureau, as well as by workers in state and private laboratories. They attempted to culture it for release against Japanese beetles which had been ravaging field crops, fruits, and vegetables, from New Hampshire southward to North Carolina and westward to Ohio. Other approaches, such as trapping, burning, and spraying with chemicals, had been inadequate.

Treatment with milky spore of experimental plots resulted in more than 90 percent mortality two months after application. Equally high kills were found in areas where the disease had been established naturally.

In 1939, a program was launched from the Moorestown laboratory, in cooperation with state and federal agencies, to colonize milky spore disease in areas where it did not occur. Within a decade, more than 166,000 pounds of spore dust had been applied to nearly 122,000 colony sites, and nearly 93,000 acres were treated in Eastern states.

How does milky spore disease act? When a healthy grub becomes infected, the spores give rise to slender vegetative rods which grow and multiply in the blood by repeated divisions. Within a few days, the normally translucent blood of the grub becomes milky in appearance. Ultimately the grub dies. The spores which have filled its body cavity are released in the soil, taken up by other grubs, and they in turn become infected. The process is self-perpetuating and cumulative.

During the rod stage, the disease organism is quite short-lived. But the spores are durable, resisting excessive dryness or moisture, cold or heat. They can remain alive in soil for many years, although their potency is reduced by long exposure to strong sunlight or ultraviolet rays.

Bacillus popilliae is only one of several milky diseases which attack the grubs of Japanese beetles and a few close relatives such as May and June beetles. Most likely these organisms have occurred naturally in our native white grubs before invasion by Japanese beetles. *Bacillus popilliae*, known as "type A," is the most widespread and important of the various milky diseases, and it can be cultured on several media, although not on artificial ones. Because of this problem, Dutky developed a technique to obtain spores by using the grub itself as a culture medium. Thousands of healthy grubs are dug out of fields every fall, stored in cold cellars, and removed when needed. Each grub is inoculated hypodermically with approximately a million "type A" spores from milky grubs. They are held individually in cross-section boxes, with soil and sprouted grass seed serving as food, at 86°F. for ten to twelve days, during which time each grub develops some two billion spores. The grubs are ground up and mixed with a filler such as talc to standardize the spore dust. Theoretically, if no loss occurs during processing, only twenty-three grubs, containing some two billion spores each, could produce a pound of spore dust. The product is stable and it has been stored dry for as long as ten years without noticeable deterioration.

Spore dust is not applied to the soil as a complete coverage, but usually is distributed in spots. At times a modified rotary hand corn planter has been used which, when tripped, drops small quantities of the dust. In treating a small yard, the gardener can apply the dust with a teaspoon to the top of the ground, subsequent rainfall washing it into the soil. It should not be applied on frozen ground or on a windy day. Experimentally, good results were obtained when the powder had been spread with fertilizer or other filler.

Eventually milky spore disease will spread out from the area originally treated. This will be achieved by any natural or artificial movement of topsoil containing the spores, by the movement of diseased grubs through the soil, and by birds and animals that feed on the diseased grubs. Experimentally, it has been found that live spores are still present in the droppings of birds that have fed on diseased grubs.

Milky spore disease may be purchased. Samples of the dust produced commercially are tested at the Moorestown laboratory several times yearly to ensure the maintenance of standards. The dust has been used successfully by individual gardeners to treat small yards, as well as on large areas such as golf courses and parks. In some places, garden clubs and other organizations have initiated community projects for the purchase and distribution of the dust.

Since grubs contract milky spore disease and die over a long period of time, the gardener who looks for infected grubs in the soil discovers only those that are milky at that particular time, but fails to find traces of ones which have already died of infection and decomposed. Once the disease has been established, it is not necessary for the gardener to re-introduce it. In newly treated places, the disease is not immediately as effective as it will eventually become.

Although milky spore disease kills grubs in the soil, it does not prevent beetles invading from untreated areas. For this reason a community program of soil treatment with the disease is desirable. If the infestation is serious, supplementary control measures can be taken. The gardener can remove all ripening and rotting fruit, clean out host weeds and non-economic or non-ornamental plants, keep plants and trees in a healthy condition, plant trees that do not attract beetles, and delay the planting of crops to avoid the height of the Japanese beetle season. There are other control agents which destroy beetle grubs, including other bacteria, parasitic fungi, nematodes, parasitic and predaceous insects, birds, animals, and weather. Following summers of low rainfall, for example, the Japanese beetle population may be reduced.

Milky spore disease is one of the most effective factors in regulating the population of Japanese beetle as the insect spreads to new areas which may be free of its natural enemies. Any agent that slows down or checks an initial buildup helps to make the pest less destructive. Milky disease is such an agent. It can be directed to areas along the periphery of a main infestation to prevent populations from reaching the peaks attained in the older infested areas. It cannot be viewed as an immediate measure for emergency, but rather as a long-range regulator and preventive. It is a one-shot, self-perpetuating control.

Viruses. Viruses have been hailed by workers in the field as the ultimate in microbial controls. They are extremely host-specific, which means they may be limited to infecting a single insect species. Researchers look forward to the day when they may possess a virus specific for each species of insect pest. It has even been suggested that, in time, an insect pathologist may go to the shelf and mix a combination of viruses to control a specific infestation! Such a prospect is not likely in the near future, but we are beginning to make good use of these materials.

So far, viruses cannot be grown readily on artificial media but must be produced within the insect which they attack in nature. Ultimately, it is hoped that a form of tissue culture can be developed for uniform and consistent production. Despite the difficulty of culturing them, there are several examples of successful projects in which sufficient quantities of virus were obtained for spectacular pest regulation.

In 1930, an outbreak of European spruce sawfly was devastating thousands of acres of spruce in southeastern Canada. The destruction of trees, by 1938, had reached a peak. Heavy infestations had spread into neighboring Vermont and New Hampshire. By 1940, the outbreak had subsided because of a disease that eventually brought about a tremendous kill of sawflies. Canadian insect pathologists identified the helpful agent as a virus. Since then, the European spruce sawfly has been common in Canada and the northeastern United States, but is no longer a serious pest in the presence of the virus. In the future, if the spruce sawfly shows signs of buildup, entomologists have a tested weapon which can be mass-produced and applied for a strong initial attack.

In the early 1950's, in a similar manner, the European pine sawfly was spreading unchecked in Canada and parts of the

United States. Canadian microbe hunters knew that this insect was held within bounds in Europe by a virus disease. Infected larvae were obtained from Swedish entomologists and sprayed by aircraft over thousands of infested acres in Canada and America. The result was 99 percent mortality.

Although this virus has not been produced commercially, a bank of extract from insect sources has been established. This virus can be stored in suspension at least five years and remain virulent. One spraying of infested trees generally keeps the European pine sawfly under control for six or seven years, providing application is well timed in the spring. The economy of the material is striking; a spray made from four finely ground infected sawfly larvae in a gallon of water is sufficient to control an entire acre. This formulation allows some of the pests to survive, thus assuring a perpetuation of the disease.

Further success in control of the pine sawfly was achieved in 1954 with the discovery of the diseased Virginia pine sawfly in Maryland. Dead larvae were gathered and a virus was identified. A spray was developed and used at the larval season in infested pine woods, where, in a typical test, it achieved about 77 percent mortality in eleven days.

To date, one of the most spectacular of all virus diseases is polyhedrosis, a pathogen of the cabbage looper. This virus will kill the cabbage looper in four or five days, if the temperature is 70°F. or above. The fact that young caterpillars feed for several days on the lower leaves of the cabbage, before moving up to attack the head that goes to market, has made it possible to prevent appreciable damage to the crop. It is only necessary to apply the virus to the lower leaves where the eggs are laid, and the caterpillars die young.

The effectiveness of the material does not end with the death of the sprayed cabbage loopers. When they die, their body walls break down, releasing the disease in a fluid mass onto the foliage, to be further distributed by wind and rain. Each insect that dies of the disease succeeds in releasing it and increasing the concentration of the virus on the crop foliage. The control becomes so widespread that only one or two applications of the virus may provide enough to take care of these insects for an entire season. In 1959, the polyhedrosis virus gave excellent control of cabbage loopers that had nearly ruined truck farm crops.

Other virus diseases also show promise. For the first time, a virus disease has been found which appears capable of infecting spider mites. It was discovered in Whittier, California, in 1958. When tested, this virus caused infection and death of healthy mite colonies within seven to eighteen days, and appeared to be lethal to all stages of the mite's life cycle except the eggs.

Borrelina campeoles Steinhaus, a virus disease of alfalfa caterpillar, has been successful in California field experiments against this serious economic pest. By diluting dead infested caterpillars in water or talc, this pathogen has been sprayed or dusted on fields to infest alfalfa caterpillars.

The red-banded leaf roller, a major apple pest in the Northeast, is susceptible to a virus, granulosis. In field tests, spraying of the virus over apple foliage resulted in total destruction of the insects. However the virus is slow-acting, and under field conditions it may kill the insects within a month. Since the red-banded leaf roller feeds directly on the fruit, a great deal of damage might be done within this time. Granulosis might be valuable, however, in an integrated program in which several materials are combined for greatest effectiveness. Granulosis has an additional advantage as a pathogenic material: it can be produced artificially.

Dr. C. P. Clausen, distinguished entomologist who has pioneered in work with insect pathogens, feels that virus work offers great promise. In an interview, he discussed the possibilities of commercial companies entering the field and producing such sprays and dusting powders of various virus diseases. These materials could be used in any climate, and they would be exceedingly economical. Clausen estimated that millions of viruses could be produced daily at an estimated cost ranging from ten dollars to fifty dollars per million.

Some microbial materials store for future use better than others. In tests many retained their virulence very well, withstanding both dryness and cold. These can be air-dried and refrigerated, either in purified form or as dried larvae. Among viruses that have been stored in this way, some have remained virulent for over twenty-five years. On the other hand, a virus used to kill the European spruce sawfly showed loss of strength after only two years in storage. For such materials it would be necessary to maintain a fresh supply, perhaps on a yearly basis.

One of the hurdles which must be overcome is a reorientation of viewpoint by commercial producers. In the past, manufacturers of chemical pesticides have been attracted to produce broad-spectrum materials which have killing power for a wide range of insect species. Manufacturers must be educated to the value of narrow host-specific materials which in some cases may be limited to infecting a single insect species. This is the great asset of virus diseases.

Nematodes. Nematodes, or eelworms, are wormlike organisms barely visible to the eye. Of the hundreds of different types of nematodes that live in the soil, relatively few are harmful to crops. Some are actually beneficial since they are parasites and predators of other nematodes and insects. It is only recently that enough has been discovered about these creatures to recognize their usefulness for insect regulation.

One experiment in the 1930's discovered a nematode, *Neoplectana glaseri,* parasitic in the Japanese beetle. Although Dr. R. W. Glaser and his associates mass-produced this parasite, the milky spore disease, introduced at the same time, proved more effective, and was exploited more fully. The nematode remains in reserve, however, and may yet prove useful, since it can be cultured successfully on artificial media and is able to survive for long periods of time even when the Japanese beetle population is low.

Another useful nematode was discovered in the 1950's by Dr. R. S. Dutky, of milky spore fame, and Dr. W. S. Hough. This one, named DD 136, was found in codling moth larvae and has the remarkable power of carrying its own bacteria with it which it releases against its insect prey. The bacteria kill the insect, the nematodes feed on the cadaver, multiply, and leave after several generations, carrying the bacteria with them. When they are not feeding, they carry the bacteria in their guts. In a resting stage, DD 136 can be stored for long intervals at reduced temperatures.

Both in the field and in the laboratory, DD 136 proved successful against the larvae of many pests. At high humidities the nematode reduced 80 to 85 percent of tobacco budworm larvae. When used in treatment of the trunks and main branches of apple trees, the nematode achieved 60 percent or more mortality against codling moth larvae, and when applied against one brood, it remained effective against the second that appeared three months later. Its success against the pink bollworm, a cotton pest, was particularly notable, as chemicals have not been very successful in reaching these larvae which bore deeply into the cotton bolls. The tiny nematodes are able to pursue the larvae, no matter how deep they go.

Further experiments with DD 136 have been conducted in the 1960's by Dr. H. E. Welch and associates in Canada, by inoculating soil with the nematode to give resistance to damaging root maggots. DD 136, in water spray, controlled corn borers and killed almost as many cabbageworm larvae as chemical insecticides.

Use of parasitic nematodes for insect control is still in the experimental stage, but full of possible usefulness. Equally promising are the predaceous nematodes which consume insects and other nematodes. Some devour their prey whole, while others puncture or slit the body wall of prey larger than themselves to suck out the internal organs. The stoma, a mouthlike organ, dilates to form a kind of suction cup. This may be armed with one or more large puncturing teeth, or many small grasping teeth, or both. Other predaceous nematodes have hollow stylets with which they puncture the organisms on which they feed and through which they suck their food.

Species of the genus *Mononchus*, soil-inhabiting predaceous nematodes, have attracted attention as potentially useful against species of plant parasites. Several commonly occurring mononchus feed extensively, although probably not exclusively, on other nematodes. Some are capable of destroying large numbers of plant-parasitic nematodes of importance to the gardener, including those which attack onions, beets, potatoes, tomatoes, and clover.

One species, *Mononchus papillatus*, has been considered for control of sugar beet nematodes. Under laboratory conditions, it is a prodigious consumer of other nematodes. In an instance, one of these predators killed up to 83 root-knot nematode larvae in a single day. During its life span of about twelve weeks, one mononch destroyed 1332 nematodes.

Species of another genus, *Dorylaimus*, have been noted as an effective predaceous nematode in Hawaiian pineapple fields. They may be even more effective control agents than the mononchus. The possibility of using parasitic and predaceous nematodes is an attractive, yet largely unexplored, field awaiting investigation.

Fungi. Fungi were the first microorganisms used for biological control. Today it is known that insects are infected by hundreds of species of predaceous and parasitic fungi. They operate as contact insecticides and are less specific than bacteria in what they will attack. Fungi produce spores, but these are not nearly as resistant as bacterial ones. Little is known about vital factors for spore germination and infection, or the effects of an artificially created environment, but fungus diseases develop when humidity is relatively high.

Everyone is familiar with common fungi such as the mushroom or toadstool. These are massive fruiting bodies that bear the spores by which the fungi reproduce themselves. The main body, or mycelium, is composed of innumerable threads, or hyphae, which are incredibly fine. Some have filaments only ten thousandths of an inch thick. They branch and join up again to form a fine weft that permeates the upper layer of the soil and draw their nourishment from the organic matter that it contains.

Related to these familiar visible fungi are predaceous ones so small that they were only discovered microscopically in 1888. To date more than fifty species have been identified. These fungi attack small crustaceans, amoebas, and rotifers, and overwhelm nematodes many times their own size. The equipment by which they seize their prey resembles fish hooks, rabbit snares, lassoes, and other devices of the human hunter. The *Arthrobotrys* fungus, for instance, traps nematodes on small spherical knobs, facetiously called "lethal lollipops," coated with a sticky substance that dooms the nematodes on contact. They are stuck, like flies to flypaper, and once caught they seldom escape being consumed by the fungus.

One of these predaceous fungi, *Arthrobotrys oligospora Fres.*, has been used successfully against the potato root eelworm, a nematode which has been a serious pest of English agriculture. This fungus is commonly found in soils rich in decaying vegetable matter or animal manure. Dr. C. L. Duddington of Regent Street Polytechnic in London showed that the activity of predaceous fungi can be greatly stimulated by the addition of compost to the soil. Similarly, "green manure," which is vegetable matter, is also valuable. In Hawaiian experiments, when fresh green plant matter was mixed with soil, the number of harmless free-living eelworms increased. This in turn led to a greater number of predaceous fungi which were able to reduce the population of harmful eelworms.

Duddington recommends that if manure is unavailable, green manure will encourage predaceous fungi already present in the soil. Furthermore, he suggests soil inoculations with cultures of suitable fungi, believing that this technique raises no difficulty.

Fungi could be applied in powder form by means of a simple device attached to the tractor in front of the plow. In this manner, turning under of green manure as well as soil inoculation could be combined in one operation.

Duddington also stresses the need for good cultural controls:

> Apart from the use of organic manures, it must be remembered that predaceous fungi are, for the main part, organisms that require a good supply of air for their proper development. The normal farm cultivations that maintain and increase the aeration of the soil — adequate drainage, proper tillage and so on — are likely to benefit the fungi as much as the crop. In short the conservation of predaceous fungi in the soil may be summed up in two words — *good farming.*

In 1959 a parasitic fungus, *Catenaria vermicola,* was discovered in Louisiana on a species of dagger nematode which had been destroying St. Augustine grass. Later the fungus was found in sugarcane and rice fields in the same state. Now it is believed that this fungus is widely distributed in nature. This parasite kills a nematode by penetrating the skin and growing within the body of its host. Researchers were able to isolate the fungus and grow it experimentally on beef liver extract. When tested, it was effective against root-knot, sting, sheath, dagger, lance, ring, meadow, citrus, and stunt nematodes.

Another fungus disease, *Beauveria bassiana,* very long known, has been under study in recent years, notably in the United States and Austria. Although this fungus is only three thousandths of a milligram in size, it is a fierce killer of insects but harmless to other organisms. Its spores destroy insects by bodily contact or ingestion. Experimentally, this disease organism has controlled the European corn borer. The spores of the fungus, mixed with sterilized dry cornmeal, achieved 91 percent mortality of first generation corn borers. An extensive study has been completed to develop a culture medium to enable the fungus to produce billions of spores. One commercial producer of microbial pathogens in the United States is interested in developing mass production methods.

A closely related species, *Beauveria globulifera*, infects many insects, including chinch bugs, beetles, aphids, leafhoppers, flies, grasshoppers, mealybugs, caterpillars, and mosquitoes. Mexican bean beetles, especially susceptible to fungus disease, may perish in all stages of development, including the egg. Experimental work shows promise, but field tests are still needed.

Beneficial fungi can also be used against plant-damaging fungi, as was shown in experiments with root wilt and root rot of strawberries. Plant pathologists at the Connecticut Agricultural Station grew two beneficial fungi on wheat seed which was then used to inoculate the top few inches of soil in field-test plots. Treated areas showed significantly healthier plants.

Molds are another kind of fungus which can be turned against other microorganisms, especially nematodes. The molds form ring traps, like rabbit snares, which they constrict in the presence of their prey. When a nematode wanders into the opening of the constriction, in less than a tenth of a second the rings inflate to three times their normal size and grip the victim, as with a stout lasso, and strangle it.

Other molds have rings which are not capable of constricting, but this handicap is ingeniously overcome. The rings tend to fuse together, forming an elaborate network of loops coated with a sticky substance. A nematode, attempting to pass through, adheres to it. The more the nematode writhes, the more it becomes entangled, and it is ultimately consumed by the mold.

Protozoa. Protozoa are microscopic organisms, many of which are parasitic and pathogenic to insects. Some are slow to develop but ultimately prove fatal to their prey. Due to the presence of spores or cysts, the infected insect may develop an opaque appearance or other discoloration, or it may show no outward signs of disease except for sluggishness and lessened appetite.

Canadian scientists have found protozoan diseases which affect spruce budworm and jack pine budworm—two caterpillars which attack spruce and fir stands from coast to coast. These studies have been of particular interest because the effects of chronic protozoa diseases are exceptionally difficult to trace.

In the case of the spruce budworm, the protozoan forms spores in the cells of the larva. These spores multiply and pack the midgut so that the larva can digest less food. This robs the larva of its capacity to grow or have energy. An infected female larva which lives to adulthood is so weakened that it produces relatively few eggs. At times the spores work fast enough to kill the larva. In such a case, the larva does not have a shrunken appearance of starvation, but a breakdown of its vital organs apparently causes death.

At present, efforts to investigate another protozoan, *Perezia pyraustae*, are in early stages, with research centered in Iowa. It was first discovered attacking borers in American cornfields in 1949. Since then it has been reported in many localities, and apparently it is present in nearly every corn borer infestation. If the spores can be spread artificially, this protozoan may be useful in regulating corn borer populations. Experiments show that it can infect the borer at all stages, from egg to adult.

CURRENT WORK ON INSECT DISEASES

The foregoing gives a glimpse of the rich variety of pathogenic materials supplied by nature to infect insects. Our knowledge and exploitation of them are still in early stages. In the United States, the University of California has pioneered in efforts to apply pathogens in practical situations. The Entomology Research Division of the Agricultural Research Service maintains an insect pathology laboratory in Beltsville, Maryland, where several scientists are exploring promising disease agents for pest control. They work in cooperation with the specialists from the

Entomology Research Division on pests of major farm crops. In addition, several insect pathologists from this center are stationed at other laboratories, working on field problems.

The United States Department of Agriculture Forest Service conducts similar research on tree protection, with laboratory work centering primarily at Corvallis, Oregon, New Haven, Connecticut, and Beltsville, Maryland. Specialists from Forest Service work with insect pathologists on field-test projects. Additional work is conducted at state agricultural experiment stations, as well as other research agencies, including those in industry and in foreign countries.

These efforts are commendable, but inadequate to meet the present and future challenges in agriculture. According to officials in the United States Department of Agriculture, *there are only one hundred entomologists and bacteriologists at universities, private institutions, state and federal research centers, throughout the world, currently involved in the study of insect diseases.* In addition, there are a few engaged by industry. This represents a very small part of the vast program for pest control. Since pathogenic materials offer promise, the present program needs expansion. If a division for biological control were to be established, the study of insect pathogens would find its proper niche within this division.

The long-range effects of microbial controls should be appreciated. Since the abundance and destructiveness of any insect in a given season is dependent, in part, on the number that overwinter, any factor which reduces them significantly is advantageous. Not all pathogenic organisms studied will find a utilitarian place in applied insect control programs. At worst, results of such investigations will enrich our knowledge of soil biology. Workers in this field hope that with more future research, live diseased insects may be utilized to infect and kill their kind. Entomologists suggest that it may be possible to breed defective insects that produce progeny incapable of surviving. Although microbial diseases may not offer a complete method of control, we must understand that no one method ever will. We must learn to use ingenuity with a diversity of approaches, and we cannot afford to ignore any approach which may achieve safe and effective control.

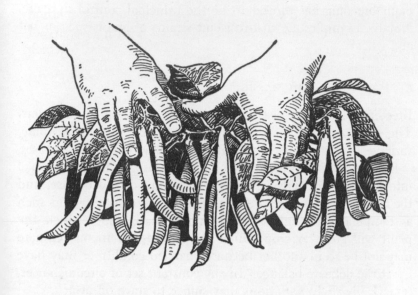

12. BREEDING PLANTS FOR RESISTANCE

The question of plant immunity is being studied more closely than ever before, and even now there are signs that in the dim future it may be possible to relegate the spraying machine to an honorable retirement.

— *Dr. A. M. Massee, East Malling Research Station, Kent, England* (1937)

WORKING with latent characteristics and useful mutations, plant breeders have been creating new fruits and flowers for over a century, developing late-ripening and early-ripening, solid fruit, long fruit, odd-color fruit, changing even the number of chromosomes in the cell. Among other factors that have challenged their ingenuity is the complex question of resistance to disease and to insect attack. Here teams of agronomists, horticulturists, and entomologists have been needed to work out resistant strains, and have worked together with such success that sometimes plant breeding has proved to be the principal control measure. Notable examples are rust-resistant strains of grains such as oat and wheat.

RESISTANCE TO DISEASES

Breeding plants to resist disease has been a boon to gardeners. The extensiveness of the practice can be seen by noting many varieties bred to resist rust, smut, rot, mildew, and other diseases.

Breeding resistant plants is a long-term program. It must take into account not only heredity, the nature of the disease, and the type of resistance desired, but the environmental factors such as temperature, length of day, and rainfall, under which the plant will grow. A crop which proves resistant in one climate may not be so in another because changed conditions may have upset the delicate balance. In any constant set of circumstances, remarkably slight variations may suffice to stave off attack.

There are different types of resistance in plants, ranging all the way from a positive immunity to the "practical resistance" in which the crop escapes although the plant itself is attacked. Then there are the "disease-escaping" plants which manage to mature earlier or later than the period when the pathogen appears. Actually these plants may be quite susceptible to the pathogen if the timing is altered. Some disease-resistant plants can endure moderate attacks but not a heavy epidemic. Most likely a moderate degree of resistance will always be more common than the rarer complete immunity.

Different approaches are used in developing resistance. One is to try to prevent the entrance into the tissues of the plant of the pathogen, which may often be stopped by some structural characteristic such as a thickened epidermis or the development of hairs on the leaves. Some varieties of plums resist brown rot because of the toughness of their skin, the firmness of their flesh, or a high fiber content. A particular variety of wheat is resistant to a rust because it has a tendency to keep the pores closed.

Some barley has a waxy coating on its leaves which makes it resistant to rust. Once the breeder knows how natural resistance works, he can try to accentuate the helpful factors.

Another line of development is based on the biochemical properties of the cell which influence the effect of the pathogen once it has gained an entrance. The invader sets up a parasitic relationship with the plant, which may dwarf it, cause overgrowths or decay, or kill it outright. The precise mechanisms of resistance in the plant cell are still being explored and breeders have little more to go by than a working hypothesis. In many instances chemical antagonisms are noted. The invading fungus may secrete toxins that begin cellular decomposition of the plant, and then secrete enzymes that further the breakdown process. Tannin, found frequently in vegetable cells, is generally toxic to the fungi. Some enzymes, abundant in unripe fruit, seems to protect it against rot. The acidity of the cell sap may also play a role in resistance, as has been demonstrated with grapes and wheat.

Other cell contents seem to account for some types of resistance. Some parasitic fungi have been found sensitive to minute differences of the amount of albumin in plants. Pigments found in red and yellow onion skins contain toxic substances which appear to be associated with disease resistance. Different levels of phenols in the cell sap of wheat varieties is important in their resistance of leaf rust fungus.

Nutritional starvation is another line of development. Nitrogen nutrition appears to be particularly significant for many pathogens. Sometimes the critical factor is a vitamin, such as the riboflavin which makes some peanut varieties resistant to peanut leaf spot. In soybeans, a lack of calcium is associated with fungus disease. There are strong indications that disease-resistant varieties may be improved by proper plant nutrition. The natural resistance of many plants when grown on a healthy soil is stronger than is generally realized.

RESISTANCE TO INSECTS

In contrast to the large number of disease-resistant varieties, there are relatively few varieties of plants which have been produced by man which have a high resistance to insects or mites. In developing insect resistance in plants, similar principles are used, but insects are less closely associated with the host plant than is a plant disease organism.

Differences in reaction of plant varieties to insect attack have been recognized for more than a hundred years. Publications have recorded approximately a hundred plant species resistant to more than a hundred insect species. But organized efforts to develop insect-resistant species began to develop only about fifty years ago.

One of the mechanisms of resistance is preference. Insects react differently to a plant's color, the light intensity, and directions of oscillations of polarized light and wavelengths. They also vary in their response to the physical structure and surface of the plant, as it will serve them for shelter, feeding, and egg laying. For example, a certain variety of onion resists the onion thrip because the angle of divergence of the two innermost leaves and the distance apart of the leaf blades on the sheath column does not provide a shelter for the insect. A similar example is found with sorghum: those varieties in which the leaf sheath does not cling tightly to the stem allow easy penetration by chinch bugs.

Several varieties of corn have been bred for repellent physical structure. Some outsmart the larvae of earworms which feed downward, following the silk into the ear tip. The resistant corn has long tight husks which prevent the entrance of the earworms. Tight husks and deepset ears of corn have also provided resistance to bird predation.

Odors and tastes which attract or repel are also factors in preference. Plant breeders have developed cabbages and marigolds without their distinctive odors which normally attract insects.

Many plants are insect-resistant due to some inherent toxic compounds. Researchers at the University of Wisconsin found a natural substance in corn, toxic to the corn borer, which might be used to advantage. Toxic materials were found inside the cells of zia alfalfa grown in New Mexico, and this strain showed less damage from the spotted alfalfa aphid than all other strains.

Plants may be bred with natural resistance through dietary controls. Breeders are trying to exploit insect resistance based on the lack of some nutrient essential to the insect but not to the plant. For instance, they have worked to produce cotton plants with a smaller yield of nectar, since feeding insects are attracted to this sweetish secretion. Lowering the amino acid content of the sap, and possibly raising the sugar content, may give control of the pea aphid. The yellow mealworm must have one of the B vitamins in its diet. The pale western cutworm dies unless it gets the proper balance of amino acids, the muscle building proteins, in its food. By stepping up the major and minor minerals and other nutritional factors, it may be possible to produce crops that are good for man and livestock, but distasteful or harmful to insect pests.

Another resistance mechanism is antibiosis — adverse effects on the life history of an insect, again through nutritional control. It is known, for instance, that insects gain certain growth factors from plants, and once these have been discovered it may be possible to breed plants which lack them. Several types of corn have been found to contain substances which slow the growth rate of corn borer larvae. In addition to the growth factors, insects may be adversely affected through the death of the young, abnormal length of life, death immediately before the adult stage, restless behavior, lack of formation of proper food reserves, inability to hibernate successfully, development of smaller individuals, larvae with reduced weight, reduced egg production, fewer young produced, and a reduction in the overall population — all of which may be manipulated through plant breeding.

Still another resistance mechanism is heterosis, the ability of the plant to tolerate injury. In this case it is important to understand the nature of the plant's ability to withstand damage as well as its ability to repair damage. Some insects inject toxic materials into the plant. These are shown to consist of enzymes or to be accompanied by enzymes. By what means does the plant inactivate these enzymes or toxic materials? The answer may give another means for increasing resistance.

At present there are some crop plant seeds which are insect-resistant, and there are more in development. Those available to the gardener today include: alfalfa resistant to leafhopper, pea aphid, and spotted alfalfa aphid; barley resistant to greenbug; beans resistant to Mexican bean beetle; corn resistant to grasshopper, corn leaf aphid, rice weevil, sap beetle, European corn borer, and corn earworm; cotton resistant to thrip; sorghum resistant to chinch bug and corn leaf aphid; squash resistant to squash vine borer; sugarcane resistant to sugarcane borer; wheat resistant to grasshopper, Hessian fly, and sawfly.

The United States Department of Agriculture reports development in breeding strains of potatoes resistant to the golden nematode, flea beetle, and leafhopper; lima beans and chili peppers which are nematode-resistant. For the latest information regarding pest-resistant varieties of plants, check with your local suppliers and seed catalogs as well as state agricultural agents and colleges.

LIMITATIONS OF PLANT BREEDING

Although plant breeding offers one more possible approach to insect control, it has its limitations. The insect, as well as the plant, can adapt itself to a new situation. Plant breeders know that what is "inherited" is not a specific character, but rather the tendency of the organism to react in a particular way to a certain environment. Applied to insect resistance, the genetic factors that are inherited consist of the ability of the plant to influence the insect population, or to withstand damage under certain conditions. If this environment is changed, the plant-insect relationship called resistance may also undergo change. Hence, resistance is not permanent. A crop may be free of pests when introduced, but acquire ones other than those which occur on related plants, within a few years. This was shown to be true with rapeseed.

Insects have demonstrated that they are able to adapt to new habits of behavior. The European corn borer, for example, over a period of time, adjusted to breeding two generations yearly, instead of, as formerly, breeding only one. The Japanese beetle has also shown signs of modified behavior. During the peak of devastation from this pest some twenty years ago, grass turf in fine condition was a favorite site. Now these insects are found in rough turf and cultivated ground as well.

Although plant breeders may develop varieties of plants unsuitable as food for the target insect, nutritional requirements of insects vary within a species. This gives insects a selective advantage of readily adapting to new nutritional offerings.

The use of resistant crops is dependent on finding mutant plant forms carrying the necessary resistance. There may be times when this is incompatible with the characteristics desired in a crop plant.

Despite the dynamic forces which create limitations, plant breeding can be a useful tool. It must be fitted carefully to the control of specific insects, and into the plant improvement programs of particular crops. The results already obtained show the possibilities of using plant resistance to insects. It deserves a careful study and full exploitation for both major and minor pests.

13. INGENUITY AND IMAGINATION

Man will need to improve and change his pest-fighting tactics progressively to have any hope of maintaining a good earth. The struggle will get harder, inevitably, as agriculture changes and as insects invade new areas through the expanding networks of transport and travel. No single type of control is likely to give man an all-purpose pest destroyer. To combat different insects in different situations, man will need a variety of special-purpose weapons and methods. He will need to choose among these, and at times combine several, guided by the best recommendations that research can provide.

— *Special Report, Agricultural Research Service,*
United States Department of Agriculture, October 1961

THE VARIETY of possibilities for combatting plant diseases and insects seems limited only by the human imagination. Many ingenious methods are under investigation today, with promise of good results.

RADIANT ENERGY FOR INSECT CONTROL

Experimenters have explored twentieth-century discoveries in radiant energy for possible use against insects. Radiant energy encompasses a wide range of various wavelengths, including radio, infrared, visible and ultraviolet lights, X rays and gamma rays, energy from various atomic particles such as neutrons, alpha particles, and electrons, and sound waves of various lengths, both audible and ultrasonic. Each type of radiant energy has an effect on the molecular structure of an insect. When the energy is sufficiently intense the insect is torn apart physically.

In making use of radiant energy, we need to be sure that we are not exchanging one undesirable set of methods for another. While we may succeed in destroying insect pests without leaving chemical residue, are we at the same time destroying our foodstuffs? Although flour may appear the same after it has been exposed to high heat, is the biological quality altered? Although grain may look the same after it has been treated with radio waves, is it still viable? Is the chemistry of the crop altered as well as that of the insect pest, when ultraviolet rays are used? These basic questions deserve answers in these experimental studies.

Radio waves have been used since about 1928 in a number of studies with insects. The effect seems to be mainly due to heating. Both radio waves and infrared waves have been used against insects imbedded in grain, flour, or similar material, and in both cases the temperature of the material itself had to be raised to a level high enough to kill the insects, although the radio waves penetrated more deeply than the infrared rays.

A cathode-ray machine, with a 3 million volt capacity, has been used experimentally to release electrons against powder-post beetle larvae in wood, larvae of the confused flour beetle, American cockroach egg capsules, yellow-fever-transmitting mosquito eggs, black carpet beetle larvae, bean weevil adults and larvae, codling moth larvae and potato tuberworm larvae. Complete mortality was obtained.

More recently cathode rays have been used by the U.S. Department of Agriculture in studies for control of insects that attack stored farm products. High voltage rays used against rice weevils in stored wheat killed the weevils instantly. Lower levels of irradiation checked reproduction and killed the insects over a period of time. These methods were also successful against confused flour beetles, red flour beetles, granary weevils, and others.

IRRADIATION OF MALE SCREWWORMS

Although much work with radiant energy for insect control is still in experimental stages, one highly successful technique has been developed in this field: the irradiation of male screwworms.

The screwworm fly was accidentally introduced into Georgia in 1933, possibly through a shipment of infested cattle. A native of tropical and subtropical parts of North America, it survived the warm winter in Florida and Texas and the following summer it began migrating into other Southern states.

The larva of the screwworm is a maggot that breeds in decaying flesh. It is a parasite on warm-blooded animals, growing only in wounds and feeding on living tissues. It attacks wild animals such as deer, raccoon, fox, and rabbit, as well as domestic livestock. In a few years the screwworm became the most destructive insect affecting livestock in the South, and attempts were made to deal with the ravages of the pest. In 1938 two young entomologists in the U.S. Department of Agriculture, Edward F. Knipling and Raymond C. Bushland, were assigned the task of finding some chemical treatment for the wounds caused by the insect. Both men were dissatisfied with having to treat the ravages of the screwworm, since they felt that the solution of the problem was to prevent the insect from entering the flesh of animals.

In studying the habits of the screwworm, Knipling and Bush-land noted that the female seemed to mate only once during her lifetime, whereas the male mated a number of times. This fact led the men to an exciting possibility, If they could sterilize males, large numbers of them could be released to overwhelm native males. The sterilized ones would compete and mate with native females, but little or no reproduction would result. The men reasoned that such a program, conducted over a period of time, would greatly reduce or eradicate the pest species.

Surgery, however, at that time the only known sterilization technique, was unsuited to their needs. The idea of sterilizing insects invariably met with scoffing derision from other entomologists. The war years intervened, and the project was deferred as typhus control took precedence.

In 1946, Knipling became Chief of Insects Affecting Man and Animals Branch of the United States Department of Agriculture. Renewing his interest, he assigned Bushland to work on their sterilizing idea. In 1950, Knipling came across an article which gave new encouragement. Dr. H. J. Muller, working on genetic experiments, had sterilized fruit flies completely with overdoses of X ray. Using this lead, and working after hours, Bushland used an X-ray machine in a nearby hospital, experimenting to discover the precise amount of radiation required to sterilize male flies without damaging their sexual drive. Later he induced scientists at the Oak Ridge National Laboratory to lend him a small cobalt-60 gamma-ray source machine.

Meanwhile Knipling attempted to get financial support for the project. He approached the Atomic Energy Commission as well as scientists at large universities, but invariably encountered the same scorn. His scheme was considered "fantastic and impractical." Still determined, Knipling requested a Congressional appropriation and received a pittance. The amount was estimated as the equivalent of the financial losses incurred from screwworm damage to livestock in two hours on a hot summer afternoon.

Bushland's work with cobalt-60 gamma rays confirmed the earlier findings of the two men regarding the mating habits. Although the female mated only once, the male mated an average of five times. Researchers collected native Floridian flies and bred from them a strain of males that mated seventeen times.

Sanibel Island, two miles off the coast of Florida, was the site chosen for the field testing of the sterilized male screwworms, with additional tests in Georgia and Alabama. More than 70 percent mortality was achieved, which was higher than averages with insecticidal treatment. However, fertile flies managed to invade from neighboring areas, and once again there was a buildup. Hence the testings were not considered completely successful.

An opportunity to obtain conclusive results came in 1954, when Dutch officials from Curacao requested that the United States Department of Agriculture help rid their island of native screwworms. The pests were abundant and were attacking many goats which roamed over the land. This 170-square-mile island, some fifty miles off the coast of Venezuela, was sufficiently isolated to provide an excellent testing site.

Sterilized flies, released at the rate of four hundred males per square mile every week for a month, drastically reduced the native screwworm population. More than 80 percent of the collected egg masses were sterile. After three months a few egg masses were still found in examined animals, but none hatched. The last egg mass was found after thirteen weeks. The program of releasing treated flies ended, and screwworms failed to reappear. The Dutch hailed the results as a miracle.

The success in Curacao led to further work. In 1955–56 a research team in Florida developed mass-production techniques for greater efficiency in rearing the sterilized flies. A large cobalt-60 gamma-ray device was built especially for the work, capable of releasing fourteen million sterile screwworm flies a week. The flies were packaged, four hundred to a box, in cartons quite similar to those used for packaging frozen food. Special equip-

ment was developed for opening the boxes and releasing the
contents by air

In 1957 a pilot test was made in central Florida, with the
joint cooperation of the United States Department of Agriculture and the Florida Livestock Board. The test demonstrated
that it was possible to maintain continuous releases by air of
millions of sterilized flies per week over thousands of square
miles of land, and that the program could be effective.

After this dramatic display, Knipling and Bushland had no
difficulty in obtaining interest or financial backing for their work.
The legislatures of the Southeastern states appropriated funds,
and a $6 million federal grant was made for a three-year project
in that area. In 1958, research facilities were expanded, a huge
fly-sterilizing production plant established in Florida, and all
infested areas of the Southeast were covered. Releases were
effective, and most of Florida was free of screwworm by the end
of the year. Releases of treated flies ended the following year,
and relatively little infestation recurred in the entire Southeast,
except for a few instances in Louisiana, Florida, and some isolated regions, noted as late as June 1962.

Meanwhile the program was extended to the Southwest, with
another large screwworm-rearing plant in Texas opened in 1962.
Improved methods of rearing the flies made it possible to produce up to 130 million treated insects weekly, requiring some 75
tons of meat and some 7000 gallons of blood. However, the
program in the Southwest has encountered problems which
make it more complex than the successes achieved in the Southeast. Workers altered campaign strategy to deal with differences
in terrain, climate, and habits of the Southwestern screwworm.
Damage in the Southwest has been reduced dramatically. In
1963, infestations were only 4 percent of those experienced in
the former year during the peak season. Outbreaks which occurred were small but widely scattered, in Oklahoma, Texas,
and New Mexico, making them hard to spot and treat promptly.
Nonetheless, in view of the vast areas covered both in the South-

east and Southwest, the program for irradiation of screwworm represents a notable achievement.

Before the work was begun, annual losses from screwworm to the livestock industry in the Southeast were estimated up to $20 million, in the Southwest, as much as $100 million. Despite the heavy costs of the sterilization project, substantial savings have been realized.

Future efforts with the irradiation technique may be easier through the development of screwworm flies which have special genetic markings. Until recently, field workers had no quick effective way to distinguish released flies from the others and thus could not easily determine the progress of the irradiation program. Irradiation does not alter the appearance of the screwworm flies and they are no longer radioactive when they are recovered in traps. Dye or other markings are not sufficiently permanent for accurate identification.

Now a special colony of black screwworm flies has been developed from a naturally occurring mutation of the normally blue-green flies. Releases of black irradiated flies may prove very useful since the color provides an easily distinguishable genetic marker.

Still another research tool has been developed as an outgrowth of the technique. Radioactive chemicals increase our knowledge of the life processes of insects. When introduced into the food of insects, or applied to them by other means, radioactive materials can be traced later for identification purposes. This helps in the study of behavior, movement, habits, lifespan, responses to various stimulations under natural conditions of life, the abundance of insects, and for developing quarantine and control measures.

FURTHER DEVELOPMENTS IN RADIATION

The scientific principle for insect sterilization has been established, and its possible usefulness is being extended to many economic pests including the boll weevil, pink bollworm, cotton bollworm, codling moth, tobacco hornworm and budworm, European corn borer, sugarcane borer, and fall armyworm.

At present, growers of cotton rely heavily on chemical insecticides, and they are reported to use 40 percent of the entire output of the chemical insecticides produced. A large portion of this is used to fight the boll weevil which since crossing the Rio Grande River into Texas in 1882, has eaten through cotton worth an estimated $10 billion. Working on an Atomic Energy grant, Dr. James Brazzell discovered that the boll weevil can be sterilized after feeding on small doses of the radioactive isotope phosphorus, thus making it possible to sterilize large numbers of weevils for release. According to an official of the United States Department of Agriculture, a successful biological control of this pest could cut the use of insecticides on cotton by 75 percent. Similarly, effective programs against the codling moth on apple and the hornworm on tobacco, could drastically reduce chemical treatment on such crops currently dependent in large measure on insecticides.

The corn borer, which annually inflicts an estimated $94 million worth of crop damage, may be controlled by radiation. Current research using X ray rather than cobalt as a source of radiation has been used successfully to sterilize male corn borers. After treated males mated with untreated females, only 1 percent or less of the eggs hatched. Additional tests revealed that corn borer pupae could also be irradiated successfully.

The radiation technique may be useful with insects of medical importance. It is being used against the tsetse fly in Southern Rhodesia, and being considered for mosquitoes transmitting yellow fever and malaria, as well as against houseflies and other household pests.

Trials are in progress to irradiate various fruit flies, including the Mediterranean, Mexican, and tropical ones. With the latter, the work is complicated by the fact that the female fly mates repeatedly; a single mating with a released sterilized male does not completely destroy her reproductive potential. In addition, the long-lived male may regain some degree of fertility.

Currently a combination of biological and chemical methods is being used in pilot experiments on the Pacific island of Rota. Integration of controls shortens the time and reduces the cost of the program. The target insect is the melon fly, which attacks melons and related crops. A chemical bait is used to reduce the number of wild melon flies on the most heavily infested farms. Then irradiated male melon flies are either dropped from aircraft or released from cages on the ground. The large-scale experiment is judged successful.

The knowledge gained from sterilization and the study of insect pathogens may be combined to yield a technique superior to either of them singly. Insect diseases may be transmitted through mating. Hence, quantities of released infected male adults could reduce pest populations, even among insect species which mate only once. Many pathogens lessen or destroy the egg-laying capacity of female insects. At times, infection can be transmitted from the egg to the larva. Furthermore, some pathogens persist in plants or soil, in which cases reservoirs of the disease agent could be established through infected insects. Success with the infected male might give even better control than merely the release of sterile ones. This is especially true among species in which male insects mate several times.

There are other possibilities within the realm of genetic control. Dr. Knipling believes that an even greater reduction of insect pests is possible by using some material that would cause sterility in 90 percent of the females that escaped the sterilizing agent, thus reducing the numbers of the succeeding generation by 90 percent.

Theoretically, there are possible genetic approaches, such as rearing and releasing interracial hybrids which would interbreed freely with the pest species but produce sterile females as offspring. This was demonstrated in the laboratory by successfully breeding a Japanese strain of gypsy moth with one from North America.

Another possibility is to carry the dominant genes for an abnormally high sex ratio of males to females, as has been done with the mosquito which is a carrier of yellow fever — *Aedes aegypti*. Strains of genes could be chosen for other characteristics which interfere with the synchronization of life stages with food supply or seasons, causing a reduction in survival or fecundity.

The sterilization principle, which has been hailed as one of the outstanding scientific ideas of the century, may be extended to other areas. Plant breeders are producing mutations in seeds by exposing them to radiation in the hope that strains resistant to insects and diseases may be developed. Wildlife biologists and other scientists are investigating the possibilities of applying the technique as an effective method of regulating populations of birds, fish, and animals.

Even before the usefulness of irradiation has been fully explored, another technique threatens to supplant it. If appropriate sterilization of insects in the natural populations can be achieved, the costly program of mass rearing might be eliminated. This approach would offer far greater possibilities for preventing the buildup of insect populations than would be achieved by killing the insects. Since the spring of 1958 compounds have been tested that simulate the effects of radiation and induce sterility in insects. Out of some two thousand tested, more than seventy showed some effect on insect reproduction. Unfortunately, the ones which to date offer the greatest promise are a half dozen derivatives of aziridines, a family of chemicals hazardous to other forms of life. Chemists continue working with new materials, hoping to develop completely safe sterilants.

SOUND WAVES FOR PEST CONTROL

Sound waves show promise for safe pest control, but up to now their use has been largely unexplored. Sounds can be used to attract, repel, or kill. Sounds within the human range of hearing as well as ultrasonic ones can be effective.

All insects produce sounds, some of which are meaningful to them. Singing, for example, is important to the males who call their prospective mates. The whirring of the wingbeats of certain female insects lures males for mating. Conceivably, recordings of such attractant songs and sounds could be used in insect traps. There are other sounds which are repellent and part of an insect's signaling system, but unfortunately our own information is too limited to make use of them.

Many insects have highly developed ears, while others have different types of sound receivers. For instance, when sounds vibrate the antennae of mosquitoes, ball-shaped masses of sensitive cells at their base begin to quiver. Such reactions deserve further study for possible use.

Certain sounds made and heard by insects, as well as other creatures, are ultrasonic. Since these are above the range of human hearing they appear especially attractive for pest control. Possibly a screen of ultrasound around a patio, garden, or field might be constructed to keep certain insects away. Mammals such as dogs, cats, and rodents respond to ultrasonics, and practical controls may be developed to keep these animals away from valued flower beds.

Experimentally, ultrasonic signals sent through water killed fish and destroyed other marine life. These studies, extended to other organisms, demonstrated that fish, frogs, and rodents could be killed easily, while some insects and bacteria could be destroyed at certain frequencies and intensities. It has not yet been determined whether death results from the heat generated by the sound waves, if the organism is shattered by the intense energy, or by subtler effects of chemical changes. In view of the destructiveness of ultrasonics to these living organisms, it would appear prudent to fully explore possible adverse effects on humans before attempting to develop this technique.

The Agricultural Research Service at Beltsville, Maryland, has experimented with ultrasonic waves against newly hatched codling moth larvae, cabbage aphids, bean aphids, two-spotted mites, and yellow-fever-carrying mosquito larvae. The insects were easily shattered by the high intensity waves, but there remained the problem of avoiding injury to most of the surrounding materials.

The use of ultrasonics for insect control is currently being studied in Canada and the United States. The tympani of some night-flying moths are hearing organs that can detect the high frequency sounds of bats which prey upon them. These sensitive receivers of the moths are hidden beneath the fur on the thorax. When experimenters found that the moths would take evasive action from ultrasonics resembling bat cries, they used this to upset the moths' feeding and egg-laying habits. In one test, ultrasonic transducers were set up in a corn field, producing sounds that resembled the cry of an echo-locating bat. The experiment succeeded in reducing the infestation by the European corn borers by more than 50 percent.

These findings are significant because a large number of tympanate moths are pests of economic importance throughout the world. If the results of the field trial are confirmed by large-scale experiments, a good practical technique may be developed. The ultrasonic transducer had no apparent harmful effects on plants, other insects, or nocturnal mammals. The possibility of the moths becoming resistant to sound is unlikely, and should it occur, the moths would merely be more apt to be caught by bats. Even though much of the apparatus was specially developed, the total cost was under $100. The limitation of the technique is that insects are repelled rather than destroyed. However, if a sufficiently large area of corn is protected in this way, the infestation may be reduced by modifying the mating and egg-laying behavior of the insects.

Although the use of sound is still in an experimental stage for insect control, it has achieved some practical application against bird and animal predation. (This is discussed in Chapter 8.)

Research is being conducted on colors, air currents, light, and other forms of radiant energy to which insects respond. It has been found, for example, that under controlled conditions, if darkness is interrupted with light for only five minutes, cabbage butterfly larvae can be prevented from overwintering.

POPULATION DYNAMICS AND INSECT CONTROL

Population dynamics helps to explain what regulates the numbers of insects, and is a useful tool for insect control. With the difficulties of expressing the complex interactions, predicting the rise or fall of insect populations remained a near impossibility until 1961, when a mathematical model was constructed in Canada to explain and predict population dynamics. With the aid of a computer, the model can simulate the different types of attack and show the variety that can occur in nature. Long-term "life tables" of population can be made, resembling those of insurance companies. These studies evaluate the mortality factors which affect pests, and discover the ways in which weather, biological agents, cultural, and chemical controls act and interact.

INSECT CONTROL THROUGH ATMOSPHERE

The dynamic forces of temperature, precipitation, humidity, winds, and air pressure change the fate of insect populations. A steady spring rain may fill up pools and create breeding places for mosquitoes, or an early summer of strong rain may prevent a buildup of chinch bugs by destroying them in the nymph stage. A hot summer may increase houseflies, but a cool summer may reduce general populations of insects. Even within a brief span of a few days, weather factors may reduce insects which otherwise would have posed a serious threat. We are learning to understand and manipulate these atmospheric forces for effective insect regulation.

The Bioclimatology Section of the Forest Entomology and Pathology Laboratory in Victoria, British Columbia, was established in 1945 to investigate weather as a factor on spruce budworm population. Later the agency studied the eastern tent caterpillar, fall webworm, sawfly, and other forest pests in their relation to weather and climate. Long-range weather study is used to regulate the outbreak of insects, by correlating surveys of adult insects and eggs. For example, information on grasshopper infestation in the Canadian prairie provinces has been recorded every fall for the last thirty years and the data has been helpful in planning control measures. Short-range weather forecasting is also useful. Predictions are made by taking field samplings, studying the catch in traps, and using information about previously known habits of the insect.

One area of study, currently being conducted in Belleville, Canada, is to determine the effects of atmospheric electricity on insect behavior. It is well established that living plants possess electrical potentials and radiate electrostatic fields around them. Additional charges are added to the plants by raindrops splashing from soil, dust, and sprays. Insects detect and react to the electrical charges carried by plants and other objects, which vary in intensity. Since different electrical charges influence flight activity, flight pattern, and egg-laying habits of insects, this knowledge may have practical application in insect regulation.

Insects respond directly to temperature changes, and in many cases it is known precisely at what minimum or maximum temperature they perish. This knowledge has led to control measures using such simple and readily available materials as water vapor and heat. One example of this is the intelligent campaign waged in 1929 against the Mediterranean fruit fly invasion in Florida. Insects spread rapidly, threatening the citrus crop of the entire region. A method had to be devised which could guarantee that the shipped fruit would be free of any living stage of the fly.

Working with the knowledge that Mexican fruit-fly larvae were killed when infested fruit was heated to 100°F. or above, researchers found that if large loads of citrus fruit were evenly heated, the Mediterranean fruit flies would be killed. But how could this be done? The system had to be absolutely foolproof.

Some of the infested fruit was loaded into a cabinet designed to provide constant temperature and humidity. A mixture of saturated water vapor, air, and fine water mist was driven through the fruit. Similar experiments were carried out in Hawaii, where the Mediterranean fruit fly was attacking many other kinds of fruits and vegetables. The exact death point of the larvae was established, and when the fruit was cool, experts could not distinguish treated from untreated fruit.

The safety of the technique having been established, two cars of sterilized grapefruit were shipped to the New York market, where it was accepted and sold at premium prices. The next problem was to devise standardized equipment to handle the entire citrus crop of Florida, ripening fast on the trees. Arthur B. Hale, a commercial engineer, devised the needed apparatus and, within a month of the New York shipment, sterilized fruit went to many other markets.

The success of this venture also assisted work on the Mexican fruit fly which had long been a problem in Texas. Sterilization procedure was introduced there in the 1937–38 season and resulted in a safe crop. As the process was improved, Hawaiian fruits and vegetables formerly excluded from mainland markets were admitted, and by 1945 some Mexican fruits, subjected to the heat-vapor process, were allowed to enter the United States. By 1950, in Texas alone, a half million tons of citrus fruit had been sterilized.

In addition to providing safe, non-toxic insect control, the heat-vapor process offers additional value. When citrus fruit is sterilized, any that is thorn-pricked, bruised, lightly infested, or injured becomes brown over the injured spot, making it easy to cull them when the fruit is graded. Ordinarily injured fruit is not easily detected, and breaks down in transit, hence the sterilization technique helps reduce transportation losses.

Although the vapor-heat process was developed specifically for the fruit fly, the process offers other possibilities. It shows promise for the control of scale insects on house plants. Mites and larvae of flies on narcissus bulbs have been eliminated, as have cyclamen mites in gerbera, and mites on strawberry plants. The technique may also be helpful on nursery stock.

In 1953, scientists in the United States Department of Agriculture began experiments using hot water on plants to free them of nematodes. By the following year two treatments were perfected and are of value to nurserymen. The methods must be followed exactly to avoid damage to or destruction of plants. One is to immerse dormant plants infected with root-knot or root-lesion nematodes in 127°F. water for two minutes. The other is to immerse dormant plants infested with insects or mites as well as with root and foliar nematodes in 121°F. water for seven minutes. Treated plants show marked reductions of infestation.

Hot water treatment has proved equally valuable in combatting plant diseases. California citrus growers have used it to kill fungi on picked lemons, and a similar method has been devised for soft fruit such as peaches. Depending on the species, the picked crop is dipped in water at 120°F. for seven minutes, 130°F. for three minutes, or 140°F. for two minutes. This treatment kills brown rot and Rhizopus rot on peaches before they are placed in the hydrocooler. A similar procedure is being studied for strawberries, raspberries, and sweet potatoes.

Pasteurization of certain seeds in hot water controls black rot and black leg disease on cabbage, celery blight, and bacterial canker, fruit spot, anthracnose, small leaf spot and bird's-eye leaf spot on tomato.

Cold air is another method of dealing with insect pests. More than fifty years ago it was known that the Mediterranean fruit fly could be killed by exposure of larvae, eggs, or pupae to temperatures of 36°F. or below. Cold treatment of fruit by itself would be relatively expensive as a method of killing fruit flies. But frequently imported fruit must be kept under refrigeration to prevent spoilage, and this makes cold treatment feasible. The fruit is loaded on boats with cold storage facilities and it is precooled immediately. During the voyage it is held at the required coolness, checked by a continuous automatic recording of air and fruit temperature. Despite the tremendous quantities of imported grapes, pears, plums, and apples which are inspected upon arrival, live fly maggots are rarely encountered.

DISTURBING THE BODY CHEMISTRY

Insects grow within their hard shell-like skins. When they have outgrown one skin they merely discard it and form another. Each of these changes is called a molt, and most insects molt several times before reaching maturity. Three interacting hormones have been found which control the process of growth and molting, including one called the "juvenile hormone" which keeps the insect from passing into the next stage until it is ready.

Experimenters extracted pure juvenile hormone from a million silkworm cocoons and used this substance on insects. Some treated insects never completed the molting process but became overlarge, while others became disfigured or fractional and died after a short period of time. Juvenile hormone, applied to the skin of insects, made them molt too soon and die.

The hormones taken from any one insect worked successfully on others. Therefore the materials need to be handled cautiously so that beneficial insects are not harmed. It is believed possible that the hormone material may be made more specific by varying the molecular structure, so that it will be lethal to one species but not to another.

Work in hormone manipulation is still in experimental stages but offers promise. Dr. Lawrence I. Gilbert of Northwestern University believes that well-timed spraying with juvenile hormone of target insects in their vulnerable stages may prove to be a safe and successful alternative to insecticides.

Scientists have found compounds which simulate hormone action on insects. Some materials arrest maturing. For example, their use can produce an abnormal beetle that is half pupa and half adult. When the structure of such compounds is known, highly selective materials may become available which could prevent the insect's sexual development, or succeed in having it emerge at the wrong season, not timed with the growing stage of the plant on which it depends.

Doubtless nutrition plays a vital role in insect life, and nutritional deficiencies have been produced to regulate insect pests. The normal activity, for instance, in the diamondback moth, depends on the balance of nutrients in the leaves of the plant on which it feeds. When the proportions were changed experimentally with fertilizers, soil insecticides, nutritional, insecticidal, and fungicidal sprays, a number of metabolic and structural changes appeared in the moths. The cutworm, *Agrotis orthogonia*, has been starved to death from malnutrition when spring soil was cultivated and kept free of all plant growth for a period of time.

Insect nutrition may also play a significant secondary role in other means of regulation. Susceptibility to insecticides is affected by the kind and quantity of food eaten by insects or stored in their body tissues. Bacterial infection and virus diseases may be related to dietary factors.

Another approach to insect control is being explored with an anti-feeding compound, "24,055." This technique would prevent insects from feeding on a treated surface, without necessarily killing or repelling them. It acts rather as a feeding deterrent, and to be effective must be presented to the insects continually.

Anti-feeding compounds have been in use as mothproofing materials and animal repellants, but the possible use of such compounds for crop protection is a recent innovation.

According to findings from laboratory and field tests, the method is selective and will affect only those insect pests which feed on the crop protected. Parasites and predators who happen to walk over treated foliage or feed on the affected insects will not be killed, as they are with conventional insecticides. Honeybees and other pollinators will not be affected by toxic deposits nor will the compound inhibit their feeding. Mammalian toxicity is generally low. To date, tests with "24,055" show this compound to be effective against most leaf-surface-chewing insects such as caterpillars and beetles, including the armyworm caterpillar, Mexican bean beetle larva, Japanese beetle, cabbageworm, and asparagus beetle. It is not effective against piercing or sucking insects.

Certain chemicals set up metabolic blocks within the insect, dulling their appetites, discouraging feeding, and ultimately leading to starvation and death. In the last four years some eighty-eight of these compounds, known as anti-metabolites, have been studied as effective pesticides. Imidazole, developed as an antihistamine in human beings, seems to be the most promising for insect control. Intensive studies show it to be effective, inexpensive, and of low toxicity for mammals.

Imidazole was first used to control fabric-feeding insects, with excellent results. This led to experiments with insects infesting cereal, and with many household pests. The material may also be useful for mosquito control since it has low toxicity, compared to other insecticides, for such highly sensitive fish as rainbow trout. Many common plant pests such as aphids, mealybugs, soft and armored scale insects, thrips, and whiteflies succumbed to imidazole with oil, in water spray. Since imidazole evaporates, there is no long-lasting residue.

USING CHEMICAL DEFENSES IN INSECTS

Some insects synthesize and store cell-killing chemicals that they exude or spray on predators, without suffering ill effects themselves. These defensive substances contain additives that enhance penetration in the bodies of predators. It may be possible to utilize these substances commercially as insect repellants or insecticides. Research on these naturally occurring chemicals may uncover new ones useful in insect control.

DEATH BY DESICCATION

Moisture is a fundamental requirement for insects' survival. They can lose large amounts of fat or protein and still live, but even a small water loss can go beyond a critical threshold and prove fatal. In order to conserve this vital element, insects are endowed with a complex outer covering of at least two layers, with a cement-like layer covering a wax or greaselike substance. It has long been known that insects can be killed by very fine dusts or other dehydrating materials. At first it was suspected that the insects were killed by suffocation, but it is now understood that death results from mechanical irritation and desiccation. The dusts kill the insects by removing the waterproof layer through continuous absorption or abrasion, either of which causes abnormal water loss and leads to desiccation.

Gardeners have made use of various dry materials as desiccants. For example, rye flour sprinkled over cabbage plants in the early morning dehydrates cabbageworms and moths. Confectionery sugar has been used for the same purpose. Talc, lime, and other inert dusts stored with dried beans keep them free of weevils.

Laboratory experiments have worked out some of the principles of this method of insect control. Dusts that adhere well to the insect's body are most effective. The finer the particles, the greater their covering power. Hairy insects, or those with a soft wax outer cover, are more susceptible than smooth-bodied ones.

Silica is one of the most effective of these dusts, its insect-killing properties having been discovered in 1958. It is used in the form of an aerogel, the liquid phase of the gel form having been removed and replaced by air. This process results in a dry light particle, having the same volume as the original gel, though unlike ordinary silica gel, the aerogel remains dry.

Silica aerogel has been effective against the flour beetle, rice weevil, granary weevil, and larva of the Mediterranean flour moth. Seed grain, pelletized feed, and ground bird food (but *not* food grain) can be treated with silica aerogel instead of repeated fumigation or irradiation. One treatment gives protection for an indefinite period. It is nontoxic. However, the dust is highly irritating when breathed, and workmen handling the dust are protected from breathing it by suitable respirators and by proper ventilation.

The use of silica aerogel has been extended to household pests such as roaches, ants, silverfish, some fleas, lice, mites, ticks, field crickets, and even to protection against dry wood termites. In tests for a 100 percent knockdown kill of German cockroaches in a brief period of time, the material compared very favorably with various chemical insecticides commonly used. Commercial preparations are now available for home use. Read labels carefully. Some sorptive dusts have insecticide added to hasten knockdown, but it is possible to avoid these toxic additives and obtain the dusts without them.

Refined diatomaceous earth is another desiccant dust. This is particularly useful as a dust or spray for dairy pest control, as it is not injurious to warm-blooded animals, nor does it leave harmful toxic residues which might contaminate milk. It is also useful in stored grain, where it needs to be applied only once. At present it is the only pesticide exempt from tolerance on barley, buckwheat, corn, oats, rye, rice, sorghum, wheat, and mixtures of these grains at the time of harvest or storage. Laboratory tests to date indicate that no insect is impervious to the desiccating effect of diatomaceous earth. If it is used in the fields, applications need to be timed properly, in order to protect honeybees.

Another approach to desiccation has been the experimental treatment of soil with sugar in order to kill nematodes. Used at the rate of one part in twenty to one part in one hundred of soil, it succeeded in killing 100 percent of the nematodes within twenty-four hours. The sugar did not pass into the nematodes' bodies, but water passed out of their bodies to dilute the sugar solution in the soil.

While it is commendable that such research is being attempted, with a bold imaginative approach, and using nontoxic materials, it should be pointed out that manure and composting materials are effective nematocides. Also, in the experimental work, growth of corn and citrus was temporarily retarded, though the citrus plants in the greenhouse recovered when the sugar was flushed out of the soil with water twenty-four hours after treatment. This serves as an indication that in the long run material such as sugar in the soil may produce its own problems.

IMMOBILIZING INSECTS

Various materials have been used through the years which have kept insects under control through adhesion. Perhaps the first which comes to mind is flypaper. The long festoons were commonly seen in kitchen, barn, and stable, and there have been many other ingenious applications of the same principle.

Many adhesives have been used to immobilize crawling insects from ascending trees. To prevent damage, trunks of trees have been daubed or ringed with tar, tung oil, or a combination of powdered Manila gum copal, castor oil, and beeswax. A variety of materials have been used to make traps, coated with sticky materials, but the drawback of this technique is that it is not selective. Beneficial insects as well as pests may get caught.

Many insects or mites have been immobilized on plants by spraying water solutions containing flour, poster paste, sugar, molasses, glue, soap, or gelatine. The pests either die or are devoured by their enemies.

Some gardeners have made mixtures of equal parts wheat bran, hardwood sawdust, molasses, and water as bait for cutworms. The material is placed around plants at dusk and the cutworms feed on it during the night. Since the bait clings to their bodies and hardens, the cutworms cannot burrow back into the ground.

Recent experiments at Purdue University made use of an old-time favorite, a combination of buttermilk and wheat flour, to destroy spider mites by immobilizing them on leaf surfaces where they exploded. While it is too early to draw definite conclusions from this experiment, it was encouraging to note that the materials are nontoxic, noncorrosive to machinery, and, of course, quite inexpensive. An estimated 300,000 pounds of flour and 1500 gallons of buttermilk would take care of 1000 acres of bearing orchard, and the use of these materials would have the additional advantage of using up surplus farm products.

The experiments were conducted by Dr. G. Edward Marshall. Dr. Marshall explored nontoxic materials after he had been hospitalized as a result of experiments which had exposed him to a long series of phosphate acaricides, chemical insecticides specific against mites. Wrote Marshall: "The preliminary work from last summer suggests, contrary to the procedure in the last decade, that it is quite possible that considerably less dependence on very hazardous sprays will be necessary."

Polybutenes are a modern material which show potential usefulness in an old field. These oil derivatives are used in industry for sealing and caulking, and the making of adhesives, and moisture-proof and vapor-resistant paper. Due to their high viscosity, they have been found helpful in immobilizing insects and mites, and in preventing or controlling plant diseases caused by airborne spores.

Dr. Robert W. Fisher of the Canadian Department of Agriculture has done pioneering experiments, begun as recently as 1959, with polybutenes against insects, mites, and plant diseases. In his trials, polybutenes gave effective control of red spider mites on peach trees. This was followed up successfully in early season sprays in commercial orchards in British Columbia, New York, Indiana, and Great Britain. Polybutenes were equally effective as a chemical fungicide in preventing leafmold on tomato, in control of resistant red mites on apples in field tests, and, when combined with nickel salts, controlled wheat rust. Under current investigation, polybutenes are controlling powdery mildew on a highly susceptible variety of greenhouse roses, and mildew on cucurbits. Further possible uses may be against scales and mites on citrus crops, fungus diseases, and forest pests such as gypsy moth and spruce budworm. Polybutenes can be emulsified in water, but are not washed off by rain. In terms of costs they compare favorably with oil sprays.

Another modern industrial product which proves useful against insects and mites is the group of cellulose polymers. These materials are used as thickening agents, binders, and stabilizers in industry. Used against mites, for instance, they not only stick them to the leaves, but cause much internal disturbance as well. The materials have very low toxicity to mammals and are therefore of promise for use on food crops to control soft-bodied insects such as aphids and scale insects in their motile stages.

OTHER INGENIOUS APPROACHES

Sometimes gardeners have stumbled upon simple materials which offer help in combatting insect pests. Among these is the use of dry materials such as bran, which, when eaten by the insect, make it swell up and rupture. Bran has been sprinkled on the tops of potatoes wet with dew for the purpose of killing potato beetles. Similarly, cornmeal has been dusted on cabbage plants, causing cabbageworms to drop off.

Smoke is another material which can be useful in insect control. Mexicans have used smoke on mango trees during the fruit-maturing season to reduce infestation by Mexican fruit flies. John G. Shaw and Donald F. Starr, both from the Bureau of Entomology and Plant Quarantine, investigated this technique. Using litter from mango groves consisting mostly of leaves, they produced smudge from the smoke. The studies were made during a season of frequent rainfall in which the litter was damp and easy to keep smoldering rather than burning. The experiment showed that smoke from the burning mango leaves, and also from rice straw, greatly reduced the fruit fly population.

Frequently greenhouse gardeners have difficulty controlling aphids, ants, and mites. In such cases, the greenhouse may be safely fumigated with smoke from oak leaves which are not poisonous, do not kill soil bacteria, and leave no harmful residue. You can make your own smoking device in a pail. Place newspapers at the bottom and above them place a metal grating. Put a layer of straw above the grating to act as a buffer and then place watered oak leaves on top. Light the newspaper, and the oak leaves will smolder rather than burn, producing thick smoke. Close the greenhouse door tightly and smoke the leaves for a half hour. Other useful plants for smoking are stems and leaves of canna plants and the leaves of peppergrass.

At present, the United States Department of Agriculture has begun to plan research, seeking new physical methods to control insect pests. For example, a team of scientists, using highly refined techniques, is attempting to control four species of flies most objectionable on dairy farms through light and other forms of radiant energy, audible and ultrasonic sound, air currents, and geometric patterns.

In the past, we have depended mainly on pesticidal treatment for post-harvest storage of crops, with heavy fumigations of grains in granaries, and chemical treatment of fruits and vegetables to retard deterioration. New and more sophisticated control measures offer possibilities of reduced dependence on toxic materials. Among items recently developed is a multi-ply, heat-sealed kraft paper bag, the outer layer of which is treated with an insect repellant that protects the bag and its contents against insects, without contaminating. Research is currently being conducted on methods of storing agricultural commodities safe from insects and diseases by using controls such as cold, heat, aeration, and light in lieu of pesticides. Induced low temperatures can be used to help protect grain, feeds, and seeds from insect attack. Cold winter air recirculated through grain keeps it below the temperature required for insect activity.

Controlling the composition of the air appears promising for protecting stored commodities. Air containing less than 2.5 percent oxygen stops insect and fungus activity. Short exposures to nitrogen or carbon dioxide affect the metabolic functions of insects, thus making them more susceptible to insecticidal and fumigant action. Within airtight storage facilities, a controlled atmosphere can be created, either by normal combined respiration of grain, or by replacing a portion of the air with nitrogen or carbon dioxide. Pretreatment of stored commodities with one of these gases may make it possible to control insects with considerably less pesticide. Control of storage atmosphere has reduced the need for chemical protection of certain fruits and vegetables. A technique has been developed in which fresh peaches, exposed briefly to hot water to retard decay, no longer require chemical treatment.

As basic research progresses in other areas, it may yield new tools for insect control measures. Future discoveries about genetics, cells, nutrition, viruses, proteins, enzymes, and a host of other subjects concerning plants and animals may also succeed in furnishing useful information about insects.

Nontoxic approaches have application to large-scale farming operations as well as to the small garden. The developments described indicate in some small measure what can be achieved when problems are met with ingenuity and imagination.

APPENDIXES

LIST OF SUPPLIERS OF MATERIALS

ORGANIZATIONS INTERESTED IN
   GARDENING WITHOUT POISONS

LIST OF SOURCES

APPENDIX A

THE FOLLOWING are some of the plants attacked by cottony cushion scale:

acacia	geranium	pepper
alfalfa	grape	pine
almond	lemon	poinsettia
apple	magnolia	pomegranate
apricot	maple	potato
boxwood	white oak	quince
buckeye	orange	rose
castor bean	peach	sunflower
chrysanthemum	pear	English walnut
cypress	pecan	willow
fig		

The following are some of the well known pests of economic importance parasitized by trichogramma:

armyworm	carpenter moth
fall armyworm	codling moth
bagworm	dagger moth
cotton bollworm	gypsy moth
pink bollworm	hawk moth
European corn borer	hummingbird moth
peach tree borer	Io moth
squash borer	luna moth
tobacco false budworm	Oriental fruit moth
imported cabbageworm	polyphemus moth
cankerworm	promethea moth
fall cankerworm	regal moth
alfalfa caterpillar	rosy maple moth
eastern tent caterpillar	royal moth
forest tent caterpillar	tussock moth
cutworm	wax moth
corn earworm	nymphalidae
tomato fruitworm	prominents
grassworm	datanas
tobacco hornworm	pterophoridae
tomato hornworm	giant silkworm
inchworm	skipper
lasiocampidae	spanworm
bean leaf roller	swallowtail
cotton leafworm	fall webworm
cabbage looper	alfalfa worm
Angoumis grain moth	California oak worm
brown-tail moth	measuring worm
	overflow worm

APPENDIX B

AMONG the shrubs which will provide food for birds are:

black alder	mountain holly
Korean barberry	Tartarian honeysuckle
blackberry	juniper
highbush blueberry	autumn olive
chokecherry	rose (especially multiflora)
silky cornel	sassafras
dewberry	snowberry
red osier dogwood	spicebush
elderberry	staghorn sumac
black haw	viburnums
hawthorn	

Among low shrubs are:

bayberry	fragrant sumac
coralberry	

In addition to shrubs, there are particular trees and vines which provide good bird food and shelter:

apple	hackberry
mountain ash	white mulberry
gray birch	Allegheny serviceberry
Oriental bittersweet vine	tupelo
red cedar	white oak
wild cherry	woodbine
flowering crabapple	plum
box elder	

Suitable bird food might include:

bread	peanut butter
crushed or cracked corn	peanuts and other nutmeats
eggshell	sorghum
fruit	suet
grits	sunflower seed
hempseed	wheat grain
millet	

APPENDIX C

PLANT THESE together for protection:

beans: near potatoes, against Colorado potato beetles

chives or garlic: near lettuce or peas, against aphids

garlic: near roses, against blackspot, mildew, and aphids

geraniums: among roses or grapes, against Japanese beetles

white geraniums or odorless marigolds: near corn, against Japanese beetles

certain marigolds: near cucurbits against cucumber beetles

nasturtiums: near beans, against Mexican bean beetles; near broccoli, against aphids; near cucurbits, against striped cucumber beetles and squash bugs

parsley: near roses, against rose beetles

potatoes: near beans, against mexican bean beetles

radishes: in hills of cucurbits, against striped or spotted cucumber beetles

rosemary, sage, thyme, nasturtium, catnip, mint, hemp, or *hyssop:*
near cabbage, against white cabbage butterflies

soybeans: near corn, against chinch bugs and Japanese beetles

tansy: around cabbage plants, against cabbageworms and cutworms

tansy, garlic, or *onions:* around peach trees, against borers

tomatoes: near asparagus, against asparagus beetles

APPENDIX D

RECIPE FOR Soap:

Heat three quarts of melted fat to lukewarm and strain. This is about five pounds and two ounces by weight. It may be composed of bacon drippings, clarified meat scraps, lard, etc. Dissolve one can of lye in one quart of cold water. When this is lukewarm, stir the fat into it, and immediately add one cup of ammonia and two tablespoons of borax which have been dissolved in one half cup of warm water. A teaspoonful of oil of citronella may be added. Allow this mixture to cool. It will harden, and may be cut into cakes, or flaked for soap solution.

Recipe for miscible dormant oil spray:

For each gallon of light grade oil use two pounds of soap as an emulsifier. (Fish oil soap is good, if obtainable.) Mix and heat the two, bring to a boil, and pour back and forth until thoroughly blended. Dilute in twenty times or more its volume in water. Use it as soon as possible. Cover the entire tree thoroughly in one spraying.

Essential oils effective against mosquitoes and mosquito larvae:

In tests using extracts of essential oils, 100 percent kills were made using oil of sandalwood, elecampane, bayberry leaves, pumpkin seeds, and black mustard; 95 percent kills with oil of basil, garden sage, sweet basil, sweet marjoram, balm of Gilead, and caraway; 90 percent kills with oil of rosemary, cypress, and hydrangea; lesser kills with oil of patchouli, butternut, rhubarb, tupelo, prickly ash, comfrey, and others. In addition, there are many other plant materials which are toxic to mosquito larvae.

THE FOLLOWING plants have been used as herbal tea sprays, after being prepared in water solution:

burdock against grubs of June beetle
camomile against damping off in greenhouse and coldframe
chive against leaf and fruit scab
garlic and onion against late blight on potato and tomato, and brown rot of stone fruit
gooseberry against mildew
horsetail (*Equisetum arvense*) against mildew and other fungi, especially on grapevines, vegetables, fruit trees, rosebushes
horseradish against fungi
hyssop against bacterial diseases
stinging nettle against plant lice
wormwood against leaf-eating caterpillars on fruit trees and aphids

BOTANICALS which have been used to control household pests:

Cucumber juice, *cucumis sativus*, was used to banish wood lice and cockroaches, by strewing the green peel on the floor for three to four nights. On the Gold Coast, the angel's-trumpet, *Datura arburea*, was pounded and smeared on floors to kill lice and other vermin. Indians of southern Mexico swept the floors and walls of their huts with bloodflower, *Asclepias curassavica*, in the milkweed family, to repel fleas and vermin.

Botanicals which have been used to protect garments from insects:

A wide variety of plants have been used to repel moths, including oils of cade (*Juniperus oxycedrus*), lavender, costmary, wormwood and clove; leaves of fennel, patchouli, sweetflag, fern, bracken and rosemary; flowers of male breadfruit tree; black pepper; Irish moss; citron, alcoholic solution of coumarin and hemp; extract from broom seed, cinchona, lupine, tung oil, elecampane. The wood of cedar has long been recognized as a moth repellant. Greeks and Romans painted the backs of parchment manuscripts with oil of cedar wood to prevent attack. Chests, closets, cedarwood chips, and impregnated paper have been used to store woolens.

In addition to moth repellants, botanicals have been found usefull against other insects which destroy cloth. These include camphor and powdered clove against carpet beetle larvae. Clothing has been treated with a soapy emulsion of anise oil, or bayberry oil to ward off insects.

Botanicals which have been used to relieve domesticated animals of insects:

Freshly cut pumpkin or squash leaves, a decoction of black walnut leaves soaked overnight, or an infusion of pignut leaves, rubbed on horses or cattle, repelled flies. Sometimes yellow wild indigo was placed in harnesses to keep horses free of flies. Concentrations of potato water rubbed on cattle, and clove on chickens and dogs, were used to repel lice, and a water solution of wormwood was used to bathe small animals and rid them of fleas. In Brazil a tincture of cocoa leaves is considered a remedy for poultry lice, while cocoa shells, used as bedding for dogs, are credited with repelling fleas.

APPENDIX E

BAIT FOR codling moth traps in apple orchards:

1. Fill a small ice cream cup two-thirds full of sawdust. Stir into it a teaspoonful of glacial acetic acid. Add enough liquid glue to saturate the mixture completely. After one or two days the cup should be dry. Suspend it in a mason jar which is partly filled with water.

2. Fill a quart jar one-fourth full of a 10 percent solution of molasses in water. Hang it near the center of the tree. When trapped moths fill the jar almost solidly, remove them and renew the solution.

3. Mix one gallon of molasses with three cakes of yeast and one ounce of oil of sassafras. Dilute this mixture in five gallons of water and fill jars half full. Check traps daily.

4. Mix ryania and mustard, and add to a molasses bait.

For codling moth control, suspend at least one baited trap in each large tree. Place it so that it does not jar against the branches, and provides ready entrance for the moths. Cover the openings of jars with small screenings, with ⅛- to ¼-inch holes, to prevent bees from entering.

Bait for ants:

Ants can be lured into small paraffin-lined pillboxes or cans baited with sugar, water, bacon rind, fat, or meat. Drop filled traps into a pail of boiling water.

A homemade fly trap:

A fly trap can be easily made with wire screening rolled into a cylinder twelve to eighteen inches in diameter and twenty-four inches high. Inside the open end place a screen-wire cone that reaches nearly to the top. Set the trap on one-inch legs over a shallow pan containing bait such as stale beer, a solution of one part blackstrap molasses to three parts water, milk, fruit wastes, or meat in water.

Bait for grasshoppers:

Grasshoppers can be attracted to bait of molasses, citrus fruit, lemon or vanilla extracts, apple flavorings, beer, vinegar, saccharin, salt, calcium chloride, soap, and other materials.

Waste materials as diluents:

chopped ground alfalfa
bagasse (wastes from sugarcane or sugar beet)
ground beet pulp
citrus meal
ground corncobs, chopped cornstalks, and cornmeal
cottonseed hulls
ground flax fiber
oat hulls
ground peanut shells
pea bran
pear and apple pomace
peat moss
sawdust
soybean meal
coarse wheat bran, rolled wheat, ground wheat screenings, and low-grade wheat flour

Of all, coarse wheat bran seems to be the most successful.

A homemade mechanical electric light trap to catch codling moths:

The device consists of a fifteen-watt blacklight bulb and two rotors turned by a fractional horsepower electric motor. After the insects are attracted to the light, they are hit by the whirling rotor blades. The motor is geared down to one thousand r.p.m. to prevent overheating. Each rotor is made of two heavy strands of wire mounted on the end of a drive shaft, resembling an X. The blades are rigid enough to kill, but not heavy enough to create a visible barrier which would repel. Such a mechanical trap is useful in capturing other insects as well. More than five hundred horn-worm moths have been captured nightly in such a mechanical trap.

A homemade electrocuting trap to catch pests of fruit trees:

Set together three rectangular electric flyscreens to form a tri-angular column, connected by joints. Stand the column on a frame with three legs; top with a roof. Attach to the underside a trans-former and socket with a bulb. The transformer can increase the voltage of current to about 3000 volts which is needed to operate the flyscreen. A number of night-flying insects are attracted and fall into the screen tray from which they must be emptied each morning. Since trees in a fruit orchard limit and absorb some visible light, set such traps at the borders.

APPENDIX F

THE FOLLOWING insects are affected by *Bacillus Thuringiensis*:

armyworm

cabbage looper

eastern tent caterpillar

salt-marsh caterpillar

walnut caterpillar

European corn borer

tomato fruitworm

grape leaf folder

tobacco hornworm

tomato hornworm

cotton leaf perforator

red-banded leaf roller

brown-tail moth

grape-berry moth

gypsy moth

orange-striped oak moth

artichoke plume moth

western tussock moth

celery leaf tier

fall webworm

sod webworm (lawn moth)

California oak worm

melon worm

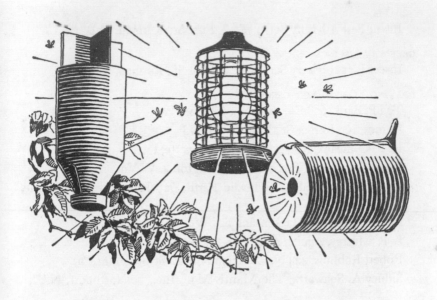

LIST OF SUPPLIERS OF MATERIALS

THIS LIST is for the convenience of the reader. It is not necessarily complete, nor does it imply any endorsement of either a product or the technique it represents.

CHAPTER 2: THE VITAL ROLE OF INSECTS

LADY BEETLES

California Bug Co., Rte. 2, Box 335, Auburn, Cal.

Greenberg Control Co., Rte. 4, Box 1891, Oroville, Cal.

Paul Harris, Ladybug Sales, Box 1495, Marysville, Cal.

Insect Pest Advisory Serv., 762 S. First St., Kerman, Cal.

H. A. Mantyla, Rte. 2, Box 2407, Auburn, Cal.

G. C. Quick, 367 E. Virginia Ave., Phoenix, Ariz.

Robert Robbins, 424 N. Courtland St., E. Stroudsburg, Pa.

L. E. Schoor, 646 Elm St., Yuba City, Cal.

VEDALIA
Insect Pest Advisory Serv., 762 S. First St., Kerman, Cal.

GREEN LACEWINGS
Insect Pest Advisory Serv., 762 S. First St., Kerman, Cal.

PRAYING MANTID EGG CASES:
Ted P. Bank, 608 Eleventh St., Pitcairn, Pa.

Burnes, 109 Kohler St., Bloomfield, N.J.

H. P. Comeaux, Rte. 2, Box 259, Lafayette, La.

Little Gem Farm, Box 9024, Huntington 4, W.Va.

Mantis Unlimited, Glenhardie Farm, 625 Richards Rd., Wayne, Pa.

Mincemoyer, 104 Hackensack St., Wood Ridge, N.J.

L. R. Murray, Aguila, Ariz.

Robert Robbins, 424 N. Courtland St., E. Stroudsburg, Pa.

Sidney A. Schwartz, The Mantis Man, Inc., E. Northport, N.Y.

TRICHOGRAMMA
Gothard, Inc., Box 332, Canutillo, Texas. Trik-O.
Insect Pest Advisory Serv., 762 S. First St., Kerman, Cal.

FROGS
Nu-Tex Frog Farm, Box 4029, Corpus Christi, Texas

CHAPTER 4: FROM THE GROUND UP

SOIL-TESTING KIT
Edwards Laboratory, Box 318, Norfolk, Ohio
La Motte Chemical Products Co., Chestertown, Md.
Sudbury Laboratory, Sudbury, Mass.

GENERAL SUPPLIERS OF ORGANIC SOIL CONDITIONERS
Badger Soil Serv., Inc., 3691 Fond du Lac Rd., Oshkosh, Wisc.

Bedford Organic Fertilizer Co., Ltd., 2045 Bishop St., Montreal, Quebec, Can. Vitalite.

Benson-MacLean, Bridgeton, Ind.

Bi-Or-Ganic, Box 225, Van Buren, Maine

Blenders, Inc., 6964 Main St., Lithonia, Ga.

Brooks, Van Baron Rd., Caribou, Maine

Brookside Nurseries, Darien, Conn.

Clapper Co., W. Newton, Mass.

Deer Valley Farm, Guilford, N.Y.

Degler, 51 Bethlehem Pike, Colmar, Pa.

Dickinson Co., 9940 Roselawn, Detroit 4, Mich.

Earp Laboratories, Inc. 20 West St., Red Bank, N.J.

Eaton, Rte. 2, Wallingford, Conn.

Fanning Soil Serv., 4951 S. Custer Rd., Monroe, Mich.

Alvin Filsinger, Rte. 3, Ayton, Ontario, Can.

Garden Fare, 68 Newbury St., Hartford 6, Conn.

Hallett, Woodhaven Rd., Orchard Pk., N.Y.

Herzberg, Wells, Minn.

Nat'l Soil Conservation, Inc., Medford, N.J.

Natural Development Co., Perry Hall, Md.

Carleton W. Neier, 6730 South Dr., Melbourne, Fla.

Normal Soil, Inc., Box 162, Hinsdale, Ill. A man-made virgin soil, using nature's own raw materials.

North East Soil Serv., Wolfboro, N.H.

North Olmsted Feed and Supply, 27100 Lorain Rd., N. Olmsted, Ohio

Odlin Organics, 753 Dennison Dr., Southbridge, Mass.

Quaker Lane Products, Box 100, Pittstown, N.J.

Re-Vita, Inc., 1372 Peachtree St. N.E., Atlanta 9, Ga.

Soft Phosphate, Inc., Box 31, Medina, Pa.

Squanto Peat Products, Box 177, Oakham, Mass.

Ward Brokerage Co., 314 Baumer Rd., Johnstown, Pa.

Webb Super-Gro Products, Flemington, Pa.

Webber, Brabon Research Farm, Rte. 1, Telford, Pa.

ANIMAL WASTES

Dried Blood Meal

Brookside Nurseries, Darien, Conn.

Quaker Lane Products, Box 100, Pittstown, N.J.

Bat Guano

Brentwood Berry Gardens, Box 49801, Los Angeles 49, Cal.

Cissell Hullett Co., Wakita, Okla.

Erle Racey, 3012 Maple Ave., Dallas, Texas

Bone Meal

Archer-Daniels Midland Co., 600 Roanoke Bldg., Minneapolis 40, Minn.

Brookside Nurseries, Darien, Conn.

Consolidated Rendering Co., Boston, Mass.

Quaker Lane Products, Box 100, Pittstown, N.J.

EARTHWORMS

Bell's Worm Garden, Bell 2, Tenn.

Brazos Bait Farm, 60 Lincoln St., Waco, Texas

California Western Bait Co., Box 90244, Airport Station, Los Angeles 45, Cal.

Carter Fish Worm Farm, Plains, Ga.

Clark's Worm Hatchery, 49 Falmouth St., Attleboro, Mass.

Copps Worm Farm, Box 77, South Barre, Mass.

Frank's Worm Ranch, 541 Jauncey Ave., N. Arlington, N.J.

Gary Road Farms, Roselle, Ill.

Georgia Worm Farms, Dawson, Ga.

Hall Farm, Hilton, Ga.

Hillaire, Northville, Mich.

Jensen, Rte. 1, Box 281, Mentone, Cal.

Lindsey, Alamance Worm Ranch, Haw River, N.C.

Meeko's Worm Ranch, Rte. 6, Hot Springs, Ark.

Mill Creek Ranch, Rte. 2, Noel, Mo.

McKenzie, 2607 Cayce Dr. S., Norfolk 6, Va.

Oakhaven, Cedar Hill, Texas

Ontario Earthworm Farms, Rte. 3, Pickering, Ontario, Can.

Ozark Worm Farm, Willow Springs, Mo.

Putnam, Sunrise Ave., Amherst, Mass.

Red Box Earthworm Farm, Livingston, Cal.

Rockhaven 2, Sulphur Springs, Texas

Shady Pine Hatchery, Spring Lake, N.C.

South Worm Farm, 6417 E. 37th St., Kansas City 29, Mo.

Ver Hoven, Box 805, Hesperia, Cal.

Willing Worm Farm, 1624 N.W. 39 Terrace, Miami, Fla.

Worm Gardens, 324 David Dr., Waco, Texas

Earthworm Castings

Carter Earthworm Farm, Plains, Ga.

Excello, Kosciusko 10, Miss.

Ontario Earthworms, Rte. 3, Pickering, Ontario, Can.

Worm Castings, Gray Goose Bait Farm, Huntsville, Ark.

FEATHER TANKAGE

Brookside Nurseries, Darien, Conn.

HAIR AND HIDE TANKAGE

Brookside Nurseries, Darien, Conn.

MANURE, CATTLE

Organic Compost Corporation, Germantown, Wisc., and Oxford, Pa.

MANURE, DRIED COW

Maegeo Dehydrating Co., Lexington, N.C. Fertal-Gro.

Quaker Lane Products, Box 100, Pittstown, N.J.

Walker Gordon Farms, Plainsboro, N.J. Bo-Vung.

Wayside Gardens, 7 Mentor Ave., Mentor, Ohio

MANURE, DRIED SHEEP

Consolidated Rendering Co., Springfield, Mass., and Boston, Mass.

POULTRY HOUSE LITTER AND WOOD FLOUR

Timberlake Industries, Inc., Warren, Maine, and Westford, Mass. Endressin.

BUCKWHEAT HULLS

Conrad Fafard, Inc., Box 774, Springfield, Mass.

Larrowe Mills, Cohocton, N.Y.

CALCIUM

Lonfosco Phosphate Co., High Springs, Fla. Natural untreated calcium phosphate.

Marlo Products Co., 2690 Highway 101, San Rafael, Cal. Marl-O, derived from natural prehistoric deposits of fish, marine animals, and plants, as calcareous secretions by the plant algae chara.

CASTOR POMACE

Baker Castor Oil Co., Bayonne, N.J.

COCOA WASTES

Hershey Estates, Hershey, Pa. Ko-K-O Mulch and K-K-O Meal; cocoa shells; cocoa meal.

COMPOST ACTIVATORS

Benson-MacLean, Bridgeton, Ind.

Bio-Dynamic Compost Starter, Threefold Farm, Spring Valley, N.Y. Natural soil-building bacteria and enzymes.

Earp Laboratories, Inc., 20 West St., Red Bank, N.J.

Schiff Agricultural Enzymes Division, S. Hackensack 10, N.J. Biorg.

COTTON WASTES

Cotton Hull Ash

Brookside Nurseries, Darien, Conn.

Consolidated Rendering Co., Springfield, Mass.

Cottonseed Meal

Buckeye Cotton Oil, Div. Buckeye Cellulose Corp., Memphis 1, Tenn.

Cocke and Co., 32 Peachtree St. N.W., Atlanta 3, Ga.

Goldenrod Oil Meal Sales Co., Box 152, Memphis 1, Tenn.

Humphreys Godwin Co., Box 3897, Memphis 14, Tenn.

Nat'l Cottonseed Products Assoc., Dallas, Texas

Wayside Gardens, 7 Mentor Ave., Mentor, Ohio

FISH SOURCES

Fish Emulsions

Acme Peat Products, Ltd., 687 No. 7 Rd., Rte. 2, Richmond, Br. Columbia, Can. Liquid whale plant food, bone, and baleen.

Alaska Fertilizer Co., 84 Seneca St., Seattle 1, Wash.

Atlas Fish Emulsion Fertilizer Co., No. 1 Drumm St., San Francisco 11, Cal.

Standard Products Co., Inc., White Stone, Va. Stapco.

Dried Fish Meal
Brookside Nurseries, Darien, Conn.

Fish and Mammal Paste
Brookside Nurseries, Darien, Conn.

GRANITE

Fletcher Co. Granite Quarry, W. Chelmsford, Mass. Super Granits.

Hocking Granite Industries, St. George, Maine

Keystone Granite Quarry, Zionsville, Pa.

KELP

Brookside Nurseries, Darien, Conn.

Kel-Min Corp. of America, 301 Admiral Blvd., Kansas City 6, Mo. Kel-Min; dehydrated ocean kelp.

Norwegian Import-Export Co., Ltd., 6970 W. North Ave., Oak Pk., Ill. Algit.

Norwegian Kelpmeal, Box 185, Penngrove, Cal.

Wright Feeds, Paramount, Cal. Sea-Gro; Pacific kelp.

LEAF MOLD COMPOST
Brookside Nurseries, Darien, Conn.

LEATHER WASTES

Tyoga Products Co., Div. of Elkland Leather Co., Elkland, Pa. Elk-Organic. Tan Bark is waste material in leather-tanning process. It is made of wattle, mangrove, myrobolans, and valonia, and contains lignin, active part of humus.

LICORICE ROOT

MacAndrews & Forbes Co., Third St. & Jefferson Ave., Camden 4, N.J. Right Dress.

LIME

Benson-MacLean, Bridgeton, Ind. Limestone.

Brookside Nurseries, Darien, Conn. Limestone and gypsum rock; Aerosoil.

Lee Lime Corp., Lee, Mass. Dolomite.

U.S. Gypsum, Falls Village, Conn. Ground limestone, also known as agricultural limestone.

LINSEED MEAL

Archer-Daniels Midland Co., 600 Roanoke Bldg., Minneapolis 40, Minn.

Sherman Williams Paint Co., Cleveland, Ohio

Spenser Kellogg and Sons, 1616 Walnut St., Philadelphia 3, Pa.

MARL: *earthy deposits formed from snail shells and chara plants; takes lime out of water in which it grows*

Alexander, Box 185, Penngrove, Cal. Marl-O.

Dickinson Co., 9940 Roselawn, Detroit 4, Mich. Greensand.

Kaylorite Corp., Dunkirk, Calvert County, Md. Glauconitic greensand, natural marine potash, and other glauconite minerals.

McConnell, 200 S. Crawford Ave., New Castle, Pa. Kaylorite.

Nat'l Soil Conservation, Inc., Medford, N.J. Greensand.

MUNICIPAL COMPOSTING RECLAIMED WASTES

Altoona Fam, Room 468, Altoona Trust Bldg., Altoona, Pa.

City of Schenectady, N.Y. Orgro, sludge.

Sewcrage Comm., Milwaukee 1, Wisc. Milorganite, sludge.

Wandel Machine Co., Inc., Pomeroy, Pa. Agromat, composter of garbage for home use. Somat, composter of garbage for commercial and industrial use.

NITRATE

Chilean Nitrate Co., 120 Broadway, New York 5, N.Y. Champion.

NITROGEN

American Agricultural Chemical Co., New York, N.Y. Agrinite.

PEANUT PRODUCTS

Peanut Meal

Humphreys Godwin Co., Box 3897, Memphis 14, Tenn.

Peanut Shells
Tidewater Brokerage Co., Inc., Suffolk, Va.

PEAT AND SPHAGNUM MOSS

Acme Peat Products, Ltd., Rte. 2, Richmond, Br. Columbia, Can. Blue Whale, whale solubles impregnated sphagnum moss, reinforced with baleen whalebone and marine marl.

Annapolis Valley Peat Moss Co., Ltd., Berwick, Nova Scotia

Beemsterboer Peat and Humus Products Co., 11732 S. Yale St., Chicago 28, Ill.

Bruco Peat Moss Corp., 117 Liberty St., New York 6, N.Y.

Canadian Peat Producers, 114 Vancouver Block, Vancouver, Br. Columbia, Can.

Canadian Peat Sales, Ltd., New Westminster, Br. Columbia, Can.

Peat Moss and Sphagnum Center, Vicksburg, Mich.

Squanto Peat and Sphagnum Moss, Box 177, Oakham, Mass.

Sterling Forest Peat Moss Co., Box 608, Tuxedo, N.Y.

ROCK PHOSPHATE

American Agricultural Chemical Co., 100 Church St., New York, N.Y., and N. Weymouth 91, Mass. Agrico.

Benson-MacLean, Bridgeton, Ind.

Degler, 51 Bethlehem Pike, Colmar, Pa.

Grabar Mills, 802 Navarre S.W., Canton, Ohio

Hocking Granite Industries, St. George, Maine

McConnell, 200 S. Crawford Ave., New Castle, Pa.

Ruhm Phosphate and Chemical Co., Box 361, Columbia, Tenn.

SAND

Brookside Nurseries, Darien, Conn. Washed and screened bank sand to help heavy soils become porous.

SEAWEED

Nilson's Poultry Farm, 3217 Fairview Drive, Vista, Cal. Trident, Norwegian seaweed.

Norwegian Import-Export Co., Ltd., 6970 W. North Ave., Oak Park, Ill. Norwegian seaweed.

Sea-Born, Box 465, Greenwich, Conn.

Sea Ledge Products Co., Chebraque Island, Maine

Sea-Weed Products, Inc., 3205 44 West, Seattle, Wash.

Sidney Seaweed Products, 2543 Beacon Ave., Sidney, Br. Columbia. Can. Alginure.

Super Soil, Inc., 2740 Sheridan Dr., Tonawanda, N.Y.

Wright Feeds, 16225 S. Paramount Blvd., Paramount, Cal. Sea Gro.

ROCK SILT: *to make leafy or humus soil dense or heavier; material is in high colloidal state and holds nutrients from leaching.*
Brookside Nurseries, Darien, Conn.

SOYBEAN MEAL

American Soybean Assoc., Hudson, Iowa

Archer-Daniels Midland Co., 600 Roanoke Bldg., Minneapolis 40, Minn.

Buckeye Cotton Oil, Div. Buckeye Cellulose Corp., Memphis 1, Tenn.

Humphreys Godwin Co., Box 3897, Memphis 14, Tenn.

TOBACCO PRODUCTS

Tobacco Dust
Odlin Organics, 743 Dennison Dr., Southbridge, Mass.
Quaker Lane Products, Box 100, Pittstown, N.J.

Tobacco Stem Meal
Brookside Nurseries, Darien, Conn.

WOOD WASTES

Douglas Fir Bark
Norwesco, Box 1138, Longview, Wash. Silvabark.

Hardwood Bark Mulch
Box 455, Lancaster Rd., Chillicothe, Ohio. Paygro.

Sawdust
Brookside Nurseries, Darien, Conn.

Wood Chips
Brown Paper Co., Berlin, N.H. Grobark.

CHAPTER 5: PLANTS OUT OF PLACE

GEESE RENTED OR SOLD FOR WEEDING
Midsouth Weeder Geese, Columbus, Mo.
Stahmann Farms, Inc., Las Cruces, New Mex.

CHAPTER 6: AN OUNCE OF PREVENTION

ADHESIVES FOR BANDING AND SEALING TREE WOUNDS
Samuel Cabot, Inc., 62 S. Terminal Trust Bldg., Boston 10, Mass.
Cabot's Tree Healing Paint.
Michael and Pelton, Oakland, Cal. Stickem.
National Control Laboratory, 5315 Touhy Ave., Skokie, Ill. Crawlz
No More.
The Tree Tanglefoot Co., 314 Straight Ave. N.W., Grand Rapids,
Mich. Tree Tanglefoot.

READYMADE TREE BANDS (*with adhesive*)
Niagara Horticultural Products, St. Catharines, Ontario, Can.

CHAPTER 7: EMERGENCY MEASURES: SIMPLE SPRAYS
AND OTHER MATERIALS

MINERAL OIL SPRAYS
Maw Manufacturing Co., 1326 Wilshire Blvd., Santa Monica, Cal.
Maw Kienol.
G. B. Pratt Co., 204 Twenty-First Ave., Paterson 21, N.J. Scalecide.

DIATOMACEOUS EARTH
Desert Herb Tea Co., 736 Darling St., Ogden, Utah
Life-Guard Products, Div. of Phoenix Gems, Inc., 1701 E. Elwood
St., Phoenix 40, Ariz. Perma-Guard.

"B.D. SPRAY"
Peter A. Escher, Threefold Farm, Spring Valley, N.Y.

For other B.D. preparations for sprays, write: Bio-Dynamic Farming and Gardening Assoc., Inc., R.D. 1, Dover Plains, N.Y.

NONTOXIC SPRAYS

Old Herbaceous, Box 2086, Potomac Station, Alexandria, Va. Against greenflies, leafhoppers, slugs, mealybugs, thrips.

Vege Products, Box 66, North Olmsted, Ohio. Vege Dust; Vege Spray.

NEW JERSEY MOSQUITO LARVICIDE CONCENTRATE (contains pyrethrum)

Seacoast Laboratories, Inc., 156–158 Perry St., New York 14, N.Y.

WHITE HELLEBORE (Veratrum album)

Desert Tea Co., 736 Darling St., Ogden, Utah

Indiana Botanic Gardens, Box 5, Hammond, Ind.

Meer Corp, 318 West 46 St., New York 36, N.Y.

S. P. Penick & Co., 100 Church St., New York 8, N.Y.

Prentiss Drug and Chemical Co., 101 W. 31 St., New York 1, N.Y.

PYRETHRUM

F. W. Berk & Co., Box 500, 8 Baker St., London W1, Engl.

Biddle Sawyer & Co., Ltd., 2/4 Fitzroy St., London W1, Engl.

Cooper, McDougall & Robertson, Ltd., Berkhamsted, Herts, Engl.

George W. Parks Seed Co., Greenwood, S.C. Pyrethrum seeds for planting in home gardens to produce plants.

S. B. Penick & Co., 100 Church St., New York 8, N.Y.

Plantabbs Corp., 1105 Maryland Ave., Baltimore 1, Md. Red Arrow Garden Spray.

Pyrethrum Bureau, Inc. For names and addresses of nearest distributors, and general information:
Premier Bldg., Washington 6, D.C.
215–217 Grand Bldg., Trafalgar Sq., London WC2, Engl.
Box 420, Nakuru, Kenya

NICOTINE

Nicotine Sulfate
Andrew-Wilson, Inc., Springfield, N.J.

European Chemical Co., Inc., 124 East 40 St., New York 16, N.Y.
Stauffer Chemical Co., 638 California St., San Francisco 8, Cal.

Nicotine Fumigants for Greenhouses
California Spray Chemical Corp., Richmond, Cal.
Fuller System, 226 Washington St., Woburn, Mass. Fulex Nicotine Fumigator.
Plant Products Co., Blue Point, N.J.

TOBACCO DUST
Odlin Organics, 743 Dennison Dr., Southbridge, Mass.
Quaker Lane Products, Box 100, Pittstown, N.J.

TOBACCO STEM MEAL
Brookside Nurseries, Darien, Conn.

QUASSIA
Desert Herb Tea Co., 736 Darling St., Ogden, Utah
Indiana Botanic Gardens, Box 5, Hammond, Ind.
Meer Corporation, 318 W. 46 Street, New York 36, N.Y.
George W. Parks Seed Co., Greenwood, S.C.
Charles Siegel & Son, 5535 N. Lynch Ave., Chicago 30, Ill.

RYANIA (*Ryania speciosa*)
Hopkins Agricultural Chemical Co., Box 584, Madison 1, Wisc.
S. B. Penick & Co., 100 Church St., New York 8, N.Y.

ROTENONE AND CUBE
California Spray-Chemical Corp., Richmond, Cal. Ortho Rotenone Dust or Spray.
S. B. Penick & Co., 100 Church St., New York 8, N.Y.
Plantabbs Corp., 1105 Maryland Ave., Baltimore 1, Md. Red Arrow Vegetable Garden Dust; Red Arrow Garden Spray.

SABADILLA SEEDS
Burgess Seed & Plant Co., Galesburg, Mich. Sabadilla dust.
Meer Corporation, 318 West 46 St., New York 36, N.Y. Seeds and dust.

S. B. Penick & Co., 100 Church St., New York 8, N.Y. Activated concentrates.

Prentiss Drug & Chemical Co., 101 W. 31st St., New York 1, N.Y. Ground seeds.

Woolfolk Chemical Works, Ltd., Ft. Valley, Ga. Sabadilla dust.

OTHER BOTANICAL INSECTICIDAL MATERIALS: *aconite leaves, aloes, betony, henbane leaves, Irish moss, mandrake root, poke root, prickly ash berries and bark, etc.*

Desert Herb Tea Co., 736 Darling St., Ogden, Utah

Indiana Botanic Gardens, Box 5, Hammond, Ind.

ESSENTIAL OILS: *patchouli*

Organic-Ville, 4207 W. 3rd St., Los Angeles 5, Cal.

GENERAL INSECTICIDE

Barth's, Valley Stream, N.Y. Insect Killer, contains mineral oil, sesame oil, and pyrethrins.

CHAPTER 8: EMERGENCY MEASURES: TRAPS

BLACKLIGHT TRAPS (*Mechanical*)

Gardner Manufacturing Co., Horicon, Wisc. Big Snuffer, for indoor use only.

BLACKLIGHT TRAPS (*Suction*)

Ampsco Corp., 1281 S. Front St., Columbus 6, Ohio. Spinsect, with disposable bags.

Farmington Manufacturing Co., 30711 Grand River Ave., Farmington, Mich.

First Lighting Products, Inc., Box 8, Toledo 5, Ohio

Hol-Dem Electric Fencer Co., 5555 Highway 5 West, Minneapolis 24, Minn. Hol-Dem.

McDonough Power Equipment, Inc., McDonough 4, Ga. Snapper, with bag.

Onamia Corp., 7711 6th Ave. N., Minneapolis 27, Minn. Lura Light.

Penetray Corp., Toledo 5, Ohio. Penetray Motorized Insect Trap, indoors or outdoors; bag must be emptied.

Sing Sing Bug Chair, Inc., Oak Park 37, Mich.

Spectrum, 5020 Market St., Youngstown, Ohio. Spectrum, disposable bags.

Vita Green Farms, Inc., Box 878, Vista, Cal. Holiday Bug-Lite, kills insects; 4 blades at 1500 rpm; machine allows insects to fall to the ground, hence unlimited capacity.

BLACKLIGHT TRAPS (*Electrocuting Grids*)

Detjen Corp., Pleasant Valley, N.Y. Screens, traps, lanterns, panels.

Electro-Lads Manufacturing Co., Dearborn, Mich. Grid plus black light.

Gardner Manufacturing Co., Horicon, Wisc. Bug-Shok Lantern; Bug-Shok Electric Fly Trap. Fly trap is a panel; can be used at night and also during day, with bait in tray; also screens.

Insect Electrocutor Co., Box 53, F. Western Hills Station, Cincinnati 38, Ohio. Panel and bait; night use only.

LIGHT TRAPS (*Suction*)

R. C. Nichols, Box 113, Wilton, N.H. Florida Bug Trap.

Scott-Mitchell House, Inc., 415 S. Broadway, Yonkers, N.Y.

ELECTRIC FLY REPELLANT

Breezette, 2918 Gilroy St., Los Angeles 29, Cal. Overhead electric fan, forms invisible barrier; for indoor use or on patio; portable.

CARNIVOROUS PLANTS

Armstrong Associates, Inc., Box 127, Basking Ridge, N.J. Venus flytrap.

Clinton Nurseries, Clinton, Conn. Venus flytrap.

Cupboard, Box 61–0, Terre Haute 12 P, Ind. Cobra lily.

Peter Pauls Nurseries, Building 2, Canandaigua, N.Y. Insect-eating plants.

Spencer Gifts, Spencer Bldg., Atlantic City, N.J. Venus flytrap.

CHAPTER 9: CONTROLLING UNWELCOME BIRDS AND ANIMALS

NETTING FOR BERRY CROPS, FRUITS, AND VEGETABLES

Chase Organics, Gibraltar House, Shepperton, Middlesex, Engl. Scaraweb, does not trap birds but frightens them; plastic; rots away after a few months; holes instantly repairable; forms a spider's web of rayon threads over seed beds, fruit trees, soft fruit bushes, vines.

Joseph Hein, Eton Rd., Thornwood, N.Y. Cheesecloth.

Fred Howe, c/o Packaging Products Dept., Union Carbide Plastics Co., Div. Union Carbide Corp., 270 Park Ave., New York 17, N.Y. Variety of polyethylene nettings in different mesh sizes and colors, flat and tubular.

Lumite Div., Chicopee Manufacturing Corp., Cornelia, Ga. Netting, variety of mesh sizes.

Dr. R. Maag, Ltd., Chemical Works, Dielsdorf, Zurich, Switz. Agrolam, similar to Scaraweb.

O. W. Stewart, 200 Elm St., RFD 1, Kingston, Mass. Protect-O-Net, plastic-coated netting.

Visinet Mill, Div. Bemis Bros. Bag Co., 2400 S. Second St., St. Louis 4, Mo. Netting, variety of mesh sizes.

Vitacultural Research Station, Oxted, Surrey, Engl. Scaraweb.

WHIRLING, SPINNING, AND SHINY MATERIALS TO REPEL BIRDS

Burgess Seed & Plant Co., Galesburg, Mich. Flying disks.

Comfort Specialty Co., 200 S. Seventh St., St. Louis 2, Mo.

B. M. Lawrence & Co., 244 California St., San Francisco 11, Cal.

Sunset House, Sunset Bldg., Beverly Hills, Cal. Scram-Disks.

COMPOUNDS TO PREVENT BIRDS FROM ROOSTING

Aegis Laboratories, 6817 S. Stony Island Ave., Chicago 49, Ill. No Roost — paste, spray, tube coatings.

Bird-Free Co., Box W, Brookline, 46, Mass. Paste; coating.

Bird-Rid Laboratories, 4817–4819 Cottage Grove Ave., Chicago 15, Ill. Paste; coating.

Burgess Seed & Plant Co., Galesburg, Mich. Dirty Bird, aerosol.

Burr Chemical Co., 3379 Auburn St., Rockford, Ill. Cartridge for caulking gun; coating.

International Pest Controls, Inc., 635 Seventh Ave., Marion, Iowa. Paste; tube; spray; coatings.

Neil A. MacLean Co., 1536 Industrial Way, Belmont, Cal., and 9846 E. Alpaca St., El Monte, Cal. Coating.

National Bird Control Laboratories, 5315 Touhy Ave., Skokie, Ill. Aerosol, cartridge for caulking gun; spray; coating.

National Bird Repellant Co., Box 154, Station B, Hamilton, Ontario, Can. No-Roost; paste; spray; tube coating.

Sentinel Laboratory, 213 E. Jefferson St., Springfield, Ill. Cartridge for caulking gun; coating.

Tanglefoot Co., 314 Straight Ave. N.W., Grand Rapids, Mich. Tree Tanglefoot; paste; aerosol coating.

METAL PROJECTORS TO PREVENT BIRDS FROM ROOSTING

Bird Scat Co., Box 447, Logansport, Ind.

G. A. Harvey & Co., Ltd., Woolwich Road, London S.E.7, Engl.

Nixalite Co. of America, 1722 First Ave., Rock Island, Ill.

Stanley's Pigeon & Bird Repellent Service, 523 W. 184 St. New York 33, N.Y.

ELECTRONIC BIRD REPELLER

Electropel, Inc., 491–495 Bergen St., Brooklyn 17, N.Y. Electropel.

LIVE BIRD TRAPS

Allcock Manufacturing Co., 148-A Water St., Ossining, N.Y. Havahart, for small creatures and sparrows.

Animal Trap Co. of America, Lititz, Pa. Verbail, for hawks and owls.

Breck's, 250 Breck Bldg., Boston 10, Mass. English sparrow traps.

Russell S. Davis, Clayton, Ill. For small birds and pigeons.

Dodson Bird House Co., Box 551, Kankakee, Ill. Sparrow traps.

Johnson's, Waverly 13, Ky. Sparrow traps.

Ridgewood Box Mill, Detroit Lakes, Minn. Elevator-type traps for sparrows and starlings.

Charles Siegel & Son, 5535 N. Lynch Ave., Chicago 30, Ill. Pigeon bobs and pigeon trap entrances.

OWL EFFIGY:

Breck's, 250 Breck Bldg., Boston 10, Mass.

Spencer Gifts, Spencer Bldg., Atlantic City, N.J.

C. H. Symmes Co., Box 165, Winchester, Mass.

AUTOMATIC ACETYLENE EXPLODER

W. V. Clow Seed Co., 1401 Abbott St., Salinas, Cal. Zon.

B. M. Lawrence Co., 244 California St., San Francisco 11, Cal. Zon.

James McBride, 66 Second St. N., Sconey Creek, Ontario, Can.

Reed-Joseph Co., Highway 1 North, Greenville, Miss. Scare Away Model M 2.

Salt Lake Stamp Co., 380 W. 2nd St. S., Salt Lake City, Utah. Salasco.

BIOSONIC DEVICES FOR BIRD AND ANIMAL CONTROL

Bio-Sonics Control Co., 4236 E. Turney St., Phoenix 18, Ariz. Procedure tailored to meet particular needs.

ELECTRIC BEACONS

Franklin's Electric Service, 118 E. Main St., Calipatria, Cal. Revolving lights or beacons.

Trippe Manufacturing Co., 133 N. Jefferson St., Chicago 6, Ill. Tripp-Lite, revolving light beam.

ANIMAL REPELLANTS

Breck's, 250 Breck Bldg., Boston 10, Mass. Dog-Shun.

Chaperone, Box 1419, Sudbury, Mass. Chaperone Repel-O-Rope; rope and also aerosol.

Niagara Horticultural Products, St. Catharines, Ontario, Can. Staoff, rabbit repellant of rosin and alcohol; and Dog Staoff, nicotine dog repellant for evergreens and shrubs.

WINDMILL MOLE AND GOPHER CHASER

Walter Drake, 45 Drake Bldg., Colorado Springs, Col. Device makes drumming noise in ground, allegedly drives animals away; two devices enough for city lot.

LIVE ANIMAL TRAPS

Allcock Manufacturing Co., 148-A Water St., Ossining, N.Y. Havahart, small creatures.

Farmer Seed and Nursery Co., Faribault, Minn. Automatic mouse trap, does not kill, traps up to twenty mice at one setting.

Kness Manufacturing Company, Albia, Iowa. Ketch-all Mouse Trap; no bait necessary; trap is wound up with a key, and will trap up to fifteen mice; mice are not harmed.

MOLE TRAPS

Nash Mole Traps, Scotts, Mich.

SQUIRREL AND CAT GUARD

Breck's, 250 Breck Bldg., Boston 10, Mass. Tree guard of flexible steel foils, rust-proof sections; fits any tree up to 24" around, yet allows tree to grow; prongs keep animals from passing.

POWDERED ALOES AND CAYENNE PEPPER (*capsicum*)

Desert Herb Tea Co., 736 Darling St., Ogden, Utah

Indiana Botanic Gardens, Box 5, Hammond, Ind.

CHAPTER 11: THE USE OF INSECT DISEASES

BACILLUS THURINGIENSIS

Bioferm Corp., Wasco, Cal. Distributed by Stauffer Chemical Co., N.Y., Thuricide.

Grain Processing Corp., Muscatine, Iowa. Pasporin.

Nutrilite Products, Inc., 5600 Grand Ave., Buena Park, Cal. Distributed by Pennsalt Chemical Corp., Philadelphia, Pa., and Ferry Morse Seed Co. Biotrol; Bio-Guard.

Rohm and Haas Co., Washington Sq., Philadelphia 5, Pa. Distributed in the Northeast by Eastern States Farmers' Exchange, Inc., 26 Central St., West Springfield, Mass., and Hubbard-Hall Chemical Co., Box 233, Portland, Conn. Bakthane.

BACILLUS POPILLIAE DUTKY (*milky spore disease*)

Fairfax Biological Laboratory, Clinton Corners, N.Y. Doom.

Hydroponic Chemical Co., Copley 21, Ohio. Japonex.

CHAPTER 13: INGENUITY AND IMAGINATION

ANTIMETABOLITE (*Imidazole*)

Shulton, Inc., 697 Rte. 46, Clifton, N.J. Imutex.

DESICCANT DUSTS

A. S. Abbott Co., Los Angeles, Cal. Tri-Cal-Phos.

Godfred L. Cabot, Inc., Boston, Mass. Silica Cab-O-Sil M5.

Chemical Additives Co., Vernon, Cal. Colloidal attapulgite clay Hi-dry; Attasorb RVM; Diluex A.

Columbia-Southern Corp., Pittsburgh, Pa. Silica Gel Hi-Sil X 233.

Davison Chemical Co., Baltimore, Md. Dri-Die SG 67.

E. I. du Pont de Nemours and Co., Wilmington, Dela. Silica Valron-Estersil.

Eagle Chemical Co., Chicago, Ill. Silica Sil; Sil-Gel; Bentonite clay Des—852.

Great Lakes Carbon Corp., Los Angeles, Cal. Diatomite Dicalite 476.

Johns-Manville Co., Los Angeles, Cal. Calcium silica: Micro-Cel-E; Diatomite; Celite 209.

Monsanto Chemical Co., St. Louis, Mo. Santocel; silica aerogel; precipitated silica; bentonite clay.

Tamms Silica Co., Tamms, Ill. Silica: Multicel; Dustex; Tamsil.

United-Heckathorn, Richmond, Cal. Silikil.

DIATOMACEOUS EARTH (*See listing in Chapter 7*)

CELLULOSE

The Dow Chemical Co., Midland, Mich. Methocel.

Union Carbide Chemical Co., 270 Park Ave., New York 17, N.Y. Cellosize.

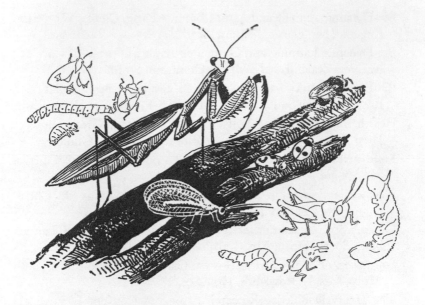

ORGANIZATIONS INTERESTED
IN GARDENING WITHOUT POISONS

THE FOLLOWING organizations will be of interest to gardeners in the United States:

Bio-Dynamic Farming and Gardening Assoc., Inc., RD 1, Dover Plains, N.Y.; Mrs. Josephine Porter, Sec.

Natural Food Associates, Atlanta, Texas; Joe D. Nichols, M.D., Pres.

School of Living, Lane's End Homestead, RD 3, Brookville, Ohio; Mrs. Mildred J. Loomis, Dir. of Educ.

Soil and Health Foundation, Emmaus, Pa.: Mr. J. I. Rodale, Pres. Also publications of Rodale Press: *Compost Science* and *Organic Gardening and Farming*

The Louis Bromfield Malabar Farm Foundation, Lucas, Ohio

The following organizations outside the United States will be of interest to English-speaking gardeners.

Bio-Dynamic Agricultural Assoc., Broome Farm, Clents, Worcester, England; Mr. David Clement, Sec.

Bio-Dynamic Farming and Gardening Assoc., Duart Rd., Havelock N., New Zealand, N.I.; Mr. P. Crompton Smith

Bio-Dynamic Information Centre, "Kawana," 234 Boundary St., Roseville, New South Wales, Australia; Mr. Robert H. Williams

Health Through Living Soil Assoc., Ezintabeni, Grosvenor Rd., Diep River, Cape Province, South Africa; W. P. Gilmore

Land Fellowship, 55 Pleasant Blvd., Toronto 7, Ontario, Canada; Mr. Spenser Cheshire, Sec.

New Zealand Organic Compost Soc., Inc., 27 Collins St., Christchurch, New Zealand; R. E. Betteridge, Nat'l Sec.

Organic Soil Association of Southern Africa, Box 7736, Johannesburg, South Africa; Mrs. Kathleen Parnell, Hon. Sec.-Treas.

Soil Assoc. of South Africa, Box 83, Claremont, Cape Prov., South Africa, Mrs. N. Rowlands, Hon. Sec.

The Henry Doubleday Research Assoc., 20 Convent Lane, Bocking, Braintree, Essex, England; Lawrence D. Hills, Hon. Sec.

The Living Soil Assoc. of Tasmania, Nat'l Mutual Bldg., 119 Macquarie St., Hobart, Tasmania; Mr. A. J. Honey, Sec.

The Soil Assoc., 8F Hyde Park Mansions, Marylebone Rd., London, N.W.1, England; Mrs. C. Miller, Sec.

Victorian Compost Society, Box 2605, W. Melbourne C.1, Victoria, Australia, Mr. H. A. Ackerly, Sec.

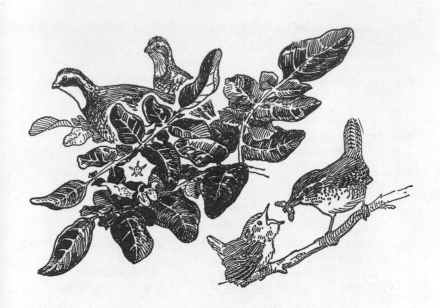

LIST OF SOURCES

CHAPTER I
THE REALITIES OF BIOLOGY

Pages 9–10. Elton, Charles S., *The Ecology of Invasions by Animals and Plants*. New York: Wiley, 1958.

Page 9. *Destructive Nematodes Found on Used Farm Tractors from England*. Release No. 2749–63, U.S. Dept. of Agric., Aug. 15, 1963.

Page 12. Clarkson, M. R., *Hearings*, 88th Congress, Subcom. on Reorganization and Internatl. Organizations, Sen. Com. on Gov. Operations, July 23, 1963.

CHAPTER II
THE VITAL ROLE OF INSECTS

Pages 13–25. *Insects, Yearbook of Agric.*, U.S. Dept. of Agric., 1952.

Page 14. Bastin, Harold, *Freaks and Marvels of Insect Life*. New York: A. A. Wyn, 1954.

Page 14. Osmundsen, John A., "Chemicals in Insects Suggested as 'Hidden' Antibiotics Sources," *New York Times*, Oct. 26, 1963.

Page 15. Westcott, Cynthia, and Peter K. Nelson, *Handbook on Biologi-*

cal Control of Plant Pests. New York: Brooklyn Botanic Garden, Vol. 16 (1960), No. 3.

Page 15. Forbes, Allan W., *Our Garden Friends the Bugs.* New York: Exposition, 1962.

Page 21. Chant, D. A., "An Experiment in Biological Control of Tetranychus telarius in a Greenhouse Using the Predacious Mite Phytoseiulus persimilis Anthias-Henriot," *The Canadian Entomol.,* Vol. 93, No. 6 (June 1961).

Page 22. Eisner, T., and J. Meinwald, "Chemical Defenses of Arthropods," address before Symposium on New Approaches to Pest Control and Eradication, Amer. Chem. Soc., Div. of Agric. and Food Chem., Atlantic City (Sept. 1962).

CHAPTER III

BIRDS AND OTHER CREATURES IN THE GARDEN

Pages 27–29. Clement, Roland C., "Birds and Insect Control," *Handbook on Biological Control of Plant Pests,* pp. 95–96.

Pages 27–29. Cottam, Clarence, and Francis Uhler, *Birds as Factors in Controlling Insect Depredation.* U.S. Fish and Wildlife Service Leaflet 224 (1950).

Pages 27–29. Kalmbach, E. R., "Birds, Beasts and Bugs," *Insects, Yearbook of Agric.,* U.S. Dept. of Agric., 1952, pp. 724–31.

Pages 28–31. Baker, John H., ed., *The Audubon Guide to Attracting Birds.* New York: Halycon, 1943.

Pages 28–31. Hausman, Leon Augustus, *Beginner's Guide to Attracting Birds.* New York: Cornerstone Library, 1962.

Pages 28–31. Terres, John K., *Songbirds in Your Garden.* New York: Crowell, 1953.

Page 32. Campbell, Charles A. R., *Bats, Mosquitoes and Dollars.* Boston: Stratford, 1925.

Page 35. Wakeland, Claude, *The High Plains Grasshoppers.* U.S. Dept. of Agric. Technical Bulletin 1167 (1958).

Page 35. Graham, Edward H., "Wildlife in the Small Woodland," *Yearbook of Agric.,* U.S. Dept. of Agric. 1949, pp. 561–64.

CHAPTER IV

FROM THE GROUND UP

Page 39. Rodale, J. I., ed., et. al., *Encyclopedia of Organic Gardening.* Emmaus, Penn.: Rodale Books, 1959.

Page 39. Rodale, ed., et. al., *How to Grow Vegetables and Fruits by the Organic Method.* Emmaus, Penn.: Rodale Books, 1961.

Pages 42–43. Waksman, Selman A., *Humus: Origin, Chemical Composition and Importance in Nature.* Baltimore: Williams & Wilkins, 1938.

Pages 42–43. Anderson, M. S., *Fertilizer or Organic Matter for Soil Improvement*. Soil and Water Conservation Branch, U.S. Dept. of Agric., Beltsville, Md.

Pages 42–43. Balfour, Lady Eve B., *The Living Soil*. London: Faber & Faber, 1951.

Page 42. Turner, F. Newman, *Fertility Farming*. London: Farber & Faber, 1951.

Page 42. Kühnelt, Wilhelm, *Soil Biology, with Special Reference to the Animal Kingdom*. London: Faber & Faber, 1961.

Pages 42–43. Duddington, C. L., *The Friendly Fungi*. London: Faber & Faber, 1957.

Page 43. *Physiology of Fusarium Root Rot of Squash*. New Haven, Conn., Agric. Exp. Station Bulletin 500 (Nov. 1946).

Pages 44–46. Balfour, *The Living Soil*.

Pages 44–46. Slankis, Visvaldis, "The Role of Auxins and Other Exudates in Mycorrhizal Symbiosis of Forest Trees," *The Physiology of Forest Trees*. New York: Ronald, 1957.

Pages 44–46. Slankis, "On the Factors Determining the Establishment of Ecototropic Mycorrhiza of Forest Trees," *Recent Advances in Botany*. Toronto: Univ. of Toronto Press, 1961.

Pages 44–46. Slankis, "Mycorrhiza of Forest Trees," Forest Soils Conf. (Sept. 8–11, 1958). Forest Biol. Lab., Sci. Service, Canada Dept. of Agric.

Page 46. "Root Exudates," *Rural Research* No. 33 (Sept. 1960). Commonwealth of Australia Scientific and Industrial Research Organization.

Pages 46–47. Oostenbrink, K. K., and S. J. J. Jacob, *Tagetes, Enemy of the Pratylenchus Species*, trans. C. C. Carter. Bocking, Braintree, England: Henry Doubleday Research Assn., 1957.

Page 47. *Interim Report on the Control of Potato Eelworm*. Bocking, Braintree, England: Henry Doubleday Research Assn., April 1960.

Page 47. "Tagetes minuta against Pests and Weeds," Henry Doubleday Research Assn. *Newsletter* No. 11 (Aug. 1961), pp. 8–13.

Pages 48–50. Voisin, André, *Better Grassland Sward, Ecology Botany and Management*. London: Crosby Lockwood & Son, 1960.

Pages 48–51. Albrecht, William A., "Physical, Chemical and Biochemical Changes in the Soil Community," *Man's Role in Changing the Face of the Earth*. Chicago: Wenner-Gren Foundation for Anthropological Research, Univ. of Chicago Press, 1956.

Page 48. Heinze, Hans, "Harmonische Abwehr von Krankheiten und Schädlingsbefall im Pflanzenbau; Bearbeitet nach dem Autoren-Referat eines Vortrages von Dr. C. J. Briejèr," *Lebendige Erde*, No. 6 (Nov.–Dec. 1962), pp. 250–55.

Pages 48–50. Haseman, Leonard, "Influence of Soil Minerals on Insects," *Jour. of Econ. Entomol.*, Vol. 53, No. 1 (Feb. 1946), pp. 8–11.

Page 49. Maltais, J. B., "The Nitrogen Content of Different Varieties of Peas as a Factor Affecting Infestations of Macrosiphum pisi," *The Canadian Entomol.*, Vol. 83 (1951), pp. 29–33.

Pages 49–50. Dahms, R. G., "Ovipositing and Longevity of Chinch Bugs on Seedlings Growing in Nutrient Solutions," *Jour. of Econ. Entomol.*, Vol. 40, No. 6, pp. 841–45.

Page 50. Rodriguez, J. G., "Mineral Nutrition of the Two-Spotted Spider Mite, Tetranychus bimaculatus Harvey," Entomol. Soc. of Amer. *Annals*, Vol. 44, No. 4 (Dec. 1951), pp. 511–26.

Page 50. Rodriguez, J. G., and L. D. Rodriguez, "The Relation between Minerals, B-Complex Vitamins, and Mite Populations in Tomato Foliage," Entomol. Soc. of Amer. *Annals*, Vol. 45, No. 2 (June 1952), pp. 331–38.

Page 50. LeRoux, E. J., "Effects of Various Levels of Calcium, Magnesium, and Sulfur in Nutrient Solution on Fecundity of the Two-Spotted Mite, Tetranychus telarius, Reared on Cucumber," *Canadian Jour. of Plant Sci.*, Vol. 39 (Jan. 1959), pp. 92–97.

Page 50. LeRoux, "Effects of Various Levels of Nitrogen, Phosphorus, and Potassium in Nutrient Solution, on the Fecundity of the Two-Spotted Spider Mite, Tetranychus bimaculatus Harvey, Reared on Cucumber," *Canadian Jour. of Agric. Sci.*, Vol. 34 (March–April 1954), pp. 145–51.

Page 50. Chabousson, Francis, "Sur Deux Cas de Pullulations de Tetranyques en Corrélation avec les Taux d'azote et de Potassium dans les Feuilles, Influence de Certains Traitements Insecticides," *Revue de Zoologie Agricole et Appliquée*, Nos. 7–9 (1960).

Pages 51–52. Howard, Sir Albert, *An Agricultural Testament*. New York: Oxford Univ. Press, 1943.

Pages 51–52. Howard, *Farming and Gardening for Health or Disease*. London: Faber & Faber, 1945.

Page 52. *Haughley Experiment, Report of the First Twenty-five Years*. New Bells Farm, Haughley, Stowmarket, England: 1962.

Pages 52–53. *Malabar Farm Newsletter*, No. 41 (Aug. 1962). Lucas, Ohio: Louis Bromfield Malabar Farm Foundation.

Pages 53–54. Mader, Donald Lewis, *Effect of Humus of Different Origins in Moderating the Toxicity of Biocides*. Emmaus, Penn.: The Soil and Health Foundation, 1961.

Pages 54–55. *Grass, Yearbook of Agric.*, U.S. Dept. of Agric., 1948.

Pages 54–57. *Soil, Yearbook of Agric.*, U.S. Dept. of Agric., 1957.

Pages 54–57. Sykes, Friend, *Humus — And the Farmer*. London: Faber & Faber, 1946.

Pages 54–57. Sykes, *Modern Humus Farming*. London: Faber & Faber, 1959.

Pages 55–57. Rodale, ed., *et. al.*, *The Complete Book of Composting*. Emmaus, Penn.: Rodale Books, 1960.

Page 56. Gottas, H. B., *Composting: Sanitary Disposal and Reclamation of Organic Wastes.* Geneva: World Health Organization, 1956.

Page 58. *Natl. Agric. Chem. Assn. News and Pesticide Review,* Vol. 21, No. 1 (Oct. 1962), p. 7.

Pages 59–60. Wiley, John S., *Studies of High-Rate Composting of Garbage and Refuse.* U.S. Dept. of Health Educ. and Welfare, Savannah, Ga.

Pages 59–60. Black, Hayse H., "Industrial Waste Treatment," *Sewage and Industrial Wastes,* Vol. 26. Industrial Waste Section, U.S. Pub. Health Service.

Pages 59–60. Brown, H. D., *Disposal of Cannery Waste in Ohio.* Columbus, Ohio: Ohio State Univ.

Page 59. Herber, Lewis, *Our Synthetic Environment.* New York: Knopf, 1962.

Page 60. Reineke, L. H. *Uses for Forest Residues.* Madison, Wisc.: Forest Products Lab., U.S. Dept. of Agric.

Page 61. Dunn, Stewart, *The Influence of Waste Bark on Plant Growth.* Durham, N.H.: Univ. of New Hampshire, Agric. Exp. Sta.

Page 61. Dunn, *The Influence of Lignin and Other Waste Materials on Plant Growth.* Durham, N.H.: Univ. of New Hampshire, Agric. Exp. Sta.

Page 61. Gessel, Stanley P., *Composts and Mulches from Wood Waste.* Seattle, Wash.: Univ. of Washington, Dept. of Forest Soils.

Page 62. Walton, G. P. and R. F. Gardiner, *Cocoa By-Products and Their Utilization as Fertilizer Materials.* U.S. Dept. of Agric. Bulletin 1413 (1926).

Page 62. Toth, S. J. and W. H. Kelly, "Complete Study of Farm Uses for Organic Wastes," *New Jersey Agric.,* July–Aug. 1956. New Brunswick, N.J., Agric. Exp. Sta.

Page 62. Holder, Ralph C., *Fishery Feed Products.* Washington, D.C.: Natl. Fisheries Inst.

CHAPTER V

PLANTS OUT OF PLACE

Pages 66–85. Martin, P., B. Rademacher, Gerhard Grummer, Horst Beyer, and P. J. Welbank, *The Biology of Weeds.* England: Blackwell Scientific Publications, 1960.

Pages 66–85. Cocannouer, Joseph A., *Weeds: Guardians of the Soil.* New York: Devin-Adair, 1954.

Pages 68–69. Pfeiffer, Ehrenfried E., *Weeds and What They Tell.* Dover Plains, N.Y.: Bio-Dynamic Farming and Gardening Assn., 1962.

Pages 70–72. Elton, *The Ecology of Invasion by Animals and Plants.*

Pages 70–72. Albrecht, "Soil Fertility — A Weapon Against Weeds," *The Organic Farmer,* Vo. 3, No. 11 (June 1952).

Page 71. Kalmbach, "Rodents, Rabbits, and Grasslands," *Grass, Yearbook of Agric.*, U.S. Dept. of Agric., 1948, pp. 248–56.

Pages 72–73. Faulkner, Edward H., *Plowman's Folly*. Norman, Okla.: Univ. of Oklahoma Press, 1943.

Pages 72–73. Faulkner, *A Second Look*. Norman, Okla.: Univ. of Oklahoma Press, 1947.

Pages 72–73. Faulkner, *Soil Development*. Norman Okla.: Univ. of Oklahoma Press, 1952.

Pages 72–73. Stout, Ruth, *How to Have a Green Thumb without an Aching Back*. New York: Exposition, 1955.

Pages 72–73. Stout, *Gardening without Work for the Aging, the Busy and the Indolent*. New York: Devin-Adair, 1961.

Pages 73–75. Voisin, *Better Grassland Sward, Ecology Botany and Management*.

Pages 73–78. Holloway, James K., and C. B. Huffaker, "Insects to Control a Weed," *Yearbook of Agric.*, U.S. Dept. of Agric., 1952, pp. 135–40.

Pages 78–79. Goddard, R. J., "Weeding Cotton with Geese on Ames Plantation," *Tennessee Farm and Home Sci.*, Progress Report No. 44 (Oct., Nov., Dec. 1962), pp. 23–24. Agric. Exp. Sta., Univ. of Tennessee.

Pages 78–79. Tanner, James C., "The Man with the Hoe Gives Way to Geese in U.S. Cotton Fields," *Wall St. Jour.*, Feb. 21, 1963.

Page 80. "Tagetes minuta against Pests and Weeds."

Page 80. "The Tagetes Experiment, Successes against Weeds," Henry Doubleday Research Assn. *Newsletter*, Oct. 1962, pp. 17–39.

Page 80. *1962 Campaign against Witchgrass Gets Underway in the Carolinas*. Release No. 2785–62, U.S. Dept. of Agric. Aug. 6, 1962.

Pages 81–82. Pechanec, Joseph F., Charles E. Fisher, and Kenneth W. Parker, "How to Control Noxious Plants," *Yearbook of Agric.*, U.S. Dept. of Agric., 1948, pp. 256–59.

Pages 82–84. Pound, Charles E., and Frank E. Egler, "Brush Control in Southeastern New York: Fifteen Years of Stable Treeless Communities," *Ecology*, Vol. 34, No. 1 (Jan. 1953).

Pages 82–84. Egler, "Human Ecology and Connecticut's Two Roadside Bulletins," *Ecology*, Vol. 41 (Oct. 1960), pp. 785–90.

Pages 82–84. Egler, *Herbicides, 60 Questions and Answers Concerning Roadside and Rightofway Vegetation Management*. Litchfield, Conn.: Litchfield Hills Audubon Soc., rev., 1961.

Pages 82–84. *A Roadside Crisis: The Use and Abuse of Herbicides*. Conn. Arboretum, Bulletin No. 11 (March 1959). New London, Conn.: Connecticut College.

Pages 84–85. Egler, "Roadside Ragweed Control Knowledge, and Its 'Communication' between Science, Industry and Society," *Recent Advances in Botany*. Toronto: Univ. of Toronto Press, 1961.

CHAPTER VI

AN OUNCE OF PREVENTION

Page 87. Turner, Neely, and James G. Horsfall, *Controlling Pests of War Gardens*. Conn. Agric. Sxp. Sta. Circular 159 (April 1944).

Pages 87–91. Cocannoeur, Joseph A., *Farming with Nature*. Norman, Okla.: Univ. of Oklahoma Press, 1954.

Page 88. Pimental, David, *Species Diversity and Insect Population Outbreaks*. Ithaca: Cornell Univ., June 21, 1960.

Page 88. Pimental, *The Influence of Plant Spatial Patterns on Insect Populations*. Ithaca: Cornell Univ., June 17, 1960.

Page 88. Brues, Charles T., "How Insects Choose Food Plants," *Yearbook of Agric.*, U.S. Dept. of Agric., 1952, pp. 37–42.

Page 89. Rodriguez, J. G., and R. B. Neiswander, "The Effect of Soil Soluble Salts and Cultural Practices on Mite Populations on Hothouse Tomatoes," *Jour. of Econ. Entomol.*, Vol. 41, No. 1 (May 25, 1949), pp. 56–59.

Pages 89–90. Pfeiffer, *Bio-Dynamic Farming and Gardening*. New York: Anthroposophic Press, 1943, pp. 113–26.

Pages 89–90. Gregg, Richard S., and Evelyn S. Gregg, *Companion Plant Herbs, Their Part in Good Gardening*. Dover Plains, N.Y.: The Bio-Dynamic Farming & Gardening Assn., 1943.

Pages 89–90. Hersey, Jean, "Strange Bedfellows," *Living for Young Homemakers*, June 1961.

Pages 90–91. Bailey, L. H., *Cyclopedia of American Agriculture*. New York: Macmillan, 1907.

Page 92. Wickenden, Leonard, *Gardening with Nature*. New York: Devin-Adair, 1958.

Pages 92–95. *Plant Diseases, Yearbook of Agric.*, U.S. Dept. of Agric., 1953.

Page 96. *USDA Entomologists Use Plow to Reduce Sweetclover Weevil*, Release No. 1536–63, U.S. Dept. of Agric., May 9, 1963.

Pages 96–97. *Insects, Yearbook of Agric.*, U.S. Dept. of Agric., 1952.

CHAPTER VII

EMERGENCY MEASURES: SIMPLE SPRAYS AND OTHER MATERIALS

Pages 102–3. *Organic Gardening and Farming Mag.*, June 1951. Report on water spraying of apple trees.

Pages 103–4. Chapman, P. J., L. A. Riehl, and G. W. Pearce, "Oil Sprays for Fruit Trees," *Insects, Yearbook of Agric.*, U.S. Dept. of Agric., 1952, pp. 299–339.

Page 105. Hare, W. W., and G. B. Lucas, "Control of Contact Transmission of Tobacco Mosaic Virus with Milk," *Plant Disease Reporter*, Vol. 42 (1959), pp. 152–54.

278   List of Sources

Page 105. "Skim Milk Halts Plant Vidus Damage," *Science News Letter*,
Vol. 76, No. 12 (Oct. 19, 1959), p. 181.
Page 106. Pfeiffer, "The Bio-Dynamic Treatment of Fruit Trees, Berries,
and Shrubs," *Bio-Dynamics*, Nos. 42–43 (1957).
Pages 106–7. Kayumov, S. R., "Tests against Cotton Pests of Some
Plants that Produce Essential Oils," abstract in *Review of Applied
Entomol.* (A), No. 24 (1936), p. 768.
Pages 106–7. Kayumov, "Tests of New Vegetable Poisons from Plants
that Produce Essential Oil," abstract in *Review of Applied Entomol.*
(A), No. 26 (1938), pp. 249–50.
Page 107. Cole, A. C., Jr., "The Olfactory Responses of the Cockroach
(Blatta orientalis) to the More Important Essential Oils and a Con-
trol Measure Formulated from the Results," *Jour. of Econ. Entomol.*,
Vol. 25 (1932), pp. 902–5.
Pages 107–10. McIndoo, N. E., *Plants of Possible Insecticidal Value*: A
Review of the Literature up to 1941. Bureau of Entomol. and Plant
Quarantine, U.S. Dept. of Agric., E-661, May 1945.
Pages 107–10. Jacobson, Martin, *Insecticides from Plants: A Review of
the Literature, 1941–53*. U.S. Dept. of Agric. Handbook No. 154
(1958).
Page 109. *Organic Gardening and Farming Mag.*, May 1962. Report on
onion spray.
Page 110. Rasmussen, O. Elstrup, "Healthy Orchards," *Star and Furrow*,
Spring 1958. Bio-Dynamic Agric. Assn., England.
Page 110. Timonin, M. I., "Antifungal Activity of Pentatomid Scent
Gland," *Annual Report* (year ending March 31, 1962), Canada Dept.
of Forestry, Forest Entomol. and Pathol. Branch. Pub. Ottawa.
Page 110. Pirone, Thomas P., and F. Malekzadeh, "An Antibacterial
Substance from Cauliflower Seeds," address before Am. Phytopatho-
logical Soc., at joint meeting of Am. Inst. of Biol. Sciences, Pacific
Div., and Am. Acad. for the Advancement of Sci. Oregon State Univ.
Aug. 1962.
Page 111. Weisberger, Austin S., and Jack Pensky, "Tumor-Inhibiting
Effects Derived from an Active Principle of Garlic (Allium sativum),"
Science, Vol. 126, No. 3283 (Nov. 29, 1957), pp. 1112–14.
Page 111. *Organic Gardening and Farming Mag.*, Nov. 1954. Report on
aqueous onion extract.
Pages 111–12. Simons, John N. and Ronald Swidler, "Compounds from
Succulents as Natural Inhibitors of Virus Diseases in Crops," Release,
Stanford Research Inst., Southern Calif. Lab., May 7, 1962. South
Pasadena, Calif.
Page 112. Bier, John E., "Tissue Saprophytes and the Possibility of
Biological Control of some Tree Diseases," paper presented at Annual
Meeting of Canadian Inst. of Forestry, Vancouver, Oct. 1962.
Pages 112–16. Dethier, Vincent G., *Chemical Insect Attractants and
Repellants*. Philadelphia: Blakeston, 1947.

Page 112. Martin, H., *The Scientific Principles of Crop Protection.* London: Edward Arnold, 1959, 4th ed.

Page 115. Lathrop, F. H. and L. G. Keirstead, "Black Pepper to Control Bean Weevil," *Jour. of Econ. Entomol.*, Vol. 39, No. 4 (Aug. 1946), p. 534.

Pages 115–16. Metzger, F. W., and D. H. Grant, "Repellency to the Japanese Beetle of Extracts Made from Plants Immune to Attack." U.S. Dept. of Agric. *Technical Bulletin* 299 (1932).

Page 115. Metzger, F. W., "The Toxicity of the Common Castor Bean Plant in Respect to the Japanese Beetle," *Jour. of Econ. Entomol.*, Vol. 26 (1933), pp. 299–300.

Page 115. Ballou, C. H., "Effects of Geranium on the Japanese Beetle," *Jour. of Econ. Entomol.*, Vol. 22 (1929), pp. 289–93.

Page 115. Thibault, J. K., Jr., "Vegetable Powder as a Larvicide in the Fight Against Mosquitoes. A Preliminary Note," *Jour. of Am. Med. Assn.*, 1918, pp. 1215–16.

Page 116. *Boll Weevil Repellent Extracted from Cotton Plant,* USDA *Reports,* Release No. 1091–63, U.S. Dept. of Agric., Apr. 2, 1963.

Pages 116–19. Bottger, G. T., and Martin Jacobson, *Preliminary Tests of Plant Materials as Insecticides."* Bureau of Entomol. and Plant Quarantine, U.S. Dept. of Agric., E-797, 1950.

Pages 116–19. Busbey, Ruth L., "Plants that Help Kill Insects," *Insects, Yearbook of Agric.*, Separate No. 2276, U.S. Dept. of Agric.

Pages 116–19. Feinstein, Louis, "Insecticides from Plants," *Insects, Yearbook of Agric.*, U.S. Dept. of Agric., 1952, pp. 222–29.

Pages 116–19. Jacobson, *Insecticidal Plants,* Special Report 26 (1953), Bureau of Entomol. and Plant Quarantine, U.S. Dept. of Agric. Insecticide investigation.

Pages 116–19. McIndoo, *Plants Tested for or Reported to Possess Insecticidal Properties.* U.S. Dept. of Agric. Bulletin 1201, 1924.

Pages 116–19. Roark, R. C., "The Examination of Plants for Insecticidal Constituents," *Jour. of Econ. Entomol.*, Vol. 35 (1942), pp. 273–75.

Pages 116–19. Schreiber, A. F., "Vegetable Insecticides," abstract in *Review of Applied Entomol.* (A), Vol. 4 (1916), p. 59.

Page 117. Arena, Jay M., "Insecticides from Botanical Sources," *Poisoning, Chemistry, Symptoms, Treatments.* Springfield, Ill.: Charles C. Thomas, 1963, pp. 65–78.

Page 117. Hayes, Wayland J., Jr., "Botanical Insecticides," *Clinical Handbook on Economic Poisons.* Atlanta: U.S. Pub. Health Service, 1963, pp. 74–76.

Pages 119–21. Glynne Jones, G. D., "Pyrethrum in Kenya, the Story of a Natural Insecticide," *The* [London] *Times Review of Industry,* April 1962, pp. 5–22.

Page 120. Jacobson, "Herculin, a Pungent Insecticidal Constituent of Southern Prickly Ash Bark," *Jour. of Am. Chem. Soc.*, Vol. 70 (1948), p. 4234.

Pages 121–22. Feinstein, Louis, Patrick J. Hanna, and Edward T. Mc-Cabe, "Extraction of Alkaloids from Tree Tobacco," *Industrial and Engineering Chem.*, Vol. 43, (June 1951), p. 1402.

Page 122. Roark, *A Review of Information on Anabasine*. Bureau of Entomol. and Plant Quarantine, U.S. Dept. of Agric., E-537, 1941.

Page 122. Busbey, *A Bibliography of Quassia*. Bureau of Entomol. and Plant Quarantine, U.S. Dept. of Agric., E-483, 1939.

Page 122. McIndoo and A. F. Sievers, "Quassia Extract as a Contact Insecticide," *Jour. of Agric. Research*, Vol. 10 (1917), pp. 497–531.

Page 122. Rhind, William, *A History of the Vegetable Kingdom*. London: Blackie & Son, 1855.

Pages 122–23. Roark, R. C., *A Digest of the Literature of Derris (Deguelia) Species Used as Insecticides 1747–1931*. U.S. Dept. of Agric. Misc. Pub. 120, 1932.

Pages 122–23. Roark, *The History of the Use of Derris as an Insecticide. Part II, The Period of 1919–1928*. Bureau of Entomol. and Plant Quarantine, U.S. Dept. of Agric., E-468, 1939.

Pages 123–24. Roark, *Lonchocarpus (barbasco, cube, and timbo)*: A *Review of Recent Literature*. Bureau of Entomol. and Plant Quarantine, U.S. Dept. of Agric., E-453, 1938.

Page 124. "Yerba de la pulga," *Scientific Am.*, July 1938, p. 33.

Pages 124–25. Rogers, E. F., F. R. Koniuszy, J. Shavel, Jr., and K. Folkers, "Plant Insecticides: Ryanodine, a New Alkaloid from Ryania speciosa," *Jour. of Am. Chem. Soc.*, Vol. 70 (1948), pp. 3086–88.

Pages 126–28. "The 1961 Tagetes Experiment," Henry Doubleday Research Assn. *Newsletter*, April 1960, Sept. 1962, Oct. 1962.

Page 128. Roark, *Devil's Shoestring* (Cracca Virginiana L.), *A Potential Source of Rotenone and Related Insecticides*. Insecticide Div., Bureau of Chem. and Soils, U.S. Dept. of Agric., June 1934.

Page 128. Roark, *Tephrosia as an Insecticide — A Review of the Literature*. Bureau of Entomol. and Plant Quarantine, U.S. Dept. of Agric., E-402, 1937.

Page 128. Jones, Howard A., and W. N. Sullivan, "Tephrosia Extract against House Flies," *Soap and Sanitary Chemicals*, Sept. 1942.

Page 128. Lichtenstein, E. P., F. M. Strong, and D. G. Morgan, "Naturally Occurring Insecticides, Identification of 2-Phenylethylisothiacyanate as an Insecticide Occurring Naturally in the Edible Part of Turnips," *Agric. and Food Chem.*, Vol. 10, No. 1, (Jan.–Feb. 1962), p. 30.

Page 129. Beroza, Morton, and G. T. Bottger, "The Insecticidal Value of Tripterygium wilfordii," *Jour. of Econ. Entomol.*, Vol. 47, No. 1, (Feb. 1954), pp. 188–89.

CHAPTER VIII
EMERGENCY MEASURES: TRAPS

Pages 130–44. Baker, Howard, and Truman E. Hienton, "Traps Have Some Value," *Insects, Yearbook of Agric.*, U.S. Dept. of Agric., 1952, pp. 406–11.

Pages 130–44. Hienton, and J. P. Schaenzer, "Farmers Use Electricity," *Yearbook of Agric.*, U.S. Dept. of Agric., 1960, p. 75.

Page 132. Rosenfeld, A. H., "Why Not Trap-Crops that Entrap?" *Jour. of Econ. Entomol.*, Vol. 18 (1925), pp. 550–52.

Page 133. Beroza, Morton, and Nathan Green, "Lures for Insects," *Yearbook of Agric.*, U.S. Dept. of Agric., 1962, pp. 365–68.

Pages 133–34. Yothers, M. A., "Summary of Three Years' Tests of Trap Baits for Capturing the Codling Moth," *Jour. of Econ. Entomol.*, Vol. 20, No. 4 (1927), pp. 567–75.

Pages 133–34. Bobb, M. L., A. M. Woodside, and R. N. Jefferson, "Baits and Bait Traps in Codling Moth Control," *Va. Agric. Exp. Sta. Bulletin* No. 320, 1939, pp. 1–19.

Pages 133–34. Alexander, C. C., and F. W. Carlson, "A Comparison of Codling Moth Captures by Bait Trap and Rotary Net," *Jour. of Econ. Entomol.*, Vol. 36, No. 4 (1943), pp. 637–38.

Page 134. Dethier, *Chemical Insect Attractants and Repellants.*

Pages 135–36. Hall, Stanley A., Green, and Beroza, "Insect Repellents and Attractants," *Agric. and Food Chem.*, Vol. 5, No. 9 (Sept. 1957), p. 663.

Pages 135–36. Jacobson, "Synthesis of a Highly Potent Gypsy Moth Sex Attractant," *Jour. of Organic Chem.*, Vol. 25 (1960), p. 2074.

Page 136. Jacobson, Beroza, and William A. Jones, "Isolation, Identification, and Synthesis of the Sex Attractant of Gypsy Moth," *Science*, Vol. 132, No. 3433 (Oct. 14, 1960), pp. 1011–12.

Page 136. Beroza, Green, S. I. Gertler, L. F. Steiner, and Doris H. Miyashita, "New Attractants for the Mediterranean Fruit Fly," *Agric. and Food Chem.*, Vol. 9, No. 5 (Sept.–Oct. 1961), p. 361.

Pages 136–37. *USDA Isolates Cockroach Attractant in Biological Pest Control Research*, Release No. 3926–62, U.S. Dept. of Agric., Nov. 9, 1962.

Page 136. Alexander, B. H., Beroza, T. A. Oda, Steiner, Miyashita, and W. C. Mitchell, "The Development of Male Melon Fly Attractants," *Agric. and Food Chem.*, Vol. 10, No. 4 (July–Aug. 1962), p. 270.

Page 136. *New USDA Melon-Fly Lure Proves Highly Effective.* Release No. 833–60, U.S. Dept. of Agric., Mar. 31, 1960.

Page 137. *Chemical in Female Houseflies Attracts Males, USDA Research Shows.* Release No. 2699–63, U.S. Dept. of Agric., Aug. 12, 1963.

Page 137. *USDA Says Control of Cabbage Looper Is Step Nearer.* Release No. 2979–63, U.S. Dept. of Agric., Sept. 6, 1963.

Page 137. *Detection of Pink Bollworm Moths Possible with Natural Attractant.*" Release No. 4349–62, U.S. Dept. of Agric., Dec. 12, 1962.

Page 139. Grotzke, Heinz, "Electric Insect Traps," *Bio-Dynamics,* Vol. 46 (Spring 1958), pp. 17–20.

Page 140. *Tobacco Hornworm Response to Light Trap Tested.* Release No. 2174–62, U.S. Dept. of Agric., June 13, 1962.

Page 140. Taylor, J. G., L. B. Altman, J. P. Hollingsworth, and J. M. Stanley, *Electric Insect Traps for Survey Purposes.* Agric. Research Service, U.S. Dept. of Agric., No. 42–3, May 1956.

Pages 140–41. Fredericks, Eldon E., "Insects See the Light," Purdue Univ. Agric. Exp. Sta. *Report,* Vol. 2, No. 2 (Summer 1959), pp. 3–5.

Pages 141. *Light Traps Reduce Tobacco Hornworm Population 50 Percent in USDA Test.* Release No. 2665–63, U.S. Dept. of Agric., Aug. 8, 1963.

Page 143. *Experimental Machine Destroys Boll Weevils.* Release No. 1018–63, U.S. Dept. of Agric., Mar. 28, 1963.

Pages 143–44. Bastin, Harold, *Freaks and Marvels of Insect Life.* New York: A. A. Wyn, 1954.

CHAPTER IX
CONTROLLING UNWELCOME BIRDS AND ANIMALS

Pages 147–48. Mitchell, Robert T., and John T. Linehan, *Protecting Corn from Blackbirds.* U.S. Fish and Wildlife Service Leaflet No. 385.

Pages 147–48. Mitchell, "Management to Avoid Bird Depredations," *Transactions,* 25th North Am. Wildlife Conf. (Mar. 1960).

Page 148. Parker, Lansing A., "Federal Responsibilities in Bird Predations Control," *Transactions,* 25th North Am. Wildlife Conf.

Page 149. Meanley, Brooke, *The Distribution, Ecology and Population Dynamics of Blackbirds.* U.S. Fish and Wildlife Service, Patuxent Wildlife Research Center, Laurel, Md., Jan. 1961.

Page 149. Granett, Philip, "Need Research on Control of Crop Damage by Birds," *N.J. Agric.,* Vol. 45, No. 3 (May–June 1963), pp. 4–8.

Page 149. Lindzey, James S., "Research on Control of Blackbird Depredations," *Transactions,* 25th North Am. Wildlife Conf.

Page 149. *Proceedings,* Bird Depredation Conf., Rutgers Univ., New Brunswick, N.J. (Jan. 1961).

Pages 149–50. Neff, Johnson A., and Mitchell, *The Rope Firecracker,* A *Device to Protect Crops from Bird Damage.* U.S. Fish and Wildlife Service Leaflet 365 (Aug. 1956).

Pages 152–56. *Bird Control Devices.* U. S. Fish and Wildlife Service Leaflet 409, (rev. June 1960).

Pages 155–56. George, John L., "Nuisance Birds—Is Control Possible?," *Natl. Agric. Chem. Assn. News and Pesticide Review*, Vol. 21, No. 5, (June 1963), pp. 6–7.
Page 157. Liddell, Isa, "Mouse Control in Orchards," *Am. Agriculturist*, Oct. 1962.

CHAPTER X
BIOLOGICAL CONTROL

Pages 163–80. Sweetman, Harvey L., *The Biological Control of Insect Pests*. Ithaca: Comstock, 1936.
Pages 163–80. Sweetman, *The Principles of Biological Control*. Dubuque, Iowa: William C. Brown, 1958.
Page 165. Elton, *The Ecology of Invasions by Animals and Plants*.
Pages 166–69. Clausen, C. P., *Biological Control of Insect Pests in the Continental United States*. U.S. Dept. of Agric. Technical Bulletin 1139 (June 1956).
Pages 166–69. Fisher, Theodore W., "What Is Biological Control?," *Handbook on Biological Control of Plant Pests*, pp. 6–18.
Pages 166–69. Beirne, Bryan P., *The Meaning of the Term 'Biological Control.'* Belleville, Canada, Canada Dept. of Agric., Entomol. Research Inst. for Biol. Control, 1963. Typescript.
Pages 166–69. Turnbull, A. L., and D. A. Chant, "The Practice and Theory of Biological Control of Insects in Canada," *Canadian Jour. of Zoology*, Vol. 39 (1961), p. 697.
Pages 168–69. Fleschner, Charles A., "Parasites and Predators for Pest Control," *Biological and Chemical Control of Plant and Animal Pests*. Washington, D.C.: Am. Assn. for Advancement of Sci., 1960.
Pages 168–69. Clausen, "Parasites and Predators," *Insects, Yearbook of Agric.*, U.S. Dept. of Agric., 1952, pp. 380–88.
Pages 168–69. Dowden, Philip B., "A Thief to Catch a Thief," *Yearbook of Agric.*, U.S. Dept. of Agric., 1962, pp. 344–47.
Page 169. De Bach, Paul H., John Landis, and Ernest B. White, "Parasites Are Controlling Red Scale in Southern California Citrus," *Calif. Agric.*, Dec. 1962.
Pages 170–71. Decker, George C., "Insect Outbreaks," address, 5th Annual Meeting, North Central States Branch, Am. Assn. of Econ. Entomologists, Kansas City (March 23–24, 1950).
Page 171. Ullyett, G. C., "Insects, Man and Environment," *Jour. of Econ. Entomol.*, No. 44 (1951), pp. 459–64.
Pages 171–72. *Research Report 1956–1958*; and *Research Report 1960–1961*. Belleville, Canada: Canada Dept. of Agric., Entomol. Research Inst. for Biol. Control.
Pages 171–72. Beirne, "Procedures in Biological Control of Insects," *Information Bulletin* No. 1, Canada Dept. of Agric., Entomol. Research Inst. for Biol. Control, 1963.

284 List of Sources

Pages 171–72. *Proceedings*, Supp. Vol., Resources for Tomorrow Conf. Montreal, 1961. Ottawa: Canada Dept. of Agric., Feb. 1962.

Pages 171–72. *Annual Report* (year ending March 31, 1962), Canada Dept. of Forestry, Forest Entomol. and Pathol. Branch. Pub. Ottawa, 1962.

Page 172. Dowden, Philip B., "Biological Control of Forest Insects in the United States and Canada," *Jour. of Forestry*, Vol. 55, No. 10 (Oct. 1957).

Page 173. *USDA Administrator Discusses Insect Control of the Future.* Release No. 2815–63, U.S. Dept. of Agric., Aug. 21, 1963.

Page 174. Smith, Ray F., "Integration of Biological and Chemical Control: Integration and Principles," *Bulletin of Entomol. Soc. of Am.*, Vol. 8, No. 4 (Dec. 1962), pp. 188–89.

Page 174. Beirne, "Integration of Biological and Chemical Control: Desirable Attributes of Biotic Agents." *Bulletin of Entomol. Soc. of Am.*, Vol. 8, No. 4 (Dec. 1962), pp. 189–91.

Page 174. Knight, Fred B., "Integration of Biological and Chemical Control: Opportunities in Forest Entomology," *Bulletin of Entomol. Soc. of Am.*, Vol. 8, No. 4 (Dec. 1962), pp. 196–99.

Page 175. Pickett, A. D., "The Philosophy of Orchard Insect Control," Entomol. Soc. Ontario 79th *Annual Report*, 1948, pp. 37–41.

Page 175. Pickett, "A Critique on Insect Chemical Control Methods," *The Canadian Entomol.*, Vol. 81 (1949), pp. 67–76.

Page 175. Pickett, William L. Putnam, and E. J. LeRoux, "Progress in Harmonizing Biological and Chemical Control of Orchard Pests in Eastern Canada," *Contribution* 3594, Canada Dept. of Agric., Entomol. Div., Sci. Service. Pub. Ottawa, n.d.

Page 175. Pickett, *The Control of Apple Insects in Nova Scotia.* Mimeo., n.d.

Page 175. MacLellan, C. R., "Mortality of Codling Moth Eggs and Young Larvae in an Integrated Control Orchard," *The Canadian Entomol.*, Vol. 94, No. 6 (June 1962).

Pages 175–76. LeRoux et. al., *Population Dynamics of Agricultural and Forest Insect Pests*, Memoirs of the Entomol. Soc. of Canada, No. 32 (1963).

Page 176. Burnett, T., "Effects of Initial Densities and Periods of Infestation on the Growth-Forms of a Host and Parasite Population," *Canadian Jour. of Zoology*, Vol. 38 (1960).

Page 176. Chant, D. A., "The Effect of Prey Density on Prey Consumption and Oviposition in Adults of Typhlodromus Occidentalis Nesbitt in the Laboratory," *Canadian Jour. of Zoology*, Vol. 39 (1961).

Page 178. *Entomology in the Soviet Union: Report of a Technical Study Group.* Agric. Research Service, U.S. Dept. of Agric., June 1961.

Page 178. Rabb, R. L., "Integration of Biological and Chemical Control: Manipulation of the Environment," *Bulletin of Entomol. Soc. of Am.*, Vol. 8, No. 4 (Dec. 1962) pp. 193–96.

Page 178. Doiiiio, "Trends in Applied Biological Control of Insects," *Annual Review of Entomol.* Vol. 7 (1962).
Page 179. USDA *Opens New Insect Research Laboratory at Gainesville, Florida.* Release No. 2724–63, U.S. Dept. of Agric., Aug. 13, 1963.

CHAPTER XI
THE USE OF INSECT DISEASES

Pages 181–209. Steinhaus, Edward A., *Insect Microbiology*. Ithaca: Comstock, 1946.
Pages 181–84. Clausen, C. P., "Microbial Control of Insect Pests," *Biological Control of Insect Pests in the Continental United States*. U.S. Dept. of Agric. Technical Bulletin No. 1139 (June 1956), pp. 11–12.
Pages 181–84. "Use of Disease to Kill Plant Insect Pests," *Special Report, 22–74*, Agric. Research Service, U.S. Dept. of Agric., Oct. 1961.
Pages 181–84. McEwen, Freeman L., "Microbial Insecticides for Insect Control," *Handbook on Biological Control of Plant Pests*, pp. 69–75.
Pages 181–84. Steinhaus, "Infectious Diseases of Insects," *Insects, Yearbook of Agric.*, U.S. Dept. of Agric., 1952, pp. 388–94.
Page 182. Steinhaus, "Concerning the Harmlessness of Insect Pathogens and the Standardization of Microbial Control Products," *Jour. of Econ. Entomol.*, Vol. 50, No. 6 (Dec. 1957), pp. 715–20.
Page 182. Steinhaus, "On the Improbability of Bacillus thuringiensis Berliner Mutating to Forms Pathogenic for Vertebrates," *Jour. of Econ. Entomol.*, Vol. 52, No. 3 (June 1959), pp. 506–8.
Pages 184–87. Heimpel, A. M., and T. A. Angus, "Bacterial Insecticides," *Bacteriological Reviews*, Vol. 24, No. 3 (Sept. 1960).
Pages 184–87. Heimpel, A. M., "On the Taxonomy of Certain Entomogenous Crystalliferous Bacteria" *Jour. of Insect Pathol.*, Vol. 2 (1960), pp. 311–19.
Pages 184–87. Angus and Heimpel, "Inhibition of Feeding, and Blood pH Changes in Lepidopterous Larvae Infected with Crystal-forming Bacteria" *The Canadian Entomol.*, Vol. 91, No. 6 (June 1959).
Pages 184–87. Heimpel, "The Site of Action of Crystalliferous Bacteria in Lepidoptera Larvae," *Jour. of Insect Pathol.*, Vol. 1, No. 2 (1959), pp. 152–70.
Pages 184–87. Heimpel, "Investigations of the Mode of Action of Strains of Bacillus Cereus Fr. and Fr. Pathogenic for the Larch Sawfly," *Canadian Jour. of Zoology*, Vol. 33 (1955), pp. 311–26.
Pages 184–87. Heimpel, "The Application of pH Determinations to Insect Pathology," *Contribution* No. 25. Insect Pathol. Research Inst., Research Branch, Canada Agric., Sault Ste. Marie, Canada.
Page 187. Westall, E. B., "Progress Report on Microbial Insecticides," *Food Processing*, June 1961.
Pages 187–91. Hawley, Ira M., "Milky Diseases of Beetles," *Insects, Yearbook of Agric.*, U.S. Dept. of Agric., 1952, pp. 394–400.

Pages 194–96. Welch, H. E., "Nematodes as Agents for Insect Control," Entomol. Soc. of Ontario, *Proceedings*, Vol. 92 (1961), pp. 11–19. Pub. 1962.

Page 194. Welch, "Effects of Protozoan Parasites and Commensals on Larvae of the Mosquito Aedes communis at Churchill, Manitoba," *Jour. of Insect Pathol.*, Vol. 2, No. 4 (Dec. 1960), pp. 386–95.

Page 195. Welch, and Briand, L. J., "Field Experiment on the Use of a Nematode for the Control of Vegetable Crop Insects," Entomol. Soc. of Ontario, *Proceedings*, Vol. 91 (1960). Pub. 1961.

Page 195. Welch, "Tests of the Nematode DD 136 and an Associated Bacterium for Control of the Colorado Beetle." *The Canadian Entomol.*, Vol. 93, No. 9 (Sept. 1961).

Pages 195–96. Coscarelli, Waldimero, "Some Nematode Enemies," *Handbook on Biological Control of Plant Pests*, pp. 76–81.

Page 196. Christie, J. R., "Biological Control — Predaceous Nematodes," Chapter 46 in J. N. Sasser, and W. R. Jenkins, *Nematology Fundamentals and Recent Advances with Emphasis on Plant Parasitic and Soil Forms*. Chapel Hill, N.C.: Univ. of North Carolina Press, 1960.

Pages 197–98. Duddington, C. L., *The Friendly Fungi*. London: Faber & Faber, 1957.

Page 198. *Scientists Test Fungus for Control of Nematodes*. Release No. 3165–60, U.S. Dept. of Agric., Oct. 28, 1960.

Page 199. Miner, Bruce B., "Pathologists Test a New Way to Fight Fungi with Fungi," *Frontiers of Plant Sci.*, Nov. 1962, p. 7. Conn. Agric. Exp. Sta.

Page 200. *Annual Report* (year ending March 31, 1962), Canada Dept. of Forestry, Forest Entomol. and Pathol. Branch. Pub. Ottawa, 1962.

CHAPTER XII

BREEDING PLANTS FOR RESISTANCE

Pages 203–9. Smith, D. C., "The Breeder's Ways and Means," *Yearbook of Agric.*, U.S. Dept. of Agric., 1948, pp. 331–41.

Pages 203–9. Dahms, Reynold G., "Resistance in Plants," *Yearbook of Agric.*, U.S. Dept. of Agric., 1962, pp. 360–64.

Pages 203–9. Stevenson, Frederick J., and Henry A. Jones, "Some Sources of Resistance in Crop Plants," *Yearbook of Agric.*, U.S. Dept. of Agric., 1953, pp. 192–216.

Pages 204–5. Wingard, S. A., "The Nature of Resistance to Disease," *Plant Diseases, Yearbook of Agric.*, U.S. Dept. of Agric., 1953, pp. 165–73.

Pages 204–5. Coons, George H., "Breeding for Resistance to Disease," *Yearbook of Agric.*, U.S. Dept. of Agric., 1953, pp. 174–92.

Pages 206–9. Painter, Reginald H., *Insect Resistance in Crop Plants*. New York: Macmillan, 1951.

Pages 206–8. Dahms, "Use of Resistant Varieties — The Ideal Way to Control Insects," *Handbook on Biological Control of Plant Pests*, pp. 82–87.

Page 207. *Cotton Plants Bred For Low Nectar Production Prove Less Attractive to Insects.* Release No. 2658–60, U.S. Dept. of Agric., Sept. 12, 1960.

Page 208. Dahms, T. H. Johnston, A. M. Schlehuber, and E. A. Wood, Jr., "Reaction of Small-Grain Varieties and Hybrids to Greenbug Attack." Okla. Agric. Exp. Sta. Technical Bulletin T-55 (Sept. 1955).

CHAPTER XIII

INGENUITY AND IMAGINATION

Pages 211–12. Yeomans, Alfred H., "Radiant Energy and Insects," *Yearbook of Agric.*, U.S. Dept. of Agric., 1952, pp. 411–21.

Pages 211–12. Christenson, L. D., "Atomic Energy to Control Insects," *Yearbook of Agric.*, U.S. Dept. of Agric., 1962, pp. 348–57.

Page 211. Webber, Harold H., Robert P. Wagner, and Angus G. Pearson, "High-Frequency Electric Fields as Lethal Agents for Insects," *Jour. of Econ. Entomol.*, Vol. 39, No. 4 (Aug. 1946), pp. 487–98.

Page 212. "Effects of High-Frequency Electric Fields on Certain Species of Stored-Grain Insects," *Marketing Research Report* 455 (March 1961). Market Quality Research Div., Agric. Marketing Service, U.S. Dept. of Agric.

Page 212. *Cathode-Ray Exposure Kills Rice Weevils in Wheat.* Release No. 1403–62, U.S. Dept. of Agric., April 16, 1962.

Pages 212–16. Bushland, Raymond C., "Insect Eradication by Means of Sterilized Males," *Handbook on Biological Control of Plant Pests*, pp. 88–94.

Pages 212–16. Knipling, E. F., "Sterile Male Method of Population Control," *Science*, Vol. 130 (1959), pp. 902–4.

Page 215. *Screwworm Eradication Program Enters Critical State in Southwest.* Release No. 2436–63, U.S. Dept. of Agric., July 22, 1963.

Page 215. *USDA to Increase Capacity for Producing Sterile Screwworm Flies.* Release No. 1879–63, U.S. Dept. of Agric., June 6, 1963.

Page 215. *New Screwworm Rearing Plant to be Dedicated June 16.* Release No. 2050–62, U.S. Dept. of Agric., June 4, 1962.

Page 216. *Black-Colored Screwworm Flies May Aid Future Eradication Efforts.* Release No. 3887–61, U.S. Dept. of Agric., Nov. 27, 1961.

Page 217. *Sterilization Technique Demonstrated in Boll Weevil Eradication Test.* Release No. 4374–62, U.S. Dept. of Agric., Dec. 13, 1962.

Page 217. *USDA Studies Potential Use of Biological Weapon against Corn Borer.* Release No. 2799–63, U.S. Dept. of Agric., Aug. 20, 1963.

Page 217. Craig, G. B., W. A. Hickey, and R. C. Van de Hey, "An

Inherited Male-Producing Factor in Aedes aegypti," *Science*, Vol. 132 (1960), pp. 1887–89.

Page 217. *New Technique Wipes Out Oriental Fruit Flies on Pacific Island.* Release No. 3414–63, U.S. Dept. of Agric., Oct. 11, 1963.

Page 218. *Biological-Chemical Method Wipes Out Melon Flies on Pacific Island.* Release No. 2378–63, U.S. Dept. of Agric., July 17, 1963.

Pages 218–219. Knipling, E. F., *Hearings*, 88th Congress, Subcom. on Reorganization and Internatl. Organizations, Sen. Com. on Gov. Operations, Oct. 7, 1963.

Page 219. Shaw, Byron T., "New Dimensions in Insect Research," address at dedication of Insects Affecting Man and Animals Research Lab., Gainesville, Fla., Aug. 23, 1963.

Page 219. *Entomologist Foresees Biological-Chemical Approach to Insect Control.* Release No. 1094–63, U.S. Dept. of Agric., April 2, 1963.

Page 219. Bořkovec, Alexej B., "Sexual Sterilization of Insects by Chemicals," *Science*, Vol. 137, No. 3535 (Sept. 28, 1962), pp. 1034–37.

Page 219. Lindquist, Arthur W., "Chemicals to Sterilize Insects," *Jour. of Washington Acad. of Sci.*, Nov. 1961, pp. 109–114.

Pages 219–21. Frings, Hubert, "Pest Controls, Study of Sound Waves Is Current Project," *New York Times*, June 30, 1963.

Page 221. "Sounds and Ultrasonics," *Research Report 1956–1959.* Belleville, Canada: Entomol. Research Inst. for Biol. Control, p. 17.

Page 221. "Effects of Sound on Behavior," *Research Report 1960–1961.* Belleville, Canada: Entomol. Research Inst. for Biol. Control, p. 17.

Page 221. Belton, P., and R. H. Kempster, "A Field Test on the Use of Sound to Repel the European Corn Borer," *Report.* Belleville, Canada: Entomol. Research Inst. for Biol. Control, Sept. 1962.

Page 221. Wishart, George, and D. F. Riordan, "Flight Responses to Various Sounds by Adult Males of Aedes aegypti," *The Canadian Entomol.*, Vol. 94, No. 6 (June 1962).

Page 222. Watt, K. E. F., "Mathematical Models for Use in Insect Pest Control," *The Canadian Entomol.*, Vol. 93, Supp. 19 (1961), pp. 5–62.

Pages 222–23. Mills, Harlow B., "Weather and Climate," *Insects, Yearbook of Agric.*, U.S. Dept. of Agric., 1952, pp. 422–29.

Page 223. Edwards, D. K., "Influence of Atmospheric Electricity and Pressure on Insect Behavior and Development," *Annual Report*, Research project of Forest Entomol. and Pathol. Lab., Victoria, B.C. Pub. Ottawa, 1962.

Page 223. Maw, M. G., "Behavior of an Insect on an Electrically Charged Surface," *The Canadian Entomol.*, Vol. 93, No. 5 (May 1961).

Pages 223–25. Baker, A. C., "The Vapor-Heat Process," *Insects, Yearbook of Agric.*, U.S. Dept. of Agric., 1952, pp. 401–4.

Page 225. *Reducing Virus and Nematode Damage to Strawberry Plants.* U.S. Dept. of Agric. Leaflet 414, 1960.

Page 226. Richardson, Henry H., "Cold Treatment of Fruits," *Insects,* *Yearbook of Agric.*, U.S. Dept. of Agric., 1952, pp. 404–6.

Page 227. House, H. L., "Insect Diseases Resulting from Malnutrition," Entomol. Soc. of Ontario, *Proceedings*, Vol. 91, 1960. Pub. 1961.

Page 227. Leius, K., "Influence of Various Foods on Fecundity and Longevity of Adults of Scambus buolianae," *The Canadian Entomol.*, Vol. 93, No. 12 (Dec. 1961).

Pages 227–28. Wright, Donald P., Jr., "Anti-feeding Compounds for Insect Control" [Am. Cyanamid Co. Compound 24,055], *New Approaches to Pest Control and Eradication*. Advances in Chemistry Series, No. 40. New York: Am. Chem. Soc., Spring 1963.

Page 228. Pence, Roy J., "The Antimetabolite, Imidazole as a Pesticide," *Jour. of Econ. Entomol.*, Vol. 56, No. 1 (Feb. 1963), pp. 1–6.

Pages 229–30. Cotton, R. T., and J. C. Frankenfeld, "Silica Aerogel for Protecting Stored Seed or Milled Cereal Products from Insects," *Jour. of Econ. Entomol.*, Vol. 42, No. 3 (June 1949).

Pages 229–30. Tarsis, I. Barry, "Laboratory and Field Studies with Sorptive Dusts for the Control of Arthropods Affecting Man and Animal," *Experimental Parasitology*, Vol. 2, No. 1 (Feb. 1961), pp. 10–33.

Page 230. Tarsis, "Control of the Snake Mite, Other Mites, and Certain Insects with the Sorptive Dust, SG 67," *Jour. of Econ. Entomol.*, Vol. 53, No. 5 (Oct. 1960), pp. 903–8.

Page 231. *USDA Scientists Find that Mixing Sugar into Soil Kills Nematodes*. Release No. 583–61, U.S. Dept. of Agric., March 1, 1961.

Page 231. Hutson, R., "Bill-Posters' Paste in Mite Control," *Jour. of Econ. Entomol.*, Vol. 29 (1936), No. 6, p. 1173.

Page 232. Marshall, G. Edward, *A New Approach to Orchard Mite Control Through Chemurgic Materials*. Lafayette, Ind.: Purdue Univ., Dept. of Entomol., July 11, 1962. Mimeo.

Pages 232–33. Fisher, R. W., "Polybutenes — A New Control for Phytophagous Mites," *Jour. of Econ. Entomol.*, Vol. 52, No. 5 (Oct. 1959), p. 1015.

Pages 232–33. Fisher, G. C. Chamberlain, and W. G. Kemp, "Control of Powdery Mildew of Greenhouse Roses with Polybutenes," *Plant Disease Reporter*, Vol. 44, No. 4 (April 15, 1960).

Pages 232–33. "Indopol Polybutenes," *Bulletin* No. 12, Amoco Chem. Corp., 1960.

Page 233. Aller, Harold E. and J. A. Naegele, "Acaricidal Activity of Cellulose Polymers," *Jour. of Econ. Entomol.*, Vol. 54, No. 3 (June 1961), pp. 511–13.

Page 233. Aller, Harold E., "Cellosize — A New Weapon for Resistant Mite Control," *Station to Station Research News*, Vol. 8, No. 1 (April 1962), pp. 3–5.

Page 234. Shaw, John G., and Donald F. Starr, "The Effect of Smoke on the Mexican Fruitfly," *Jour. of Econ. Entomol.*, Vol. 39, No. 4 (Aug. 1946), pp. 526–28.

Page 234. *USDA Scientists Seek New Physical Methods to Control Flies.* Release No. 2558–63, U.S. Dept. of Agric., July 30, 1963.

Page 235. Shaw, Byron T., "New Dimensions in Insect Research," Address at dedication of Insects Affecting Man and Animals Research Lab., Gainesville, Fla.

INDEX